BICYCLE PLANNING

THE AUTHORS

MIKE HUDSON has an honours degree in Engineering and Management. He has written a variety of publications including *The Bicycle Planning Book* (Open Books, 1978) and *The Bicycle Warrior's Handbook* (Friends of the Earth, 1978). He worked for two years as Bicycle Campaigner of Friends of the Earth, and until recently he was their Administrative Director. He is currently studying for a master's degree in Business Administration at the London Business School.

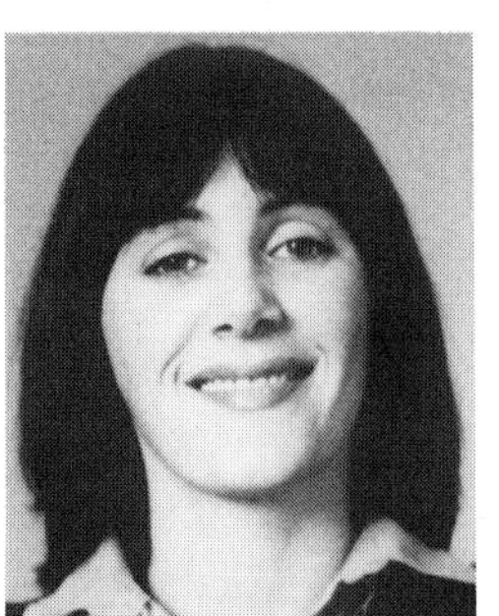

CAREN LEVY has a bachelor's degree in Economics and a master's degree in City and Regional Planning. She was a team leader of a project investigating housing in Cape Town, South Africa, which resulted in the publication of *A Comparative Analysis of Urbanism in Cape Town* (UPRU, University of Cape Town, 1977). She is currently a planning consultant in London. She has recently completed a comprehensive survey of local authority cycling policies and actions in the UK and is now preparing two research projects into different aspects of cycling for Earth Resources Research.

JOHN NICHOLSON has an honours degree in Architectural Engineering. For four years he was the Scientific Officer at the Transport and Road Research Laboratory with responsibility for bicycles. He is the author of two publications on bicycle planning. He is an associate member of the Institution of Civil Engineers. He has worked as an engineer with Bracknell Development Corporation and is now pursuing a career in traffic engineering.

RICHARD MACRORY has an honours degree in Law from Oxford. He is a barrister, author of two books on environmental law and a regular contributor to legal journals. He was for several years legal adviser to Friends of the Earth. He is a leading authority on bicycle planning law and is currently lecturer in Environmental Law and Policy at Imperial College of Science and Technology, London.

PETER SNELSON is an assistant engineer with Bedfordshire County Council. Since 1974 he has worked on the design and implementation of bicycle facilities in Bedford. He has had a number of research papers published in transport periodicals and has lectured to a variety of technical and academic organisations. He is a founder member of the Association of Bedford Cyclists.

Finally, every member of the team is a regular cyclist.

BICYCLE PLANNING

Policy and practice

MIKE HUDSON In association with

Caren Levy, John Nicholson,
Richard Macrory and Peter Snelson

THE ARCHITECTURAL PRESS · LONDON

ACKNOWLEDGMENTS

It is not possible to produce a book such as this about a rapidly developing subject without help from many people. All of us have had contact with a variety of experienced and talented people whose work and thinking has influenced the shape and content of this book. Sincere thanks are therefore due to everone who received our letters and phone calls, and to those who didn't, but whose writing has influenced our thought.

Amongst those who helped, four people deserve particular mention. John Franklin, an active member of the Cyclists' Touring Club, Don Perkins, a Divisional Planner with Milton Keynes Development Corporation, and Peter Trevelyan of Alastair Dick and Associates all spent many hours preparing invaluable comments on the original draft. Peter Trevelyan also gave a great deal of his practical experience on the evaluation and monitoring of bicycle facilities. Jack Sach of the Geelong Bike Plan also deserves sincere thanks for sending an endless stream of information, publications and photographs from Australia.

Special thanks are also due to the following whose photographs appear in this book; without your pictures the book would be dull indeed: John Aizlewood, Robert Bell, Bicycle Forum, The Bicycle Manufacturers Association of America, British Cycling Bureau, Eric Claxton, Cleveland County Council, Cornell University, Echte Nederlandse Fietsersbond, Friends of the Earth, Geelong Bike Plan, Lester Hillman, Rinus de Hilster, Adrian Hudson, Richard and Jean Hudson, the Japanese Bicycle Promotion Institute, Peter Knotley, Middlesbrough Borough Council, Milton Keynes Development Corporation, Park-a-Bike, W. R. Pashley Ltd, Pedley Equipment Company, Phil Portlock, T. I. Raleigh Industries, Rally Racks, The Royal Dutch Touring Club, City of Sheffield, Tilcon Group, Transport and Road Research Laboratory, Peter Treveleyan, Rob Van der Plas. We are also very grateful to Borin van Loon, who prepared the line drawings.

Credits are due to the many people who typed various sections of the draft and in particular to Monique Hayat who typed most of the final manuscript.

On a personal note, I would like to take this opportunity to record my deepest appreciation for the tremendous work put in by the co-authors, all of whom gave so much of their valuable time, enthusiasm and expertise to make this book possible. Particular credit is also due to their supporters/wives for putting up with 'the book' and many lost evenings and weekends.

The acknowledgments would be incomplete without giving special thanks to Maritz Vandenberg of The Architectural Press and to my wife Di. Without your enthusiasm, encouragement and support, this book would never have been published.

Mike Hudson *September 1981*

First published in 1982 by The Architectural Press Limited, 9 Queen Anne's Gate, London SW1H 9BY

ISBN: 0 85139 058 7

Set in 10pt VIP Plantin
Printed by Mackays of Chatham

Contents

Preface

During the last ten years the sale of bicycles has leapt dramatically in almost every developed country of the western world. In many, annual sales of bicycles now exceed those of cars. This renewed interest in the bicycle has been fuelled by unprecedented rises in the costs of all other forms of transport, increased demand for quick, reliable, door-to-door transport and the growing aspiration for health and fitness.

It has led to a rapid increase in the use of bicycles which has been particularly marked in urban areas. In London, for example, the use of bicycles is currently increasing by 20% a year.

Behind this shift in personal travel habits lie more fundamental changes. Ten years ago rapidly increasing affluence was the perceived future. Economic growth was accelerating and government activity was expanding at an uprecedented rate. Wholesale redevelopment of rundown urban areas, the construction of new motorways and shopping centres and the separation of industrial, residential and shopping areas were all priorities. Local planning departments were growing rapidly to cope with the work.

Today, relative austerity is the perceived future. Reduced economic growth, the ravages of inflation, and the social and environmental costs of the more extravagant developments of the 70s have combined together to create a new set of priorities. Rehabilitation, energy conservation, more equitable and less disruptive provision of transport and the improvement of the environment are now the priorities in many countries.

These new priorities are likely to remain on the political agenda for many years to come. If western economies begin to grow rapidly again, developments are likely to be more sensitive to social and environmental concerns; and if they do not grow, the priorities of austerity will remain. In short, whether the western economies become rich or poor, the new priorities are relatively permanent, and they have created a context in which the bicycle can play an increasingly important role. However, the art and science of planning for cyclists is still relatively new. Many people involved with the subject, and, more importantly, those who are not even aware of it, currently do not have access to the ideas and information which have been gathered around the world. As a result the confidence of decision-makers is lacking, and much valuable work goes unnoticed. In some cases, time and money are wasted on taking inappropriate measures for cyclists.

This international guide to bicycle planning is designed to draw together the experiences of many countries. To prepare it we have variously travelled to Holland, Germany, France and America, and have studied reports from practically every country which has made attempts to accommodate or encourage cycling. The differences between them are immense. Some countries have always given cyclists greater consideration, whilst others practically forget that they exist; in some, people cycle mainly for recreation, in others, mainly for utilitarian journeys; some have a history of mixing cyclists and pedestrians and in others it is almost forbidden. These differences between countries are complicated by the wide spectrum of strongly held views within each country. The subject of 'what to do about cycling' raises issues on which everyone has an opinion!

Our brief was to write a practical manual and not an academic thesis which compares and contrasts the differences between countries and individuals. To meet this objective we have often had to condense a great deal of material into a few short paragraphs. It is inevitable that measures tried in one country will not necessarily be appropriate in another. This book should therefore be treated firstly as a menu, from which ideas can be picked, and secondly as a guide to the ways in which the various ideas chosen can be woven together to create practical policies and proposals for the development of bicycle travel. It should not, however, be used as an alternative to government regulations and advice.

Writing this book has strengthened our conviction that the bicycle has the potential to play a significant role in the future of urban transport. Our hope is that it inspires you to play a part in the increasingly important task of making cycling safe and attractive.

Definitions of key words

This section is designed to guide readers through the jargon which we have been unable to avoid. The descriptions given are not legal definitions, and some are not widely accepted definitions, since these do not always exist. They are, however, clear descriptions of the meanings of the words as they have been used in this book.

Where a word used in the UK has an approximate equivalent in the USA, this has been put in brackets after the UK term.

Advisory cycle route (Bike route). A highway cyclists are advised to use, which is also used by motor vehicles. Advisory cycle routes are often created on residential roads with low motor vehicle flows (see section 6.2.1).

Bicycle. The term bicycle technically refers to a machine which has two wheels; the term cycle refers to a machine which has any number of wheels and therefore includes tricycles. In this book we have used the word bicycle to mean bicycle, tricycle or any other vehicle powered by the the legs of the rider.

Bicycle facilities. Any facility provided with the intention of assisting cyclists. The term includes cycle routes, bicycle parking facilities, provisions for bicycles on public transport services and other physical constructions designed to assist cyclists.

Bicycle network. A network of routes for cyclists which provides safe, continuous and convenient travel throughout a specified area. The term includes separate routes for cyclists, cycle-pedestrian tracks and those parts of the existing street system which meet a specified set of criteria (see section 3.5.1).

Bicycle parking facilities. Any facility provided for parking bicycles. This generic term includes bicycle lockers, storage areas, stands and racks (see Chapter 9).

Bicycle parking racks. Bicycle parking facilities which grip one wheel of the bicycle. This is the traditional parking facility.

Bicycle parking stands. Bicycle parking facilities which grip one wheel or the frame of the bicycle, but do not completly enclose it.

Bike rodeo. An event at which games and competitions on bicycles are organised.

Carriageway (Roadway). That part of the highway over which the public have a right of way in or on vehicles (see section 13.1 for the legal definition).

Carriageway markings (Pavement markings). Signs, instructions or delineation markings painted on the surface of the highway.

Casualty. A person who is injured or killed in an accident (and whose accident is reported to the police).

Contra-flow cycle lane. A lane in the carriageway of a one-way street for the sole use of bicycles travelling in the opposite direction to all other vehicles.

Cost-effective. A proposal is cost-effective if its implementation enables economic, social and environmental objectives to be met at an acceptable cost.

Cost-efficient. A proposal is cost-efficient if its implementation enables selected economic objectives to be met at the lowest cost (ie, if it produces the highest rate of economic return).

Cycle. See 'Bicycle'.

Cycle lane (Bike lane). A section of the carriageway (roadway) marked for use by cyclists only.

Cycle/car parking lane. A lane in the carriageway designaged specifically for travel by bicycle and the parking of cars.

Cycle-pedestrian track. A route for cyclists and pedestrians only.

Cycle route (Bikeway). A generic term for any route used by cyclists. It is often understood to mean routes for cyclists only and cycle-pedestrian routes. We have adopted a wider definition of the term to incorporate all routes used by cyclists including routes formed from parts of the existing street system.

Cycle track. A route designated for use by cyclists only. Cycle tracks can either run beside an existing carriageway or be completly independent of the carriageway.

Cycleway (Bike path). A cycle track which is independent of an existing carriageway.

Cycling corridor. A street or band of streets on which there are significant flows of cyclists.

Desire line. A straight line drawn on a map between two points to indicate a desire for a journey to be made between those two points. Desire line diagrams are used to summarize the desires for movement between specified zones, the lines between identical zones being grouped together so that the composite width of a group of lines is in proportion to the total number of desired movements.

Footpath. A highway not beside a carriageway over which the public have a right of way on foot only.

Footway (Sidewalk). A path for pedestrians beside the carriageway (commonly known in the UK as the pavement).

Freeway. A restricted access highway (often known as a motorway in the UK) usually excluding bicycles, mopeds, pedestrians and other catagories of people and vehicles.

Highway. A route over which the public have a right of way in motor vehicles, on bicycles, on animals and on foot. Where an all-purpose road is provided, the term includes the carriageway, the footway (sidewalk) and cycle tracks which run beside the carriageway. Footpaths and cycleways are also highways. (See 13.1.3 for UK legal definition and 13.2.2 for US legal definition).

Highway authority. A body which has legal responsibility for the construction and maintenance of certain highways. In the UK the Department of Transport is the highway authority for trunk roads and County Councils are the highway authority for non-trunk roads.

Island. A construction or marking on the carriageway used to separate opposing flows of vehicles.

Island refuge. An area in the middle of the carriageway protected physically, or by carriageway markings, and designed to assist cyclists crossing wide or busy roads.

Linking elements. Parts of a bicycle network which are specifically designed either to link different routes together (eg, a bridge) or which link routes used by cyclists with routes used by other modes of transport.

Local authority. This term has been used to describe any form of local government, including municipalities, county councils, district councils, etc. It also includes state government where appropriate.

Mode of transport. A means of transport. The term includes walking, cycling and the use of cars and public transport.

Moped. The UK definition is a motor cycle with a maximum design speed not exceeding 30 mph and a kerbside weight of less than 250 kg and an engine of under 50 cc capacity (see section 13.1.3 'Definitions').

Motor vehicle. Any vehicle powered by a motor. The term does not include bicycles and should not be confused with the term 'vehicle', which does include bicycles.

Multi-modal trip. A trip which is made by two or more modes of transport.

Origin/destination survey. A survey designed to ascertain the origins and destinations of journeys (see section 4.5 'Collecting local data on bicycle use').

Peak period. The period of the day during which the most traffic flows on a road. It is normally taken to be one hour and occurs on most roads either between 7.30 am and 9.30 am or between 4.30 pm and 6.30 pm.

Provisions for cyclists. This term includes all the measures which can be taken to improve cycling conditions, including route improvements, special bicycle facilities, education programmes, route map publication, etc.

Recreational trip. A trip which has no particular destination.

Residential precinct. A residential area in which the residential functions clearly predominate over provisions for motor vehicles. The design and layout of streets converted into residential precincts express the fact that motor vehicles are subordinate to pedestrians.

Road. The term is generally synonomous with the term highway. In the UK its legal definition also includes other roads to which the public has access (eg, hotel driveways – see section 13.1.3 'Definitions').

Road user. A person who uses a road. Note that the term includes pedestrians.

Roadway. See 'Carriageway'.

Screen line. An imaginary line drawn across part of a traffic study area, across which the total number of movements of any particular kind are determined, in order to check the estimated traffic flows across the same line.

Segregated cycle route. A route on which cyclists are segregated from all other modes of transport. Segregation can take various forms including physical barriers and carriageway markings.

Sight line. An imaginary line drawn from the eyes of a road user to a point which obstructs his/her vision in a direction which requires clear vision.

Sight stopping distance. The distance necessary for a cyclist to stop safely after visually perceiving a condition or object.

Squeeze point. A location on a busy road where the carriageway suddenly narrows causing cyclists to move into the path of motor vehicles. Squeeze points are created by, among other things, bridges over roads, central islands and poor road layouts.

Traffic management. The promotion of a more efficient movement of traffic within a given street system by re-directing the flows of traffic, controlling the intersections and regulating the times and places of parking.

Traffic Regulation Order. In the UK, this is the legal authority used by a highway authority for authorizing one or more traffic management measures. The measures are specified in the order and the process for introducing the order is specified in the Road Traffic Regulation Act 1967 (see section13.1.6 'Traffic Regulation Orders').

Trip. A journey made between two points for one or more purposes.

Trip attractor. A location at which trips finish (eg, place of work, school, etc).

Trip generation. The trips which are made on a route as a direct result of the provision or improvement of that route. Note that this is not the standard definition of trip generation used in traffic modelling.

Trip generator. A location from which a trip starts.

Trip stage. Part of a trip made by one mode. For example a commuter who cycles to the station and takes the train to work has made one trip in two trip stages.

Utilitarian trip. A trip made for a specific purpose.

1 Introduction

If the bicycle is defined as a two-wheeled machine capable of being steered, then the first patent on a bicycle was granted in Paris in 1818. Called a hobby (or dandy) horse and powered by riders pushing their feet along the ground, this machine caused a sensation wherever it went. It was capable of travelling at a speed of 16 kph (the maximum speed of a stage coach at the time) and achieved some remarkable feats, amongst others, beating a stage coach from London to Brighton by more than half an hour.

The potential of the hobby horse as a means of transport was quickly recognised:

> *Clergymen used the new machine to visit their parishioners, and to travel between scattered congregations. Postmen with their letter bags sailing in the wind rode the dandy horse; young swells of the period used it, not only for exercise but for the purpose of making calls.*
>
> (*The Velocipede*, 1869)

However, the principle of pushing had its limitations and soon became dated when the first two-wheeled machine which could be pedalled was patented in 1866. The results of this development were dramatic; almost overnight the velocipede became a craze and a huge social phenomenon in England, France and the USA.

The invention was timely, coming during a period of unparalleled social change which was fuelled by the industrial revolution and the development of the railways. People needed a means of transport for local journeys and the velocipede fulfilled this need for twenty-four years until 1880, when Humber produced the first diamond frame safety bicycle. This was the true forerunner of the modern bicycle incorporating most of the features used today.

The impact of these new machines first began to be felt when mass production techniques made them widely available. Houses for workers no longer needed to be built beside the factories, people could travel out of towns into the countryside and those who could not afford to travel by train had an independent means of transport. The use of bicycles flourished and by 1899 the Cyclists' Touring Club in Britain had over 60,000 members (the largest number it has ever had). Bicycles rapidly became established as an essential part of urban and rural life. They were used for many purposes including the transport of soldiers in the First World War, the carriage and delivery of goods, for vending ice creams at holiday resorts, by police and other public services, and, most importantly, as an accepted means of daily transport.

The bicycle remained a significant means of transport until the early 1950s. However, since then usage has declined dramatically in many countries of the world. The major cause of this dramatic decline was undoubtedly the increasingly widespread use of the private motor car. Faster, capable of carrying greater loads and more prestigious, its influence grew rapidly. Roads were improved and, as journey times decreased, people began to travel further and more often, so generating the need for new roads. Mass production brought down prices and made cars available to a wider section of the community, dual carriageways were built to satisfy the demand for road space and when these could no longer cope, the concept of the special way for motorised vehicles was created – the motorway or freeway.

As cars became faster and more numerous they posed increasing threats to cyclists. This was compounded by road systems which were designed primarily for motor vehicles with little consideration being given to the needs of cyclists. Faced with these problems many cyclists gave up and became motorists, adding further to the problem. By the 1960s all the indications suggested that the bicycle was at the end of its life and that nothing should be done to make cycling safer because there would eventually be no cyclists left on the roads.

Nothing could in fact have been further from the truth. The revival which began in the early 1970s has been fuelled by rapid rises in the real cost of transport and a new awareness of the importance of personal health. However, as new cyclists took to the roads it soon became clear that thirty years of planning for motor vehicles had resulted in a road network which just did not cater for the humble bicycle.

Today, cyclists have to face a frightening range of actual and perceived dangers on the road. The fact that cyclists in many countries have organised themselves into a new and more militant breed of action groups indicates the magnitude of the problem and the strength of cyclists' feelings.

The first attempts to tackle these problems had in fact been made many years earlier in the 1930s when cycle tracks had been built alongside the new dual-carriageways. However, these early tracks were much disliked by cyclists in many countries because they were frequently broken by driveways and service roads, they were seldom maintained to the same standard as the roads and, most importantly, they put cyclists back onto the road system just where the dangers are greatest – at road junctions.

Some of the early responses to the 1970s' bicycle revival were embodied in proposals for the creation of systems of separate routes for cyclists. Such an approach was wholly appropriate in new development areas and a number of notable segregated networks of cycle-pedestrian facilities have been created. However, it was considerably more difficult to implement in existing urban areas, particularly in conurbations, where the pressure for space was greatest. But it was in just such areas that the growth in cycling was greatest.

By the mid 1970s the limitations of the segregated facilities approach began to emerge in the USA and Australia. Education of cyclists then became an important issue. The problem should be tackled, it was thought, by teaching cyclists and motorists to improve their road behaviour so that the street system could be shared more safely. However, towards the end of the 1970s the limitations of this approach, and in particular the short-lived effects of such education, became apparent.

As bicycle use continued to increase at the end of the decade, it became clear that a realistic basis for planning the future of the bicycle was required. With the hindsight of the successful and unsuccessful experiments of the 1970s, an integrated approach to planning for cyclists began to emerge. Such an approach recognises that each of the solutions previously advocated (special facilities, education and use of the existing road network) has a role to play, but that none is sufficient on its own to create a safe and attractive cycling environment.

There are two prerequisites to the successful application of the integrated approach. The first is that the activities and skills of different professions can be brought together to develop plans and proposals which make realistic use of the resources available. The second is that there is the political will to grasp the opportunities which are available. The proposals set out in this book are remarkably cheap compared with other aspects of transport planning. But they do nevertheless require a small change in the priorities for expenditure. Without such a change, the ideas and examples presented will be no more than fantasies tried in a few places in the world; with it, they could quickly become part of the accepted infrastructure and behaviour of modern society.

WHY PLAN FOR CYCLISTS?

It is a cheap way of providing mobility
Cost effectiveness is an important criterion for determining the priorities for investment. Money spent on removing the constraints on cycling can significantly increase the availability of transport for a large section of the community. The provision of routes for bicycles gives people 'freeways' for the price of footpaths.

It makes efficient use of space
In congested urban areas, space is a valuable resource. Bicycles take up little space when moving; the capacity of a road is increased approximately ten times if bicycles are used instead of cars. Futhermore, bicycle parking does not rank in the same class as car parking; between 10–15 bikes can be parked in one car parking space.

It contributes to energy conservation
Energy conservation is now a priority in most countries. The American Department of Transportation has adopted policy measures designed to increase the use of bicycles for commuting from 900,000 per day in 1979 to 1.5–2.5 million by 1985, giving an annual saving of 16–25 million barrels of oil.

It keeps people fit and healthy
Regular cycling reduces body weight, reduces heart disease, lessens tension, improves sleep and therefore reduces the cost of health services. It has also been shown to increase people's efficiency at work.

It is an equitable means of transport
More people can afford the running costs of a bicycle than any other means of transport and the capital cost is less than a week's wages in most developed countries. The bicycle is a simple piece of machinery to understand and maintain, and thus gives people greater control over their lives.

It can cut death and injury on the roads
The annual toll of deaths and injuries to cyclists is appalling. Many are killed and injured through no fault of their own. Cheap and well tried measures can be used to save lives and injuries.

It is a quick means of transport
Door to door travel times for urban journeys between 4 and 6 kilometres (the vast majority of urban journeys) can be quicker by bicycle than any other means of transport

It is a reliable means of transport
Bicycles are less likely to break down than other means of transport and are unhindered by traffic jams.

It provides mobility to practically everyone
Many of the old, the young and people from the other minority groups who will never be able to use cars, can ride bicycles.

It is a benign means of transport
The bicycle is noiseless, pollution-free and does not significantly encroach upon other people's lives.

2 Urban transport planning and the bicycle

This chapter is designed to put planning for cyclists into the context of urban transport planning, where it ultimately belongs if cycling is to become a widely acceptable way of travelling.

While transport planning to date has played a leading role in revolutionizing personal mobility, it has done so for certain groups of people only and increasingly at the expense of a desirable quality of urban life, both social and environmental. The identification of the reasons for this by many urban transport planners and engineers, has led to a re-evaluation of the goals and the techniques of the discipline. Four points stand out as being important. Firstly, an underlying emphasis on increasing personal mobility rather than accessibility dominated the goals and objectives. Secondly, this emphasis on personal mobility was embodied largely in a concern for one mode of transport, the private car, with a high proportion of transport expertise and funding being channelled into provision for it. Thirdly, the close relationship between transport planning and land-use patterns was not fully appreciated. Fourthly, since 1973–4, the rapid rise in the cost of energy has added a new dimension to urban transport planning.

The fortunes of the bicycle as a serious mode of transport were directly linked to these developments. However, with the recognition of the need for wider economic, social and environmental goals and for a more integrated approach to urban transport planning, a positive framework now exists, within which cycling can be developed as an important mode of urban movement.

2.1 THE FUNDAMENTAL PRINCIPLES OF PLANNING FOR CYCLISTS

Systematic planning for cyclists has only really emerged in the UK, North America and Australasia over the past ten years. The actions taken have varied from the development of education and publicity programmes to the complete segregation of cycle traffic epitomised in demonstration routes in Tilburg and The Hague, Holland.

From the problems and experience of planning for cyclists to date, six principles have emerged as fundamental to the success of any venture:

- Since bicycle journeys are made on general purpose roads and can be combined with bus and railway journeys, it is crucial that plans to improve cycling conditions are integrated into all transport plans.

2.1 The segregation of all modes of transport (Tilburg, Holland)

- A prerequisite for integrated bicycle planning is the support of an appropriate administrative framework. Such a framework must allow for co-ordination between government departments, between different levels of governments, and between planners and public interest groups concerned with cycling.
- The aim of planning for cyclists is not a product, eg a cycle track, but safe and efficient travel by bicycle. The implication of this is that, given the cost and space constraints in most urban areas, and the trade-offs between modes which must occur in integrated urban traffic management, the provisions will generally require both the use of the existing transport infrastucture and the construction of special facilities for cyclists.
- The co-existence of cyclists and drivers on the roads requires that both are sensitive to and recognise a common set of rules. Thus, schemes for training, education and enforcement are as important as physical planning and design (fig 2.2).
- The maintenance of bicycle facilities and the monitoring and assessment of their performance must ensure continuing safe and efficient travel for cyclists. Planning for cyclists is an on-going process.
- A 'bicycle perspective' must permeate any planning for

2.2 Enforcement is an important consideration in the design of routes for cyclists

cyclists. The bicycle has its own characteristics, its own set of constraints and opportunities which planners must consider. Moreover, this must be supplemented with the recognition that cyclists do not form a homogenous group, but are people of a very wide range of age, cycling ability, experience and traffic judgment, and who are cycling for a variety of different purposes.

2.2 PLANNING FOR CYCLISTS WITHIN THE EXISTING INFRASTRUCTURE

The existing urban infrastructure reflects the interaction of many forces, both planned and unplanned. This section identifies important infrastructure constraints and opportunities which will affect planning for cyclists, and looks at the possible impact of increased cycling on other modes.

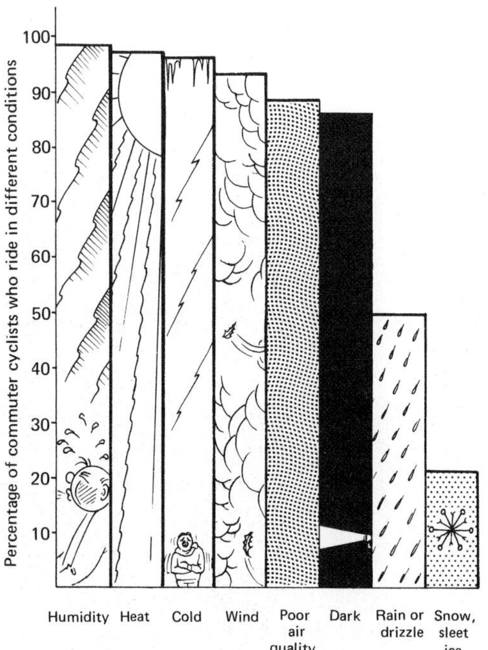

2.3 The effect of weather on commuter cycling (Source: *Washington DC Regional Bikeway Study*)

2.4 In many Chinese cities bicycles are an important mode of transport, due in part to the proximity of land-uses (Shenyang, China)

2.2.1 Physical constraints

The natural constraints of climate and especially topography, play an important role in moulding the patterns of an existing urban infrastructure. Cycling is particularly sensitive to these influences, and where neither are conducive to travelling by bicycle, provision for cyclists is unlikely to be a planning priority. However, two factors must be kept in mind.

Firstly, hilly topography will be less significant for younger and fitter cyclists and for cyclists undertaking work rather than recreational trips. Thus, the characteristics and distribution of both population and topographical conditions may indicate that, despite low use, there is a potential for cycling which could be realised.

Secondly, climatic conditions will affect both the level and frequency of cycle use through the year. In Sweden, despite low cycling levels during the severe winters, and daily fluctuations of up to 50% due to variable weather, 20 to 30% of adults and 90% of children cycle during the summer months. The cost of facilities is justified despite daily and annually fluctuating levels. Furthermore, cycle routes can be located so that the built and natural environment provide maximum protection from wind and rain.

Built constraints in the existing urban infrastructure also affect bicycle planning. As the separation of land-uses became a favoured planning objective, supported by a style of transport planning which encouraged the dispersion of city growth, so the distance between many activities increased beyond cycling range. In addition, planning for other modes without consideration for cyclists has resulted in a transport infrastructure which contains many deterrents to cyclists. Both of these factors have the effect of suppressing bicycle use. This has two implications for bicycle planning.

Firstly, the role of the bicycle in current travel patterns, indicated by the modal split, is often not a true indicator of the potential for bicycle use, and it would be a misleading basis on which to assess the need for facilities for cyclists. Secondly, town planning, transport planning and planning for cyclists are closely interrelated, and although it is not possible to produce rapid changes in urban structure, policies which encourage cycling today could show significant results in the long term.

2.2.2 Multi-modal travel

The bicycle is traditionally regarded as a short trip mode. However, its potential is greatly increased if proper links are provided with public transport services. The bicycle provides greater accessibility at either end of the journey and public transport provides greater speed over the length of the journey. Links with public transport include bicycle storage and hiring facilities at bus and railway stations and carrying facilities for bicycles on buses and trains. Providing for easy bicycle access to or from the train or bus should be an integral part of an overall plan for cycling.

'Bike and ride' schemes are operating in various forms in many countries. In Holland, hiring and storage facilities can be found at major railway stations throughout the country with reduced hiring charges available to train users. British Rail permits the free carriage of bicycles outside peak hours on all trains except the new high speed trains, on which bicycles have been prohibited. The US city of San Diego, California, started carrying bicycles on buses because of bicycle access problems across a bridge designed for high speed vehicular traffic. Buses on certain routes now have racks for five bicycles on the back with unloading stops approximately every four miles. No charge, other than the normal fare, is levied. A similar scheme is now operating in Seattle, Washington.

2.2.3 The impact of increased cycling on other modes

The desirable impact of increased cycling on other modes would be to reduce car-use for short distance trips, and by extending the range of the bicycle through multi-modal travel, to reduce the use of the car for long distance trips. The degree of the impact will depend on such factors as the size and structure of the urban area, the level of car and bicycle ownership and the level of public transport services. It has been shown that increasing the number of cyclists by improving the street system can be achieved at the expense of the car (fig 2.6).

The fear is often expressed that over short distances, the bicycle becomes a competitor with public transport. However, in the context of positive multi-modal travel planning, the promotion of cycling can enhance public transport services. For example, given a limit of ten minutes cycling to a bus or train stop, the potential capture area from that stop can be expanded from 2km² to 32km² (fig 2.7). The potential increase in users of the combination of bicycle and public transport from this enlarged capture area depends on the population density and the level of bicycle use within it, but the boost to public transport from such co-ordinated planning is potentially enormous.

City	Percentage change in	
	Bicycle usage	Automobile usage
Västeras	+30	−20
Malmö	+25	−15
Uppsala	+17	n.a.
Göteborg	+15	−10

2.6 Percentage changes in automobile and bicycle use following traffic measures in favour of cycling in Swedish towns (Source: *Pedestrians and Cyclists*, OECD, 1979)

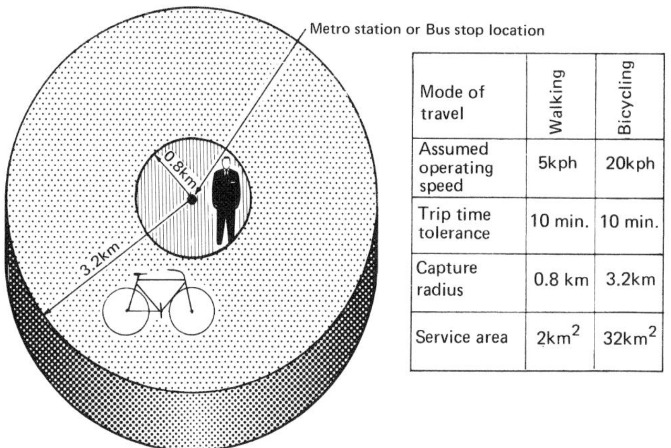

2.7 The use of bicycles significantly increases the catchment area for public transport

2.5 An example of multi-modal travel. Parking facilities at Delft railway station

2.8 Special bicycle facilities on the Demonstration route in The Hague, Holland

2.9 Delft is an outstanding example of local authority innovation and expertise in the provision of facilities for cyclists

2.3 GOVERNMENT POLICIES

Some governments have taken steps towards accommodating the cyclist in transport plans. This section looks at how governments can promote cycling in transport policies, and briefly examines the way some governments have done so.

2.3.1 Roles of central governments

> *If funding is the key to implementing bicycle transportation program, then the full integration of bicycling into all governmental planning processes is the key to initiating and sustaining them.*
>
> (*Bicycle Transportation for Energy Conservation*, 1980)

The establishment of a framework within which planning for cyclists can be integrated into 'all governmental planning processes' is the major task of a central government. Such a framework should include:

- A clear definition of the responsibilities and of the mechanism for co-operation between different government departments whose actions need to be co-ordinated.
- A clear division of responsibilities and mechanisms for co-operation between national, regional and local governments.
- Mechanisms for considering public interest groups and other organisations in the planning process, particularly at the local level. In addition to these, it may be necessary to set up other administrative mechanisms which will ensure the integration of bicycle programmes in the local, city and/or regional plans of the area.

Within this context, central government can actively pursue two roles. On the one hand, it can act as 'facilitator', providing the legal, financial and administrative framework and mechanisms to support developments at the local level, by the public and private sectors. For example, a centralised research and information unit on bicycles and bicycle planning would probably best be co-ordinated by a central government agency. On the other hand, central government can also act as 'direct intervenor', assuming responsibility for selected projects. The underlying motivation for this role would be for demonstration and experimental purposes.

Whatever the policy pursued, it is quite clear that central governments cannot merely endorse the bicycle and at the same time expect it to become a serious mode of urban transport.

2.3.2 The framework set by different governments

Three countries have been selected to illustrate different policies adopted by governments concerned with the provision of facilities for cyclists.

Holland

One of the earliest and boldest moves taken by a government was that of the Dutch Government in 1975. In that year, the Multi-Year Plan for Passenger Transport was passed, making provision for the Ministry of Transport to plan, implement and monitor two 'demonstration projects' for cyclists, located in The Hague and Tilburg. The projects would demonstrate the provision of special cycling facilities constructed to high standards in two different urban contexts. It was hoped that this would encourage local authorities to provide more and better facilities in their areas. Moreover, the projects would be 'experimental' and would test various propositions about the design and impact of cycling facilities with a series of before and after studies. Both the schemes are complete, and the first reports are available. There is little doubt that the experience gained from these projects is an invaluable contribution to all countries interested in promoting cycling. However, some of the limitations of the role of central government as 'direct intervenor' became apparent. In particular, difficulties were experienced with the participation of various public interest groups, for example local shopkeepers.

As a traditional cycling society, a framework for the provision of facilities for cyclists existed in Holland prior to 1975. This emphasised the provision of bicycle facilities by local authorities with central government in the role of 'facilitator'. In support of this, thc Multi-Year Plan for Public Transport 1975 also increased state subsidies for bicycle facilities to local authorities from 50 to 80%. The provision for cyclists on this basis is widespread in Holland, with a town like Delft providing an outstanding example of local authority innovation and expertise.

Another aspect of Dutch policy which highlights the potential for integrated planning is the residential precinct. After six years of experiment, in 1976 the Dutch Ministry of Transport made legal provision for a set of design rules and traffic regulations for the construction of residential precincts. This technique is applied mainly to residential streets, which are redesigned in such a way that the residential function of the street clearly predominates over the traffic function. (For more details of this technique see section 6.2.1 'Advisory cycle routes'.)

The UK

Until 1977, the perceived dangers of cycling led the UK Department of Transport to take a neutral stance on cycling as a serious mode of urban transport. In 1976, a government consultation document of transport policy made little attempt to encourage provisions for cyclists: 'real encouragement of [bicycle] use for journeys to work in crowded city centres would need to be accompanied by extensive and sometimes costly segregation measures' (Para 11.3). However, following considerable pressure from cycling organisations, the transport policy document which emerged from the consultation was more encouraging: 'There is scope for many more practical initiatives and for local authorities, generally to take account of both pedestrian and cycle schemes which have been shown to be successful' (Para 129).

To date, the strongest feature of UK government action on bicycles has been the co-ordination of research and information on bicycle planning and the provision of a small amount of money for selected experimental elements in bicycle schemes. These experimental facilities have been monitored by the Transport and Road Research Laboratory. The information function has included the publication of government advice on the provision of bicycle facilities – *Ways of Helping Cyclists in Built-Up Areas* – and a supplementary film *Freewheeling*, which bring together some information on the planning and design of bicycle facilities. In 1981 the government published a consultation document of cycling which set out some issues about bicycle planning and sought the views of interested parties on questions relating to government policy. However, much has still to be done before the UK government even fully embraces the role of 'facilitator'.

'BICYCLE TRANSPORTATION FOR ENERGY CONSERVATION'

This report was required by the National Energy Conservation Policy Act of 1978, the relevant section of which reads as follows:
'(a) The Congress recognizes that bicycles are the most efficient means of transportation, represent a viable commuting alternative to many people, offer mobility at speeds as fast as that of cars in urban areas, provide health benefits through daily exercise, reduce noise and air pollution, are relatively inexpensive, and deserve consideration in a comprehensive national energy plan.'
'(b) Not more than one year after the date of enactment of the Act, the Secretary of Transportation shall complete a study of the energy conservation of potential bicycle transportation, determine institutional, legal, physical and personal obstacles to increased bicycle use, establish a target for bicycle use in commuting, and develop a comprehensive program to meet these goals. In developing the program, consideration should be given to educational programs, federal demonstrations, planning grants, and construction grants. The Secretary of Transportation shall submit a report to the President and to Congress containing the results of such a study'.

The USA
The early response of the Federal Highway Administration to the growth of cycling at the beginning of the 1970s had two components. Firstly, the FHWA drew together available information on planning and design practices which had evolved at the state level in a publication entitled *Bikeways – State of the Art, 1974*. Linked to this study was a research project designed to improve the quality and consistency of bicycle facility planning which resulted in the publication *Safety and Locational Criteria for Bicycle Facilities*. Attention in the early days was focused closely on the provision of segregated routes for cyclists.

2.10 In Stevenage, UK, the cycle routes were built alongside roads to benefit from incidental funding

The second aspect of FHWA policy was the Bikeway Demonstration Program, which provided 80% federal funding for constructing bicycle facilities in urban areas. The programme generated ideas for 495 construction projects from 50 states, at an estimated cost of $141 million. In the end, 41 projects were selected for the $6 million of federal funds appropriated for the programme. An important criterion for making the grants was the proposed evaluation of the feature being funded.

At state level, Oregon and California can be singled out as leaders in this field, with the towns of Eugene and Davis implementing wide-ranging bicycle programmes. Major studies of cycling were also undertaken in Washington DC and in New York City.

More recently the main contribution of federal government has been financial. Section 141(c) of the Surface Transportation Assistance Act of 1978 provided federal funds to state and local governments for projects enhancing the use of bicycles. In 1980, the US Secretary of Transportation published one of the most impressive statements of government policy for cycling, which is also a fine example of central government acting as 'facilitator'. Developed in response to the requirements of the National Energy Conservation Act of 1978, *Bicycle Transportion for Energy Conservation* includes a 'Comprehensive Bicycle Transportation Program'. At the same time, the Department of Transportation also issued a detailed note on the implementation of the bicycle grant programme authorized by the 1978 Surface Transportation Assistance Act. However, there have been problems with the appropriation of funds for bicycle provisions.

It is as yet too early to judge its performance, but this comprehensive policy statement sets up a sound framework for the development of the bicycle as an urban commuting mode in the USA. This has recently been complemented by the publication of a draft document entitled *Design and Construction Criteria for Bikeway Construction Projects* which draws together experience to date to form the basis for future government advice.

2.4 TRANSPORT BUDGETS AND FINANCE FOR BICYCLE PLANS

The test of government policies promoting cycling is the availability of funds. This section looks at the methods of funding which have been used in various countries, and the lessons that can be learned from them.

2.4.1 Sources of finance

1. The most usual method is direct subsidy from central to local governments specifically for the provision of bicycle facilities. The size of subsidies differs from country to country, as do the conditions for the type of bicycle facilities that qualify for funding. In the USA the federal government will give a 75% subsidy to states for 'independent' bicycle projects (ie, a bicycle scheme independent of an on-going highway project). In 1971, in the state of Oregon, legislation was passed to authorize that not less than 1% of monies received from the State Highway Fund by the State Transport Commissions, or by any city or county, was to be spent on bicycle facilities, so ensuring the continuity of the bicycle programme in the state. In the UK, the Department of Transport will contribute to the cost of selected 'experimental' or 'innovatory' schemes submitted to local authorities. Local authorities can also obtain subsidies for bicycle facilities through the Transport Supplementary Grant (TSG). Each year, local authorities submit a Transport Policies Programme (TPP) to the Department of Transport outlining their expenditure over the next 5 years on transport proposals, which can include bicycle facilities. Any expenditure agreed to by the Department which exceeds a certain threshold (based on the population in the local authority area) qualifies for a 70% TSG.

2. Central government may assume responsibility for the entire funding of a bicycle scheme entitling it to exercise full control over all aspects of the scheme. The 'demonstration route' projects in Holland are examples of this; as was the case in this instance, central governments usually undertake such ventures when it considers the objectives of the scheme to be beyond the scope of local authority responsibility.

3. A significant channel of funding is that for 'incidental' bicycle facilities, built as part of improvement schemes for other transport modes, for example motor vehicles or pedestrians. In Stevenage, UK, a new town with a classic example of a segregated bicycle network on a town scale, cycle routes were built alongside main roads to benefit from such 'incidental' funding.

The disadvantage of this type of funding is that it dictates the location of bicycle facilities. On the other hand, if the bicycle is included in the terms of reference of funding for other transport proposals, this could force consideration of the bicycle during planning for other modes.

4. Government can provide financial incentives to private organisations or firms to encourage them to contribute to or provide facilities for the development of cycling. In most countries this source of funding is largely untapped. For example, private firms could do much to encourage bicycle commuting among their staff by providing secure parking and simple showering facilities. In 1979, in Bristol, UK, a local cycle group, Cyclebag, subsidized the construction of a cycle track with their own labour. With planning permission from the local authority and materials acquired at specially low prices from private suppliers, they built a cycle track along a disused railway line, linking two urban areas in the Bristol region. However, to ensure the most efficient use of private sector resources in this way, responsibility for the co-ordination of such undertakings with other planning rests with the public sector.

5. Certain government agencies may offer funding for the development of cycling for reasons not directly related to cycling itself. For example, in the USA the Public Works Impact Program, run under the auspices of the Department of Commerce, have funded bicycle projects in areas of high unemployment (8½% and over) to create employment opportunities, while at the same time providing something of public benefit. In Middlesbrough, UK, cycle routes were constructed as part of a Job Creation Project, with the Manpower Services Commission providing 20% of the total cost. Also in the UK, one cyclists' group raised money from the Selective Temporary Employment Programme to employ people to develop publicity materials for safety education.

6. Separate grant aid schemes are usually available from or through central government agencies for the 'non-construction' phases of a project, for example, research and monitoring.

In addition to grant aid schemes, a considerable proportion of the finance required for the development of cycling falls within existing budgetary systems. Although a proportion of such money is provided by central government, there is considerable flexibility in the way local authorities can spend it. Items such as road safety education, enforcement and publicity campaigns all fall within this area.

THE PRACTICALITIES OF OBTAINING FUNDS

The experience of Curtis Yates, Bicycle Co-ordinator for North Carolina's Department of Transportation:
'Obtaining resources became the most difficult problem and the most satisfying accomplishment. No state funds were given to the Bicycle Program except for salaries and minor administration. We had to look elsewhere. That left federal and local funds, volunteer work and those little overheads items to be found in state agencies if searched out. Each of these was used to the fullest, with the majority of hard dollars coming from Highway Safety grants.'
'It is easy to become discouraged in a program where no funding is directly obtainable; however, there are many ways to accomplish a task. Persistence may be a program person's greatest resource.'

2.4.2 Accessibility to funding

It is immediately apparent from the description of the grant aid schemes available in different countries that access to many funding sources is subject to proposals meeting certain qualifying conditions or following certain procedures. This 'categorical' nature of much funding often excludes local authorities from financial support for the specific purpose and at the time it is required. The recognition of this led to two recommendations in the US bicycle programme which would be desirable trends in the funding policies of all governments:

1. Local authorities (as distinct from state governments) should be able to apply and receive funds directly.
2. 'Current Federal policy is to utilise broader purpose grant programs intended to achieve general program objectives, while allowing state and local governments substantial flexibility as to the choice of specific means to these ends' (*Bicycle transportation for Energy Conservation*, 1980).

2.4.3 Trade-offs against other modes

As long as the benefits of the bicycle go unrecognised, provision for cyclists will be a losing contender in the competition for public funding. A motivated central government has tools at its disposal to improve the funding 'odds' for the bicycle. For example, one of the proposals in the US is to increase the federal share of funding for eligible energy conservation projects, of which bicycle projects are one, from 75 to 90%. This makes the selection of bicycle projects financially more attractive than regular highway construction programmes. However, competition for funding is not always to blame. Even with a federal authorization for £2.5m per year to be spent on independent bicycle and pedestrian projects, including a 75% share of costs by federal government, less than 10% of this allowed limit has been used. Lack of awareness of cycling issues on the part of local authority officers or

2.11 There are also environmentally motivated action groups. In 1979, Friends of the Earth organised a National Bike Rally in London's Trafalgar Square

inadequate publicity of the scheme can be blamed for this. However, the situation is usually one of money shortage with funding being one of the major obstacles to the implementation of proposals.

2.5 POLITICAL ACCEPTABILITY

2.5.1 Prevailing attitudes

The prevailing attitudes towards cycling will be an important determinant of how to promote and present programmes for the development of cycling, and will give an indication of the likely support or opposition they will receive. In particular, the attitudes of local people being affected by the proposals and those of the decision makers to whom the proposals must be presented are crucial to gauge. Prevailing attitudes are influenced not only by the traditions, interests and experiences of people, but also by what the 'experts' have promoted. The head of the Traffic Department in Delft, Holland, a town in which many new town and transport planning practices were initiated, highlights this problem in the promotion of a bicycle scheme: 'So you better start without making much noise about it. Politics might not support you, when you go acting against things you propagated before', (*The Woonerf in City and Traffic Planning*, 1979).

2.5.2 The different lobbies

An essential part of coming to grips with prevailing attitudes is to identify the lobbies representing the different interest groups involved. In most countries in Europe, North America and Australia the following 'standing' lobbies in the bicycle arena can be identified, some of them exerting considerable influence:

- associations representing the bicycle manufacturers and traders
- traditional bicycle touring groups
- the newer, usually environmentally motivated local or national action groups, campaigning on behalf of cyclists
- organisations representing other modes particularly the private car and pedestrians
- road safety organisations, especially those promoting safety for school children.

In response to proposals, local lobbies will no doubt emerge, either as branches of established organisations or as local groups formed especially to promote or oppose the particular proposal. Experience in cities like The Hague in Holland and Portsmouth, UK, show that as well as the lobbies involving local residents, local shopkeepers can be a powerful force if they judge the proposal to have an effect on their turnover.

In the face of such diversity of interests, some blind to the views of others, a clear justification and means for evaluating the proposals is essential.

2.5.3 The justification of proposals

A proposal will often have to be justified in purely economic terms, usually in competition with proposals for other modes. However, in the context of expanded transport goals and integrated transport planning, cost efficient evaluation is no longer acceptable. An estimate of the cost effectiveness of the scheme in terms of economic, social and environmental objectives is now widely used. However, this technique is only as good as the assumptions made for its particular use, for example, assumptions about future bicycle use and patterns, and about the measures chosen to quantify social and environmental factors. This technique will be discussed in more detail in the next chapter as part of the planning process for evaluating proposals.

3 Planning a bicycle network

The planning process presented in this chapter is a generalised one. The concepts have evolved out of the experience of bicycle planning over the past 10 years in Europe, America and Australia. While it deals with the specific steps involved in planning a bicycle network, in practice the contents of the steps and their sequence will ultimately depend on:

- the broader planning context, which will govern procedures, define the role of planners, engineers and the public in the planning process, and more specifically, will reflect the current priorities of transport planning and the political acceptability of planning for cyclists
- the size and nature of the locality being considered for bicycle provision
- the resources available to do the job (ie manpower, money, time).

3.1 THE DEVELOPMENT OF PLANNING CONCEPTS

Bicycle schemes in Europe, the USA and Australia today reflect the changing attitudes of planners and engineers to the planning of facilities for cyclists. Three different approaches can be traced over time.

The first is the provision of a **segregated cycle route** linking one part of the city with another, and containing access points for cyclists along its length. As a provision which enables safe and efficient bicycle access throughout existing urban areas, this kind of approach clearly has its limitations. It is, of course, easiest to implement in New Towns and newly developing areas, where the concept has naturally been extended to the provision of an entire network of segregated routes.

The second concept is the **'software'** approach, developed in response to some of the limitations of the first. The aim is to build up a network of cycle routes on secondary roads, avoiding main roads wherever possible, and supported by a variety of traffic management techniques. The limitations of the approach lie in its very conception; redirecting cyclists to secondary roads means redirecting them off major arterials which are often the most direct and continuous routes to most desirable urban destinations. However, good planning will minimize the re-routeing, and in some urban areas this may be the only alternative.

The most recent approach has developed along with the changes in transport planning, (ie, the new emphasis on integration in planning). The **'integrated'** approach to bicycle planning aims to create a network of facilities made up of the existing road system and appropriately located special cycling facilities, both operating in the context of an overall traffic management scheme for the urban areas. Such

3.1. One approach to planning for cyclists – the provision of segregated cycle routes (Tilburg, Holland)

3.2 The software approach to bicycle planning. This shows the experimental scheme in Portsmouth which was withdrawn after six months

3.3 The integrated approach to bicycle planning. Provision for cyclists in Delft, Holland, using the existing street system

schemes have been created in Delft and Groningen in Holland.

Trends all point to the continuing validity of the 'integrated' approach. With the slowing down of economic growth and increasing pressure on public expenditure, future provision of facilities will have to be competitively cost-effective in terms of planning for other modes.

3.2 THE DEVELOPMENT OF GOALS, OBJECTIVES AND CRITERIA

The first stage of any planning process is the development of goals, objectives and criteria.

3.2.1 Goals and objectives

The formulation of clear goals and objectives for a bicycle programme is essential for two reasons. Firstly, they are an explicit guide to all parties concerned – planners, engineers and the public – of the direction and proposed achievements of the programme. Secondly, they are a basis for evaluating and measuring the performance of proposals, when deriving and considering alternative strategies, and when monitoring the success of the proposals which are implemented.

Goal formulation for a bicycle programme should ideally involve both planners, engineers, elected representatives in local government, and the citizens who will be affected by the programme. However, it must be kept in mind that the more people involved in this process, the more complex it becomes. Various approaches, which are not mutually exclusive, can be pursued:

- a public meeting can be called to launch the bicycle programme, and can be used both for publicity purposes and for gaining an idea of the range of concerns the community has about bicycle provisions in their area
- interest groups concerned with cycling can be approached to take part in a meeting to formulate goals for the programme
- a team of planners and engineers can formulate goals by reviewing bicycle-related statements by interested parties in both the public and private sector; a written report of the goals and objectives can then be circulated among these groups for comment.

DEFINITION OF TERMS

Goals are generalised statements of a desired end or direction.

Objectives are specific targets for the attainment of goals, and begin to suggest ways of assessing their performance.

Criteria are qualitative or quantitative measures of the level of performance, usually requiring technical expertise.

Standards are optimum levels of performance, and are useful when dealing with issues which are commonplace and well understood, and involve no major decision making. Standards are problematic when used in complex situations which involve the interrelationships of many variables as they obscure the costs and benefits of their application. Since most stages in the process for planning for cyclists are necessarily complex, because of the need for an integrated approach, the establishment and use of rigid standards for evaluation is not, in most cases, appropriate.

3.2.2 Criteria

Once the goals and objectives of the bicycle programme have been defined, planners and engineers can develop a set of qualitative and quantitative criteria for measures of performance. Criteria for the performance of bicycle proposals often compete, in the sense that a facility designed to meet one, may not be able to meet others. The choice, balance and ranking of criteria will be dictated by the goals and objectives of the programme.

Three groups of criteria relating to planning for cyclists can be identified:

cyclists' criteria
criteria for other mode users
other criteria.

Cyclists' criteria

Safety: This is one of the basic rationales for planning for cyclists. The fundamental cause of danger is, of course, the cyclists' conflict with other modes of transport. However, beyond certain minimum standards, increasing safety levels by separating or diverting cyclists on heavily trafficked routes will only be achieved at the expense of other important criteria, for example, directness of the route or cost. A number of measures act as indicators of safety, for example, the number of accidents involving cyclists or the volume and speed of traffic along a route.

Continuity: Maintaining momentum is of the utmost importance to cyclists. To create continuity in a network, the missing 'links' in it will need to be identified. The physical constraints (a large intersection) or opportunities (a park) and the priorities given to competing criteria will determine what, if any, link is provided.

Directness: The choice of the most direct route to a destination is an important priority to 'utilitarian' cyclists (for those cycling for recreational purpose it is a lower priority). As a rule of thumb, cyclists are unlikely to ride more than 10% extra even if it involves cycling in more hazardous traffic conditions than on a safer but more circuitous route.

Convenience: Bicycle networks must allow easy access to all major destinations. This is a function of the directness and continuity of routes, but also involves making provisions at user-selected breaks in journeys, for example, secure and well located parking, bicycle hiring facilities, and a smooth change-over between modes in trips that involve multi-modal travel (see Chapter 2, section 2.2.2 'Multi-modal travel').

Clarity: The network must be unambiguous and easy to understand. This is particularly important in the design of intersections, and in the choice of signing, where confusion and hesitation because of lack of route clarity can cause accidents.

Security: When using the network cyclists must have a feeling of security about their own safety and their property. This implies that all parts of the network must be located in 'defensible space'.

Acceptable grades: The length, steepness and frequency of grades will influence the choice of routes by cyclists. Standards acceptable to cyclists have been developed in various countries based on different combinations of length of gradient and steepness tolerated by an average cyclist.

Road surface: Bicycles, especially modern light-weight machines, are particularly vulnerable to damage (mainly buckled wheels as a result of poor road surfaces).

Air quality: Different amounts of energy expended by cyclists along routes used by motor traffic will expose them to different levels of air pollution. Figure 3.4 shows the level of air pollution as a function of traffic flows and distance from the road. In the USA federal standards set inhalation of carbon monoxide levels of more than 35 parts per million (ppm) for a period of one hour or more as unacceptable.

Noise: Since bicycles are practically silent, noise is an irritating deterrent to cyclists; in particular, routes used by large numbers of heavy goods vehicles should be avoided.

Shelter: Cycle routes should be located so that the built and natural environment provides maximum protection from wind and rain.

Maintenance and cleaning: Facilities must be designed so that maintenance and cleaning are easy. Deterioration in either makes routes unattractive to cyclists and potentially dangerous.

Attractiveness and interest: Enjoyment of cycling is greatly enhanced if surroundings are attractive and interesting. However, while this may be the highest priority of recreational cyclists, it may not be as important to the 'utilitarian' cyclist. From the point of view of the impact of facilities on the environment, due care must be taken to blend facilities into their surroundings.

Criteria for other mode users

Meeting competing criteria for cyclists must, of course, be balanced with the benefits and disbenefits to other mode-users. In general terms, the safety of non-cyclists must not be impaired, and inconvenience, though unavoidable in a trade-off between mode users, must be minimized. Moreover, different groups of non-cyclists are sensitive to different issues in the provision of bicycle facilities. In particular, commercial lobbies have launched strong protests against provisions which they judge adversely to affect their turnover, for example cycle lanes which replace car parking outside their shops. Where the provision of shared cycle-

	Pollution levels (CO parts per million)	
Traffic count (Cars/hour)	**Kerb-side levels at urban intersections**	**Levels 9 to 15m from traffic stream**
Over 4,800	56	11
3,600–2,400	32	7
Less than 2,400	15	3

3.4 Air pollution levels as a function of traffic and distance from the road

3.5 Local shopkeepers can be a powerful force. In The Hague they dug up the cycle route

pedestrian facilities are planned, and in particular where an existing path is to be converted for joint use, the pedestrian lobby and representatives of the blind will need to be consulted. The potential for such conflicts needs to be examined, and solutions acceptable to all parties arrived at, as much through negotiation as design. Failure to do this may cause antagonism and may threaten the bicycle programme itself.

Other criteria

Space: In order to avoid conflict with other modes, cyclists require a minimum width of passage or clearance along a route. On major urban roads, competition for space between transport users is high; on others, 'squeeze points' due to the urban configuration or topography limit the space available for the passage of transport. In both situations, the vulnerability of cyclists in traffic means that they come off second best, or they pose dangers for pedestrians where such routes are shared. Ensuring minimum clearance for cyclists can be achieved in a number of ways depending on road and pavement widths, traffic volumes, and the importance of other criteria, eg, cost.

Cost: In the competition for funds in the transport budget, pressure will always be on planners and engineers to minimize the costs of provisions for cyclists. The size of the budget allocated to cycling will depend on the political will to implement bicycle proposals. However, it must be kept in mind that to ensure the optimum performance of proposals, there is a minimum below which costs should not fall. The provision of sub-standard facilities in order to minimize costs can result in their under-utilization, or worse still, could lead to accidents.

ROUTE CHOICE IN BEDFORD, UK

In 1978 Bedford City Council initiated a programme to make provisions for the high proportion of cyclists in the city. It was decided to submit one route for consideration by a committee, the members of which included District and County councillors and chief officers, as well as representatives of the Department of Transport and Department of Environment. To this end the five major 'radial' routes converging on Bedford Town Centre were selected. The following criteria were chosen to evaluate which one of the five radial routes should be put forward:

accidents involving cyclists, not only on the actual routes, but also in the corridor of movement that each route is designed to relieve
ease of implementation, taking into account the effects on local residents and the extent of the facilities to be provided
links with origin and destination areas
existing cycle usage
existing facilities for cyclists
alternatives to major traffic routes, offering safe and quick travel
the cost effectiveness of the proposals.

3.3 INVESTIGATION OF CONSTRAINTS AND OPPORTUNITIES

Alternative proposals for the bicycle network can be narrowed down by identifying the constraints and opportunities in the existing urban infrastructure. This section considers these in terms of both the physical infrastructure and the administrative structures necessary to implement plans.

3.3.1 Physical constraints and opportunities

The use of the existing street system for a bicycle network is desirable not only because it minimizes the construction costs of bicycle facilities, but also because, by its very nature and development, it provides the most convenient and direct routes to most urban destinations. However, the task of evaluation is a complex one, and a set of empirically-tested standards indicating acceptable performance levels for cycling in various street conditions, has yet to be developed. In theory, the evaluation of the entire street system may be desirable. In practice, cost and time constraints, scarcity of data and limited staff make such an undertaking unrealistic. A more pragmatic procedure is the evaluation of streets in the major cycling corridors. The choice of these will be based on current patterns of cycling and an estimate of the future potential for cycling. The techniques for establishing both are dealt with in detail in Chapter 4.

Each corridor will be between two to six blocks or approximately 1 km in width, depending on local conditions. The initial corridor selection may reveal missing 'links' in the network, and these streets should be added to the list of corridors to be evaluated. Corridor evaluation can take place in two phases. This section deals with the first phase. The second phase is a more detailed assessment of the alternatives generated in the initial phase, and is the subject of section 3.6 below.

The initial phase is a quick assessment which will serve three purposes at this early stage of the planning process. Firstly, it will give planners and engineers an idea of the kind of proposals that will be necessary to make the existing street system safe and efficient for cycling. Secondly, it will indicate the additional information necessary to make a more detailed analysis of the alternatives that emerge. Thirdly, it will serve as a useful basis for consultation within government and with the public, the next step in the planning process. This initial evaluation of the corridors is done in terms of selected criteria which should include:

- traffic volumes and speeds – an indicator of the potential for car/bicycle conflict
- highway/pavement widths, showing the space opportunities and constraints for bicycle facilities
- pedestrian volumes and flows – an indicator of the potential for bicycle/pedestrian conflict
- major barriers (for example, one-way streets requiring detours from the most direct routes to destinations)
- routes and intersections requiring frequent dismounting or long waits
- gradients.

Two points are important here. Firstly, this phase should include an inventory and evaluation of any existing bicycle facilities. Secondly, since accurate data may not exist, professional judgement will inevitably play an important role in the assessment. Because of this it may be decided to delete or add to some of the criteria listed above, depending on the local situation. The method can be extended to show the feasibility of the alternatives generated by rating or ranking the streets in terms of, for example, their need for upgrading to acceptable levels for cycling, or the cost and political feasibility of improvements.

The evaluation of the existing street system must be supplemented by an examination of the possibilities for bicycle parking at important urban destinations, and for the use of bicycles in multi-modal travel. The application of criteria for each will indicate the possible courses of action.

3.3.2 Organisational constraints and opportunities

An assessment of the organisations and administrative framework concerned with cycling issues is an important part of this phase. An initial assessment should survey:

- the existing government departments and administrative structures concerned with bicycles and the provision of facilities for cyclists
- the available funding sources for bicycle facilities
- the existing legal framework related to cycling
- the interest groups outside of government who are concerned with cycling (if this has not been done at an earlier stage)
- the organisations, both in and outside government, concerned with road safety training and education.

3.4 PRELIMINARY CONSULTATION

If the public and interest groups were not involved with the formulation of goals for the programme, then this is an approriate point for these groups to make an input into the largely technical procedures undertaken so far. The timing of consultation procedures in the planning process is important and will depend on the politics and sometimes the existing formal procedures.

At this stage consultation with two groups must take place: with the public, and with the representatives of government departments and organisations concerned with cycling (these having been identified in the previous phase). Public participation can be introduced through a public meeting, a public exhibition of the work undertaken so far, or a meeting of the representatives of all the public interest groups concerned with cycling in the area. The exact method will depend on the extent to which public opinion on cycling issues is developed, the politics of the situation, and any formal participation procedures that may exist. Where local bicycle groups exist, the views of cyclists with experience of local conditions are invaluable in identifying problems and in suggesting alternative ideas.

The political backing and cooperation of government and local authority departments, and where necessary other local authorities, is crucial. Consultation with a committee made up in part or completely of their representatives is a good way of doing this.

During consultations the goals and objectives, and the problems and possibilities for bicycle planning in the area should be discussed and a consensus reached as to the way they are defined and the overall phasing of the programme. The selection of a 'steering' group consisting of representatives of all interest groups, both in government and from the public, to work closely with planners and engineers in the following phases is one of the best methods of ensuring participation and cooperation in the programme.

3.5 THE COMPONENTS OF A PLAN

The nature and contribution of each component in the plan for a bicycle network is the subject of discussion in this section. The extent and relative cost of the components will depend on the locality and the political and planning conditions in which the plan is being proposed.

The physical components of the bicycle network also relate to the scale on which it is operating, ie, whether it is serving local or city-wide needs. At the local scale, the immediate domain of the family, and the origin of most bicycle trips, a fine-grained network for maximum flexibility is desirable, and will be made up largely of the existing street system. At the district and/or city scale, the network becomes progressively coarser, coinciding with the transport arterials linking important urban activities. On these more heavily trafficked routes, the need to provide special facilities for cyclists is more likely. Moreover, since these routes also coincide with the major cycling corridors, their cost can more easily be justified. Similarly, the way in which missing links in the system are bridged depends on their locality and importance in the network (see fig 3.6).

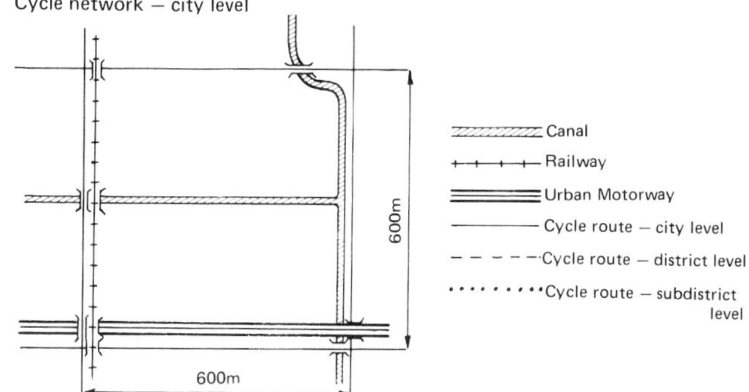

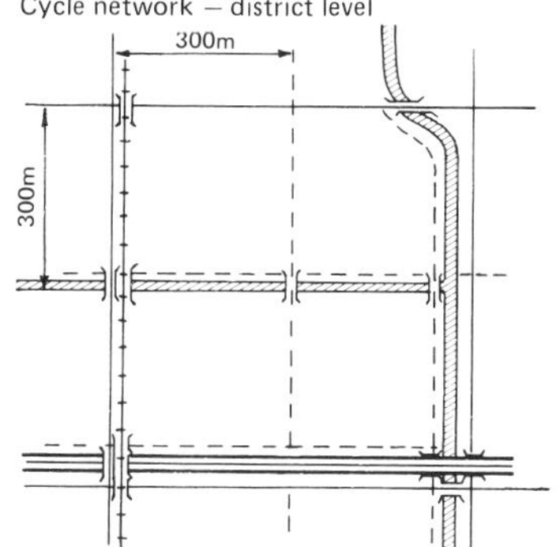

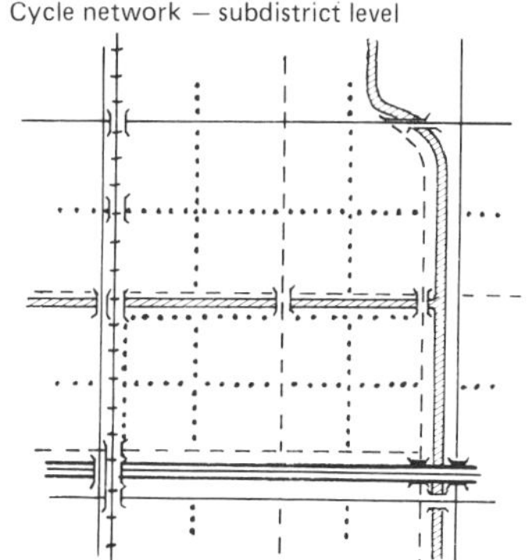

3.6 The bicycle network in Delft operating at different scales

Functional street classification	Principal purpose of street	Typical share of total urban street system mileage	Typical riding safety on roadway surface	Origins of bicycling travel	Principal non-residential bicycling destinations	Continuity of system	Need for special bikeway investment
Local	To serve adjoining land development	70%	Generally safe	Most	Few	Poor	Very low
Collector	To connect local street system with arterial system; balance between objectives of land access and traffic movement	15%	Safe to moderately unsafe	Some	Many	Fair	Moderate to high
Arterial	To serve as a corridor for traffic movement – some land access allowed	10%	Moderately to very unsafe	Some	Many	Good	High
Limited Access (expressway)	To serve as corridor for long distance traffic movement – no or very limited land access allowed	5%	Very unsafe	None	None	Good	Not recommended

3.7 A broad rating of the different components of the existing street system in terms of their potential in a bicycle network. (Source: *District of Columbia Bikeway Planning Study*)

3.5.1 The existing street system

The majority of urban streets are local and are suitable for cycling without needing costly and specially designed facilities. Streets which meet the following measures of performance will not require any special improvements to accommodate cyclists:

- a smooth road surface in good repair, particularly on the shoulder of the road
- low gradients (a maximum slope of 5% over not more than 30m is a widely accepted guideline; see fig 6.12)
- vehicle flows of less than 100 vehicles per hour
- an average speed of less than 48 kph
- travel lanes wide enough to ensure minimum clearance for cyclists (see section 6.1).
- no drainage grates with parallel openings
- no manhole covers at the edge of the road
- no major barriers to cycling
- no squeeze points
- good lighting
- a regular schedule of maintenance and sweeping.

Many streets which do not have these characteristics can be improved for cycling by simple and, usually, inexpensive means, eg, smoothing the shoulder of the road, the domain of most cyclists. More expensive techniques like road resurfacing benefit all users, so the cost can justifiably be shared between different parts of the transport budget. The range and use of these techniques is discussed in detail in section 6.1 'General improvements to the road system'.

3.5.2 Linking elements

'Every new link, even a small one, gives new possibilities and contributes to the whole, even if the chain is not yet finished' (*The Woonerf in City and Traffic Planning*, 1979). The constraints to cycling identified in the existing street system all represent gaps in the desirable bicycle network of the area. Some of these gaps can be bridged by linking elements such as specially designed intersections, gaps for cyclists in streets closed to motor traffic, tunnels or bridges.

3.8 A pedestrian and bicycle bridge provides a link in the bicycle network (Delft, Holland)

3.5.3 Elements enabling multi-modal travel

These elements enable the bicycle to be combined with three other modes of travel: walking, bus and train. Bicycle parking is the most important of these, and well located and secure parking can be cheap to provide. Other elements include bicycle hiring facilities, bicycle racks on buses and where necessary on trains. Where charges are levied for the use of these facilities, determining price is an important part of their planning.

3.5.4 Segregated cycle routes

This section introduces the framework for deciding whether segregated cycle routes are necessary in any part of the cycle network, and if so, the nature of the route that would be appropriate. The detailed design possibilities for segregated routes are described in Chapter 6.

The major impetus for segregated cycle routes is to increase safety levels. Relevant measures are the volume and speed of motor vehicles, the volume of bicycle traffic along the specified route and the extent to which the road width can be varied. The relationship between these, and the standards for each beyond which safety for cyclists is in jeopardy, define the need for segregated routes of different kinds (see figs 3.9 and 3.10). The techniques for setting such standards are an accepted part of traffic engineering.

3.5.5 Traffic management techniques

Traffic management techniques, usually employed to increase the efficiency of motor traffic, can also manipulate traffic patterns to benefit cyclists. Traffic management can make use of the following techniques to enhance cycling:

- controlling the speed of traffic
- prohibiting or restricting parking on certain streets
- applying special design concepts, eg, traffic cells (as used in Delft, Holland), to divert traffic from selected streets and to close through-routes in selected areas
- designating one-way streets on which special routes can be constructed (one-way streets without such treatment are often detrimental to cyclists because they enable increasing volumes and speeds of motor traffic along them)
- temporarily or permanently closing streets for use by cyclists only.

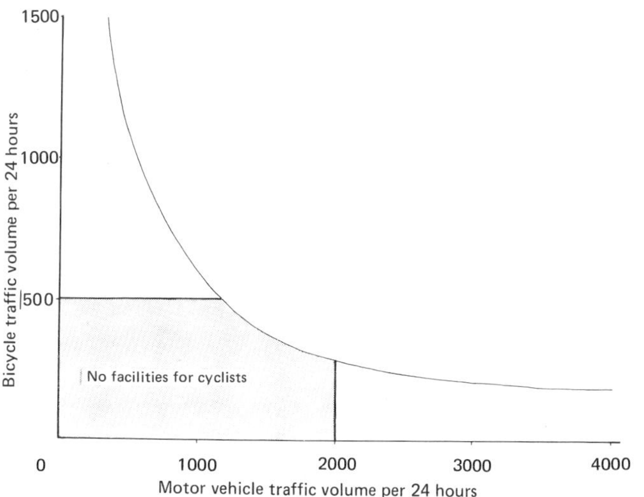

3.9 A suggested relationship between bicycle and motor vehicles for determining the need for the construction of special cycle routes (Source: Dutch Ministry of Transport and Public Works)

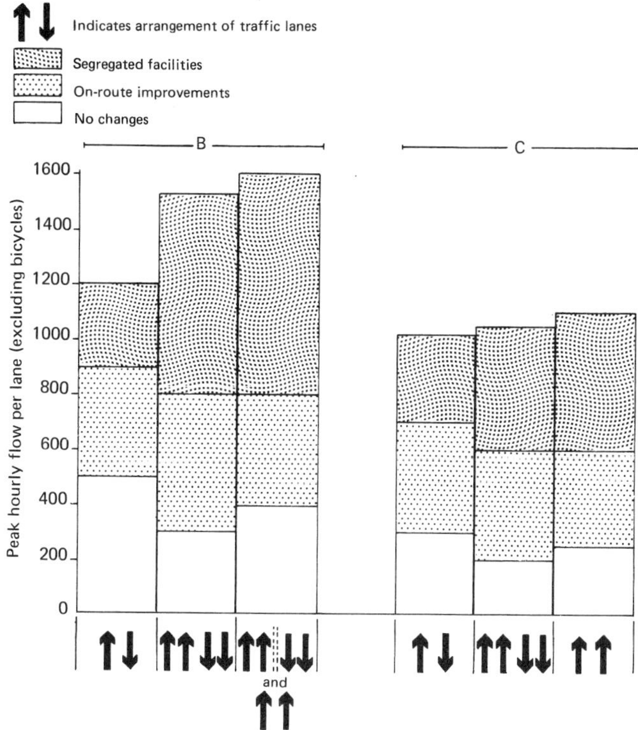

3.10 Suggested levels of provision according to total vehicle flow and class of road (All purpose roads, 4.5m clear width for bicycle/motor vehicle lanes, 3.65m width for motor vehicle only lanes.)
B No frontage access, no standing vehicles, negligible cross traffic.
C Frontage development, side roads, pedestrian crossings, bus stops, waiting restrictions throughout day, loading restrictions at peak hours.
Further reduction in the acceptable flow for given conditions should be made where there is a significant amount of parking. Given the same clear lane widths, a reduction of 30% in the values given for **C** is suggested.

An example: Groningen (population 360,000)

Objectives	• To improve city centre environment reducing noise and air pollution • To increase road safety by lessening conflict situations for weaker traffic elements
Key policy elements of plan	• Elimination of through traffic from the inner city • Better facilities for public transport and bicycles: central bus station for urban and regional network; special provision for cyclists wherever possible • Pedestrian-only streets • Creation of 4 traffic cells
General results	• 40% reduction in car traffic in the centre (80% in Grote Market), but only a small modal shift • 10% increase in cyclists to the centre • 5% rise in visits to central shops • 5% rise in pedestrians passing the central cordon (15% on Saturdays) but less concentrated in time • 10% increase in cars parked in covered or multi-storied parks but no change in total city centre parking • Some increased congestion on certain radial roads and ring road • Faster bus movement in centre
Specific environmental aspects	• Fall in central area noise level by approx 6dBA • Fewer businesses or individuals wish to revert to previous conditions as the result is environmentally safer, pleasing and less congested

3.11 A survey of traffic management techniques and their impact in Groningen, Holland (Source: Urban Transport and the Environment, Vol III, OECD, 1979)

The use of these techniques, combined with other components of the bicycle programme, has been closely related to the increased use of bicycles in some urban areas (fig 3.11).

3.5.6 Education

Until recently 'engineering, education and enforcement' were always departmentalised, with little coordination taking place between the three. Following a number of practical experiments, most notably in Geelong, Australia, the integration of existing and proposed education and enforcement programmes with planning and traffic management activities has been shown to bring considerable benefits.

Anaylsis of the problem of bicycle/motor vehicle conflicts identifies areas for education work:

- the training of all children before they are allowed to use the roads. The number of children who are killed or injured as a result of their own mistakes or ignorance indicates that current efforts are woefully inadequate
- the improvement of motor vehicle drivers' behaviour towards cyclists. Many motorists treat cyclists as second-class road users, taking advantage of the protection afforded by their vehicles to force cyclists to stop, swerve or wait, and to ride in the gutter. Since motorists and cyclists will, in general, always have to share the same road system, this attitude, which encourages a warrior-like cyclist-/motorist relationship, needs to be changed to one of compromise and conciliation.

Since some education work is already carried out in most areas, the priorities will be to identify exactly what education can hope to achieve and how a combination of a vigorously pursued education programme supported by an enforcement programme can be co-ordinated to achieve the objectives set.

3.5.7 Enforcement

Enforcement is a key aspect of integrated planning for bicycles because there are behavioural considerations to both the physical elements of proposals and education programmes.

To be successful the physical elements of any proposal must either be self-enforcing, or the enforcement agency must have the resources to police its use. Physical design and layout can play a major role in ensuring that facilities are self-enforcing. However, aspects of the problem such as vehicle parking, and the use of cycle tracks by motor cycles will require the on-going attention of the enforcement agencies.

The long term effectiveness of education programmes has also been shown to be dependent on the support of enforcement work. In particular education of children has been shown to have short-lived effects unless supported by firm but friendly enforcement.

Since both these areas of work require specialist experience and organisational support, early involvement of the enforcement agencies will be a critical factor in the success of a plan.

3.6 EVALUATING AND COSTING ALTERNATIVE PLANS

Once a plan consisting of a number of alternatives has been agreed on by the planning team in consultation with the 'steering' committee, the next step is to decide on the actual plan to be implemented.

Two stages in this process can be identified. The first is a detailed evaluation of the alternatives generated so far, arriving at a set of final proposals. The second is submitting these proposals to cost-benefit analysis as a final indicator of their impact. Given the time necessary to do this analysis, it is unlikely that it will be applied to each alternative. Cost-benefit analysis of the proposals is part of the final step in justifying the proposed scheme to the public and to decision-makers in government.

3.6.1 Evaluation of alternatives

The evaluation of the physical alternatives identified in the selected bicycle corridors will be based on further details of the conditions along these routes. These will include the following:

- volumes and speeds of traffic to establish the character of traffic flows along the routes (including an examination of lane configurations, turning movements and bus routes) and a more detailed examination of the potential for bicycle/vehicle conflict
- bicycle volumes and bicycle flows in terms of existing traffic lanes and their turning movements
- pedestrian volumes and flows – an indicator of the potential for bicycle/pedestrian conflict
- accident spots – an indicator of actual safety
- on-street parking conditions – an indication of constraints on space and the potential for bicycle/vehicle conflict
- traffic volumes on cross streets at intersections, including an analysis of their turning movements
- unacceptable sight distances and visual obstructions at intersections and along non-linear routes which impair cyclists' and motor vehicle drivers' vision of each other at critical points
- routes which are badly surfaced
- the location and design of drainage grates on the street
- routes subject to high noise levels and air pollution (one indication of this will be the volume of heavy trucks and buses along routes)
- attractive surroundings and amenities
- lighting.

Assessing the use of traffic management techniques to improve routes within the corridors will involve an analysis of related traffic movement beyond the limits of the cycling corridors.

Proposals for the location of bicycle parking and ways to enable the use of the bicycle in multi-modal travel must be integrated with the final choice of routes. Complementing the physical proposals, the education and enforcement components of the programme can also be finalised at this stage.

In order to implement the components of the proposals discussed so far, the government departments and organisations concerned in each case must be identified and final plans made for gearing up the appropriate organisational structure to ensure their co-ordination and integregation during implementation. The framework for this was set up in the first round of consultation and co-operation on many fronts may already exist, having been established during the development of the programme thus far. An important part of this is setting up channels of communication with community groups affected by the final proposals, and the general publicity and promotion of the whole programme. Since the programme will be phased over time, this will be an on-going process, with each phase requiring a particular combination of organisational, community and promotional supports.

3.6.2 Cost-benefit analysis

Once the components of the proposals have been decided, all or part of them will be submitted to cost-benefit analysis for final assessment. In essence this technique shows whether the benefits of the bicycle proposals are maximized with respect to the costs of implementing them, based on an appropriate rate of return over the life of the project.

In describing the details of application, three factors must be kept in mind:

- Cost-effective rather than cost-efficient analysis of proposals is a more meaningful tool for evaluation. Thus, this essentially cost-efficient technique must be supplemented by evaluation in terms of other non-financial targets. In the last analysis, it is only one of the tools used for assessment, and must be seen as an aid to, not a replacement for, decision-making.
- The technique is only as good as the assumptions made at each stage of its application.
- Although in principle it can be applied to assess proposals for education and enforcement, there are major problems with quantifying the related costs and benefits. For the sake of simplicity, explanation of the technique here refers only to physical proposals.

The application of cost-benefit analysis can be broken down into six stages.

1. Defining the problem

The objectives to be met by the proposals must be clearly defined. (When more than one alternative is being considered, each must satisfy the same objectives, if their evaluation is to be comparable.) This includes the definition of the geographical area from which cyclists will be drawn, based on the principal trip purposes for which the route or facility is likely to be used, and the average distance cyclists will be willing to travel (see Chapter 4 for estimation techniques).

2. Enumerating the costs and benefits

The basic problem at this stage is deciding what costs and benefits should be considered. The list of costs will include construction costs, land costs, and the cost of delays and inconvenience during construction. The latter is only one of a number of social costs that could be considered. Similarly, a reasonable cut-off point for benefits emanating from the proposals will have to be decided. Three categories of benefits can be defined: direct benefits, ie, to the cyclists; indirect benefits, ie, to other mode users; intangible benefits, ie, benefits which cannot be traded in the market place (eg, quality of life).

3. Quantifying costs and benefits

Figures for monetary costs and benefits will be relatively straightforward to identify. Difficulties arise, however, with the quantification of qualitative and value-based costs and benefits. Although attempts have been made to put monetary values to factors such as personal fitness and the quality of the environment, they introduce biases which often do not really assist in the decision-making process. The difficulties arising from this will lead to the exclusion of some of the costs and benefits in the previous step.

4. Choosing the life of the proposals

This is the amortization period, or the number of years for which costs and benefits will be calculated. It will ultimately be determined by the period for which reliable predictions for costs and benefits can be made in the future, usually between five and twenty-five years.

5. Choosing a rate of discount

Most government projects use a rate of discount of approximately 8%. The value judgement involved in estimating this is apparent; essentially it is a measure of the willingness of the present generation to change from current levels of consumption in order to benefit the consumption of future generations.

6. Calculating the cost-benefit function

This function is expressed either as the difference between total costs and benefits (B − C) or as the ratio $\frac{B}{C}$ giving the benefit per unit cost. Once the variables have been quantified, it can be calculated by substituting them into the cost-benefit formula below.

Cost-benefit formula

Total costs (C) $= K + (c_1 + c_2 + c_3 \ldots c_t)$

where K = initial capital investment

t = the life of the project

$c_{1,2,\ldots t} = \dfrac{\text{intermediate costs}}{(1+i)^t}$ where i = the rate of discount

= the discounted costs for each year of the life of the project

Total benefits (B) are calculated in a similar way, substituting benefits for costs in the formula.

It is obvious from this discussion of the method that it can be a highly complex undertaking. However, it must be remembered that making the model more comprehensive involves making additional, and increasingly questionable, assumptions. This inevitably reduces the validity of the analysis as well as making it a time-consuming process. A cost-benefit analysis using simple definitions based on limited data will often be a more valuable aid to decision-making.

3.7 CONSULTATION

Consultation at this stage is fundamental to the final choice between alternatives. Ideally, the community should be involved at two levels: through the continuing participation of the community 'steering committee' and of members of the general community who are directly affected by the selected alternatives. The latter may already be organised (eg, in residential associations), but where this is not the case, the planner or the 'steering committee' can play an active part in forming a group specifically for the purpose of discussing the alternatives, either in meetings or through a household survey. Cooperation by these groups is a first step in the implementation of the plans. Where it is not forthcoming, there are serious grounds for reconsidering the particular proposal. Where the political will is flagging, a show of public cooperation and support could be important in steering the plans through the decision-making machinery.

3.8 MAINTENANCE

The importance of the maintenance of bicycle facilities has to be reiterated. The cost of maintenance can be included in the cost-benefit analysis of the final proposals. If this is not done, then this is an appropriate point to check that facilities can be

Action checklist

1. Formulate the goals and objectives of the bicycle programme in consultation with planners, engineers, elected representatives of local government and the public.
2. Derive a set of criteria from the goals and objectives as a basis for evaluating proposals.
3. Identify the major cycling corridors and investigate within them the constraints to safe cycling and the opportunities for improving cycling conditions both within and outside of the highway in order to derive a number of alternative physical proposals.
4. Examine the existing administrative structure (see section 3.3.2) and consider the required changes for an appropriate structure for the planning and implementation of the bicycle plans.
5. Consult with the public and representatives of national and local government departments (including the legal department) and organisations concerned with cycling, reaching consensus on the goals and objectives of the programme and discussing the work done so far.
6. Set up a 'steering' group consisting of representatives of all interest groups, both in government and from the public, to work closely with planners and engineers in the subsequent phases of the programme.
7. Evaluate the alternatives generated, considering final proposals for the physical components of the plan, education and enforcement, and the appropriate administrative structure to implement and monitor the proposals.
8. Submit the final proposals to a cost-benefit analysis, providing a last assessment of the implications of the programme and an aid to decision-makers giving the final go-ahead.
9. Agree final proposals with the 'steering' group. Gain the support and cooperation of the local residents affected by the proposals.
10. Check that the physical components of the proposals can be easily cleaned and maintained.
11. Decide on the phasing of the plans (see section 3.9) and prepare plans for publication.
12. Set up a monitoring system and a 'feedback' mechanism for new input into subsequent phases of the plans.

easily and cheaply maintained after their construction. Any difficulties in this connection which become apparent are grounds for the re-evaluation of the pertinent part of the plan.

3.9 PHASING THE IMPLEMENTATION OF PLANS

The phasing of the proposals for a bicycle network is an important part of the planning process, and can dictate the momentum and ultimate success or failure of the proposals. The choice of the components for the first phases of the programme are crucial. The greater the impact and perceived success of these early phases, the greater the likelihood of continuity of the programme. This is particularly true if phases of the programme are being funded separately, a method which planners and engineers may have to exploit in order to compete for limited funding.

Moreover, each phase of the network, though integrated with the whole, must serve an essential function on its own. In the event of funding being delayed or even cut off, each completed phase must make a positive contribution so that resources will not be wasted.

In addition, phasing is essential for flexibility. It enables those concerned with bicycle provisions to take advantage of the opportunities offered by future urban development plans, and to adapt to the inevitable unplanned urban changes.

The monitoring and evaluation of a bicycle programme is critical to the future success of the programme, and fundamental to the concept of a planning 'process'. Without feedback and regular evaluation of proposals, correction of mistakes and adaptation to changing conditions would not be feasible, and could lead to the under-utilisation or disintegration of the network. The details of setting up a monitoring and evaluation system can be found in Chapter 12.

4 Bicycle use

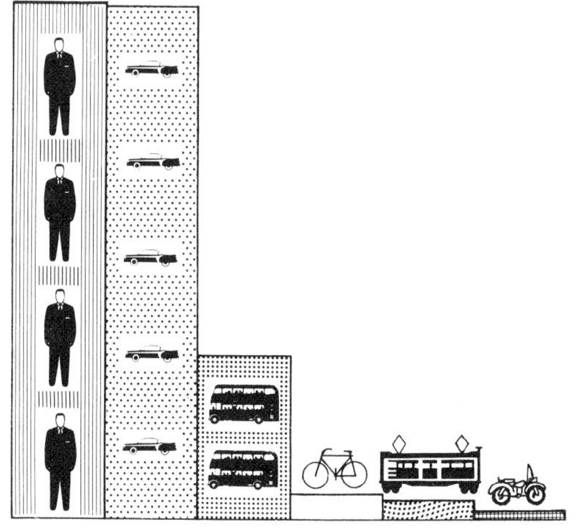

4.1 The number of trips made is the best measure of the importance of a mode. Relative use of modes in the UK (measured in journeys) (Source: *UK National Travel Survey*)

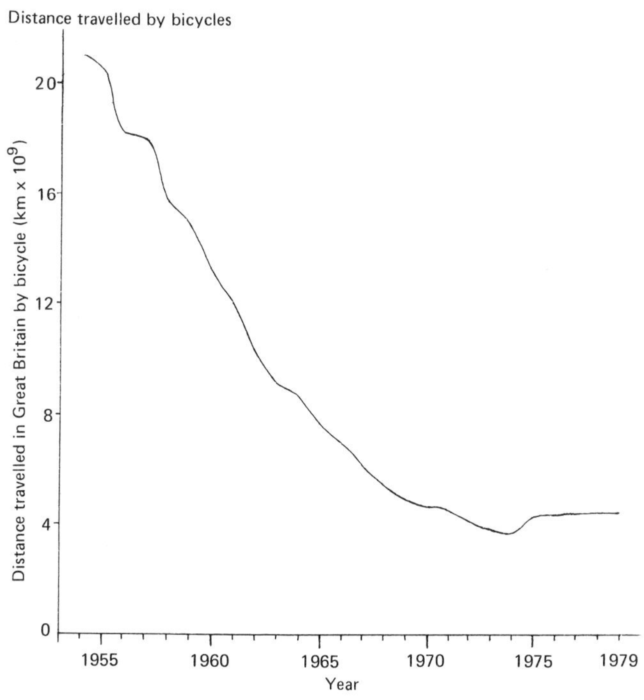

4.2 The decline in the distance travelled by bicycle has been reversed in recent years. (Source: *UK Transport Statistics*)

For many years it was generally believed that cycling played an insignificant role in transport and that bicycle usage was declining. New examinations of figures for the use of bicycles have indicated that these beliefs were ill-founded, that bicycle use has been increasing in recent years and that the levels and structure of bicycle use continue to change significantly. This chapter presents data on current bicycle use, looks at the potential for increased use, examines the factors affecting use and assesses the changes likely over the next twenty years.

4.1 CURRENT AND POTENTIAL USE OF BICYCLES

4.1.1 Levels of bicycle use

The number of *trips* made by a mode of transport, rather than the *distance travelled*, is the best measure of the importance of that mode to the individual. Someone who cycles 2km to work each day may well cover a greater distance in a year by train than on a bicycle if they make just one trip (for a holiday, for example) by train. The bicycle would, however, be a more important mode to them because it is their regular means of transport.

Many continuous records of vehicle use are, however, produced in terms of distance travelled by mode. In the UK, about twenty times as many journeys are made by motor vehicle as by bicycle, but sixty times the distance travelled by bicycle is travelled by motor vehicle. Figures for distance travelled are useful in assessing the change of use of a mode over time. The steady decline in the number of kilometres travelled annually by bicycle in the UK has been reversed since 1975 and the rate of increase in bicycle use now matches that of motor vehicle use, indicating that cycling is likely to remain an important mode of transport.

In the UK, around 7% of the population use a bicycle at least once a week and 4% of all trip stages (including walks over 1.5km) are made by bicycle. By comparison, about 30% of Danes cycle at least once a week and in Holland more trips are made by bicycle each year than by any other mode. Figures from selected European towns show the proportion of trips made by bicycle to vary from 5 to 40%. Even the lower of these figures indicates that cycling is an important method of transport in these towns; in many, cycling is more important than public transport.

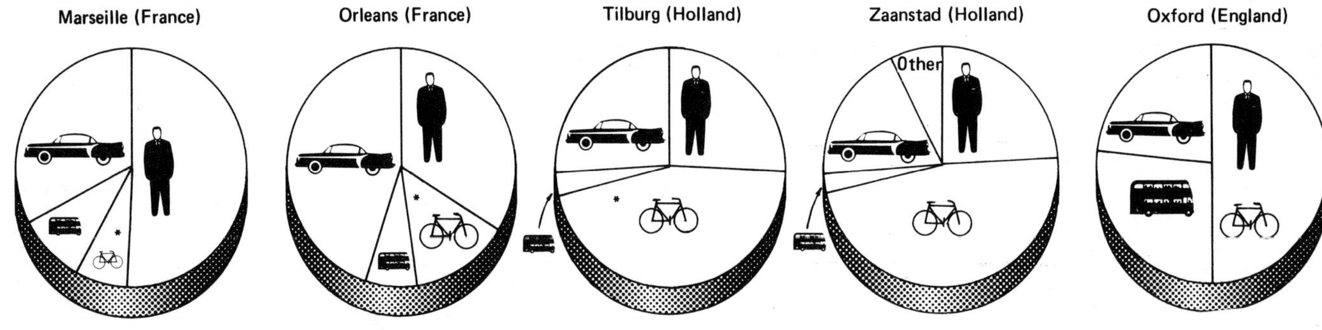

4.3 There are marked variations in bicycle use from one region to another (Source: *Background Report No. 1*)

The marked variations in bicycle use from one region to another and between towns within a region make figures for use in other areas an unreliable source of information for estimating local use. The most important sources of information will undoubtedly be local surveys. This principle applies to all aspects of use detailed in the following sections, which describe the aspects of bicycle use which a planner needs to investigate in order to gauge the potential for growth in a particular area.

4.1.2 The length of bicycle journeys

Around 40% of bicycle journeys in the UK are less than 1.5km and 80% are less than 5km in length. As more than half of all trips made by all modes (including walking) are under 5km in length, distance is not a major restriction on bicycle use, particularly in urban areas where the average trip length is shorter.

More than 80% of trips under 1.5km in length for the five main journey purposes (work, shopping, social, education and personal business) are already made by bicycle or on foot. It is therefore predominantly for trips in the 1.5 to 5km range that the choice between bicycle and other modes is critical to the level of bicycle use in a particular area. Since around 30% of trips for all five main purposes are in this distance range, there is considerable scope for change in the use of different modes.

For short trips for all five main journey purposes in the UK, the most used alternative mode to cycling is walking. For longer trips, the car is the main alternative for all purposes except education and shopping, where walking and bus are important modes.

4.1.3 The purpose of bicycle journeys

In the UK, three-quarters of all trips by all modes are for one of the following purposes: work, shopping, social, education or personal business. The same five purposes account for three-quarters of all trips by bicycle and must therefore be central to any study. Most people who do so, have to go to work or school, therefore the total number of such trips is a relatively fixed figure. If bicycle trips for work or education are to increase, it will be as a result of transfers from other modes. An increase in education trips by bicycle will be most affected by safety considerations, the availability of school buses and, if they are not free, the cost. An increase in bicycle use for journeys to work will be effected by increased costs and the availability of parking for motor vehicles.

In contrast to work and education trips, the total number of shopping, personal business and social trips may vary

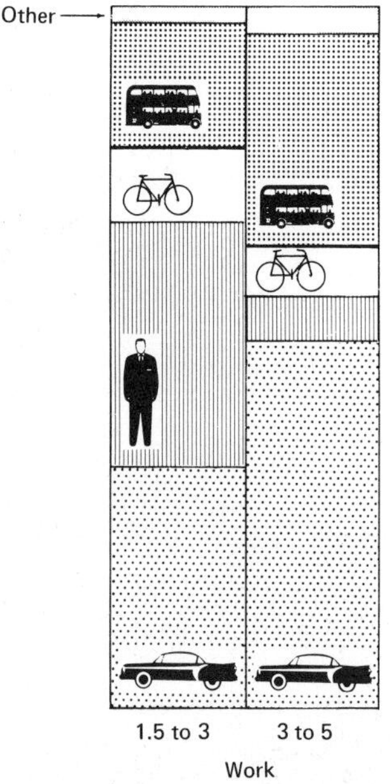

4.4 The modes most used vary according to trip length and purpose in the UK (Source: *UK National Travel Survey*)

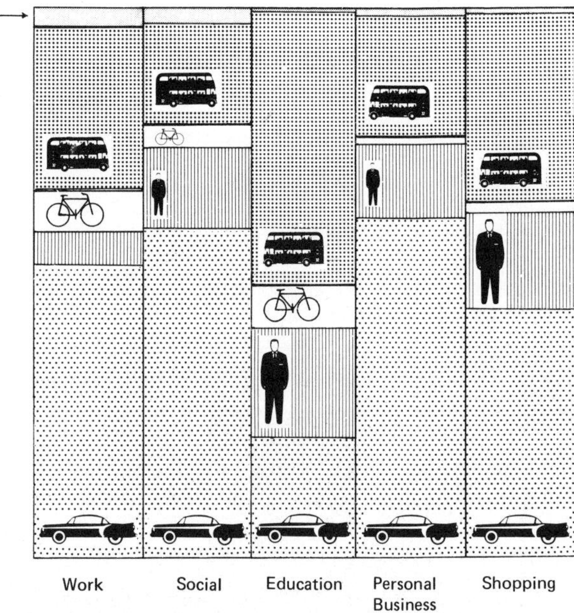

4.5 For longer trips, except education and shopping trips, car is the main alternative to bicycle in the UK (Source: *UK National Travel Survey*)

Purpose	Work	Shop	Education	Social	Personal business
% of bicycle trips for purpose (UK)	38	13	13	11	11
% of trips for purpose made by bicycle (UK)	6	3	4	3	5

4.6 There are five main purposes for bicycle journeys in the UK (Source: *Cycling as a Mode of Transport*)

SUMMARY OF UK DATA

Twenty times more journeys are made by motor vehicle than by bicycle
The rate of increase of bicycle use matches that of motor vehicles
7% of the population use a bicycle at least once a week
80% of bicycle trips are less than 5km long
One-third of bicycle journeys are made by children under 16 years of age
The choice between bicycles and other modes is predominantly for trips between 1.5 and 5km in length
Rising costs will increase bicycle use for journeys to work but not education trips, where safety is the significant factor
Most new bicycle trips which are not transfers from other modes will be shopping or social trips

considerably because there is more choice about whether, when and where to make them. Increases in real travel costs, improvements in safety or increased leisure time could all lead to increases in bicycle use for these purposes through transferred or generated trips.

4.1.4 Type of person who cycles

The proportion of men and women who cycle varies from one country to another. The British National Travel Survey shows that males in the UK make twice as many bicycle trips as females, but in Denmark more women than men cycle. Cycling is most important for those aged 16 or under in both the UK and Denmark, with around one third of bicycle journeys in the UK being made by this age group and one third of Danish cyclists being under 16 years old.
This reflects the lack of an alternative form of flexible personal transport for these young users. The groups who cycle least in the UK are women under 30 or over 60 years and men in their late 20s or over 70 years of age. Physical inability will account for the low usage among the older groups. Reasons for low usage among the younger groups are more difficult to find, especially as bicycle use is common in these groups in Holland. Such low use can only really be attributed to choice shaped by social attitudes, and as these change bicycle use may increase.

4.2 FACTORS AFFECTING BICYCLE USE

The previous sections showed that levels of bicycle use vary considerably between areas and that there is scope for bicycle use to increase in a number of ways. The following sections examine the factors which currently affect the level of bicycle use and which can be expected to have an effect over the next twenty years.

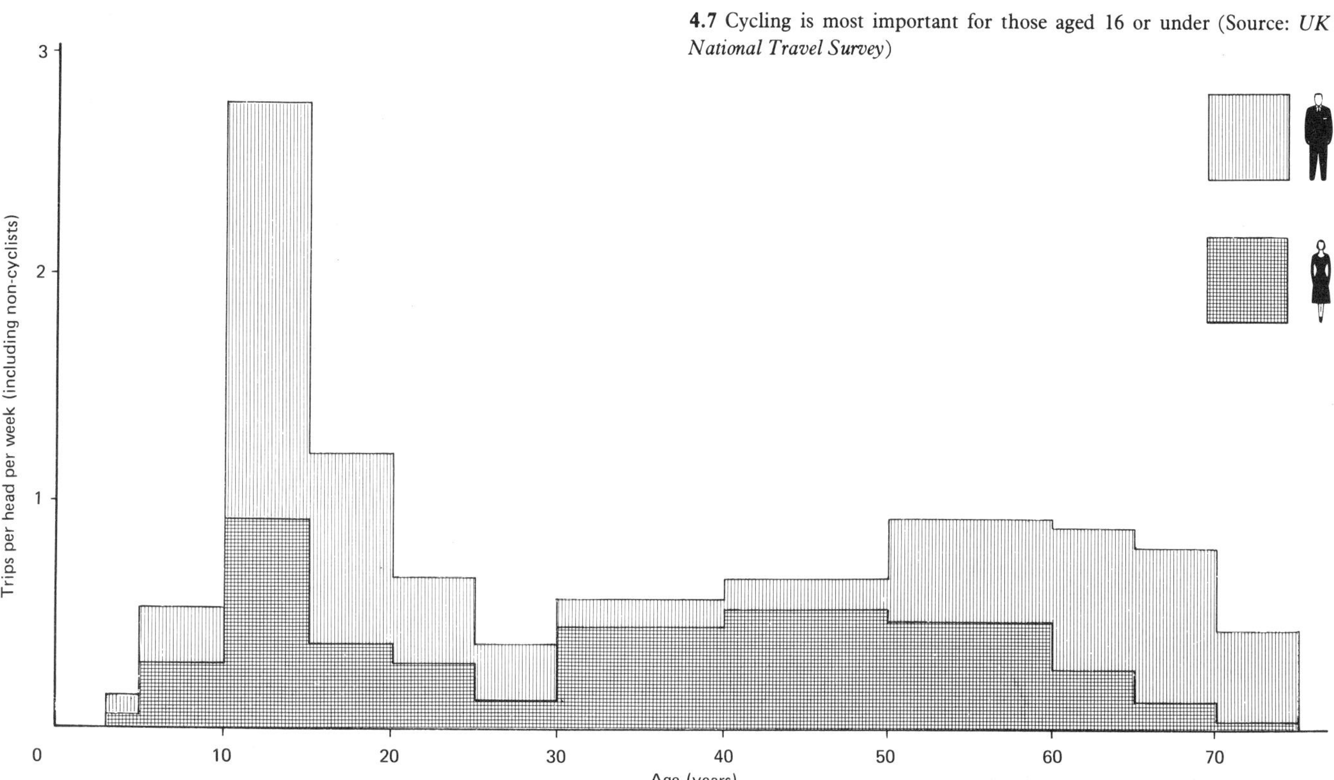

4.7 Cycling is most important for those aged 16 or under (Source: *UK National Travel Survey*)

4.2.1 Design of bicycles

There are many more ways in which bicycles are used around the world than those which are familiar to most Western people. Some of these designs are currently appearing in the West in increasing numbers. Bicycles are used for personal transport, transporting other people and goods and for recreation. In this they are no different from other forms of transport. The differences lie in the limits of performance, such as top speed and carrying capacity.

Manufacturers are recognising that bicycle use is increasing and are responding by producing more versatile designs for folding bikes, trailers and tricycles for load carrying. The stability of tricycles, for example, makes them an attractive alternative to the car when children and shopping have to be carried together and the easily-folded bike can save time and money without risking theft when gaining access to another mode of transport.

The revived interest in cycling coincided with improvements in the construction of bicycles. Materials have improved in quality, reducing the weight of popular models. Derailleur gearing systems have become more widespread, making higher speeds and gradient climbing capabilities available to more people; braking systems have been made more efficient to increase safety. Safety has been further improved by the marketing of reflective fittings and clothing and attachments such as lights and flags.

The next twenty years will undoubtedly see further improvements and innovations in design – perhaps radical changes in bicycle geometry and almost certainly improvements in the efficiency of gearing and transmission. The bicycle will thus be able to travel further and faster and carry larger loads for the same human effort and will become more competitive as a mode of transport.

Mode	Capacity		Speed (mph/kph)		Door to door journey time
	Passengers	Load (kg)	Maximum	Average	(5km)
	1	10–15	5/8	3/5	50 mins
	1 or 2	15–20	30/48	16/26	20 mins
	3	50–75	15/24	10/16	30 mins
	5	100–150	Speed limit	20/32	15 mins
	70	Not applicable	Speed limit	15/24	30 mins
	Not applicable	20,000	Speed limit	20/32	Not applicable

4.8 The difference between bicycles and other modes lies in the *limits* of performance

4.2.2 Human performance

Most of the limits of bicycle performance are determined by human factors. For a particular user, the maximum speed is determined by the *rate* at which their body can expend energy. The comfortable range is determined by the *total amount* of energy that can be expended. The maximum load that can be carried is set by the power which they can generate. In practice, speed and range tend to be considered together by users in terms of time spent travelling. For modes other than public transport, the amount of time spent travelling for a given purpose shows a greater similarity between modes than the distance travelled. This is one of the main reasons why the majority of bicycle journeys are currently under 5km in length. The previous section suggested that technical improvements could increase the range of bicycles for the same input of energy. It is also possible that over the next twenty years users will be prepared to spend more of their increasing leisure time travelling and that people will want to keep physically fitter. The average length of journey considered feasible by bicycle will therefore probably increase.

4.2.3 Topography

Steep gradients can deter cyclists, especially if they are not particularly strong or fit. In the UK, for example, bicycle use is generally higher in East Anglia, which is flat, than in Wales, which is hilly.

In a particular town which is generally hilly, however, there may be certain routes which serve major destinations and which are flat, for example along a valley. Hilly topography does not, therefore, automatically restrict bicycle use. Furthermore, in an area which is hilly, cyclists will probably accept rises on their routes which would be unacceptable to riders in flat areas who are unaccustomed to hills.

4.2.4 Weather

Few detailed surveys on the effect of adverse weather conditions on bicycle use have been undertaken. The monthly usage figures for the UK show that cycling is less common in winter, but usage by all modes is down at this time. Obviously, the comparative discomfort of cycling in the rain, wind or extreme cold will deter some cyclists if there is some alternative, more comfortable mode available. Cyclists can and do, however, take the initiative in alleviating the effects of bad weather by choosing suitable protective clothing. They can also, to some extent, choose routes away from roads where traffic generates spray (in particular heavy lorry

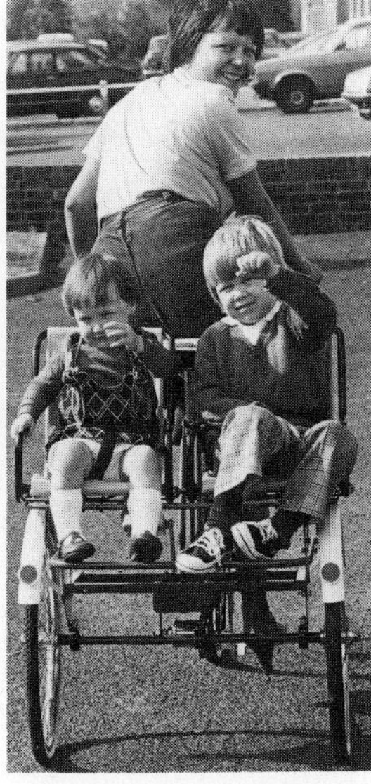

4.9 There is now a variety of designs for bicycle trailers on the market
4.10 The stability of tricycles makes them attractive when children [and shopping] have to be carried

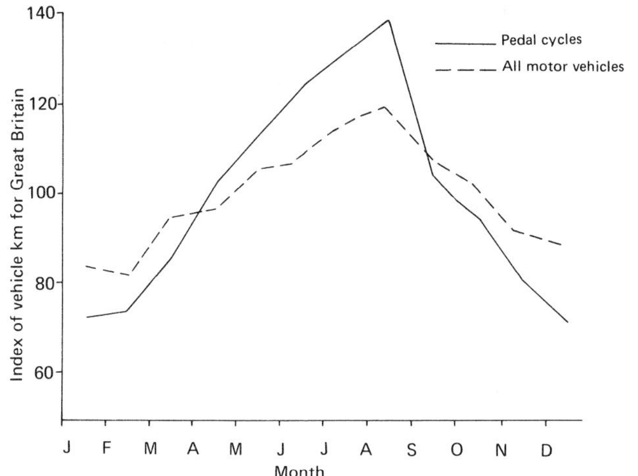

4.11 Cycling is less common in winter, but so is motor-vehicle use (Source: *Cycling as a Mode of Transport*)

routes) or in the shelter of trees or embankments, walls or buildings which provide protection from the wind. Parked bicycles can also be protected from rain or snow.

4.2.5 Type of area

The ultimate level of bicycle use that can be expected in a town or city will to some extent depend on the size of the area. In the UK, for example, the percentage of trips made by bicycle is higher in towns up to 250,000 population than in larger conurbations. There are a number of factors which probably contribute to this. In a conventional city, the commercial and industrial employment centres tend to be concentrated. As the size of the city increases, the distance from the residential areas to these centres increases and cycling becomes less attractive. This is particularly marked when the residential areas are of low density and therefore cover a large area. Furthermore, the road network to and around the employment centres is more congested as they grow in size, so conditions are more dangerous for cyclists. The deterrent of busy roads may also apply to schoolchildren who have to cycle across them to reach schools. The distance from some residential areas to the surrounding countryside where cyclists ride for recreation is also large.

Changes in the location of homes and places of work or recreation over the next twenty years could therefore lead to an increase in bicycle use if such changes reduce distances between homes and destinations.

4.2.6 Safety

Fear about cycling being unsafe is a major factor in limiting bicycle use. A National Opinion Poll survey in the UK in 1976 cited improved conditions for cyclists as the measure most likely to make people want to cycle more often. A similar study in Denmark revealed that 20% of women who did not cycle were nervous of doing so, although only 2% of men who did not cycle felt this way.

Improvements in safety will therefore not only reduce casualty rates amongst existing cyclists but would almost certainly lead to bicycles being used more, especially by women and probably by children whose parents are reluctant to allow them to cycle under current conditions. Chapter 5 discusses bicycles safety in detail and suggests how it may be improved.

4.2.7 Security of bicycles

A relatively basic bicycle costs a week's take-home pay for many people. Theft of a whole bicycle or its fittings, or vandalism of its parts, is therefore a major deterrent to an owner from continuing to cycle. One in twenty-five Danish adults interviewed about their reasons for not cycling said that they had had their bicycle stolen.

The ease with which a bicycle can be securely parked near a destination has therefore become a major consideration in deciding whether or not to cycle to that destination. Methods for improving the security of parked bicycles are discussed in Chapter 9.

4.2.8 Social attitudes

It is difficult to isolate the reasons for local or national variations in social attitudes to bicycle use and impossible to quantify them. It is nonetheless possible to quote qualitative examples. In the UK, for example, there is little difference between the medium-sized 'railway' towns of Swindon and York and other similarly structured towns like Reading and Blackburn, yet bicycle use is markedly higher in the former towns. This must to some extent be attributable to historic or social factors establishing a tradition which has survived the challenge of motorised transport.

At the national level, public and official attitudes towards bicycle use in the USA are that it is an enjoyable means of recreation and environmentally valuable. This has long been the attitude in Holland, yet in the UK appreciation of the value of bicycles is only now growing in a similar way.

The increased interest in exercise, leisure and sport; a heightened concern for the environment and the advent of the small-wheeled bicycle have all contributed to changing attitudes and the bicycle is no longer considered a purely utilitarian mode. These attitudes are weighed against the disadvantages perceived by potential cyclists before deciding whether to cycle or not. Currently the balance of favourable attitudes and costs is outweighing the disadvantages and leading to increased use of bicycles.

4.2.9 Costs to the user

The decision to rely on the bicycle, public transport, private motor vehicle or a combination of all will not be made purely on the basis of monetary cost but in conjunction with considerations of necessity, convenience, reliability, effort, time and therapeutic value. While these factors are discussed elsewhere in this chapter, it is clear that their relative importance is closely linked to lifestyle. Isolated rural households will find a private motor vehicle essential for all trips. A city dweller, on the other hand, will probably find that private transport is only needed, if at all, for leisure purposes or to make utilitarian trips easier.

The costs which are considered when choosing which mode to rely on include those incurred in, say, a year's running. These will comprise:

depreciation – the annual loss of value of the mode purchased
fixed running costs – taxes, insurance and storage
journey-related costs – fuel, maintenance and parking.

On this basis, the typical total cost per annum for a user travelling 80km per week on utilitarian journeys (work, shopping and personal business) is currently higher for a car than public transport and lowest for a bicycle.

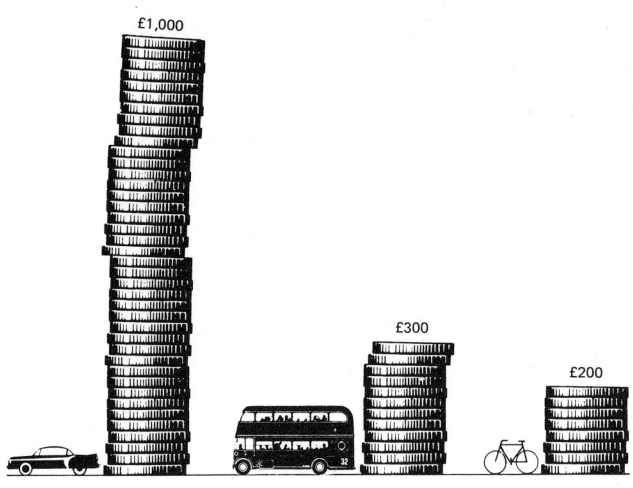

4.12 The cost of cycling is lower than other modes of transport

In making the choice of mode for a particular journey, only the journey-related costs are relevant. Currently, public transport journey costs generally exceed those of a car journey, with the bicycle again being the cheapest. Changes in the cost of a particular mode come about as a result of variations in:

labour costs
material costs
fuel costs
maintenance costs
taxation.

People change their mode of transport when there is a noticeable shift in the relative cost of modes. Such changes are usually more marked if the change in relative costs is sudden, for example the increase in both bicycle and motor cycle use following a sharp rise in fuel costs.

4.2.10 Ownership

It is impossible to obtain accurate figures for ownership of bicycles in most countries because they are not registered. Nevertheless, the most conservative estimate of bicycle ownership in the UK is that there are 7 million bicycles (compared with 14 million cars) in use, or about one bicycle for every eight people. This is on a par with ownership in France and Belgium but well below that in Denmark and Holland, where bicycle use is higher.

This link between ownership and use is also found within the UK. Ownership is highest in East Anglia and in towns up to 250,000 population and these are also the areas of highest bicycle use.

A measure of whether or not ownership is increasing can be obtained from the changes in sales figures over the years. Annual sales in the UK have increased steadily since 1970, doubling between then and 1976 (when 1.1 million were sold) and reaching 1.4 million in 1979. The upturn in sales preceded that in use by about 5 years, a fact for which there is no obvious explanation. This does suggest, however, that as long as sales and therefore ownership continue to rise (and possibly for some time thereafter) bicycle use will increase.

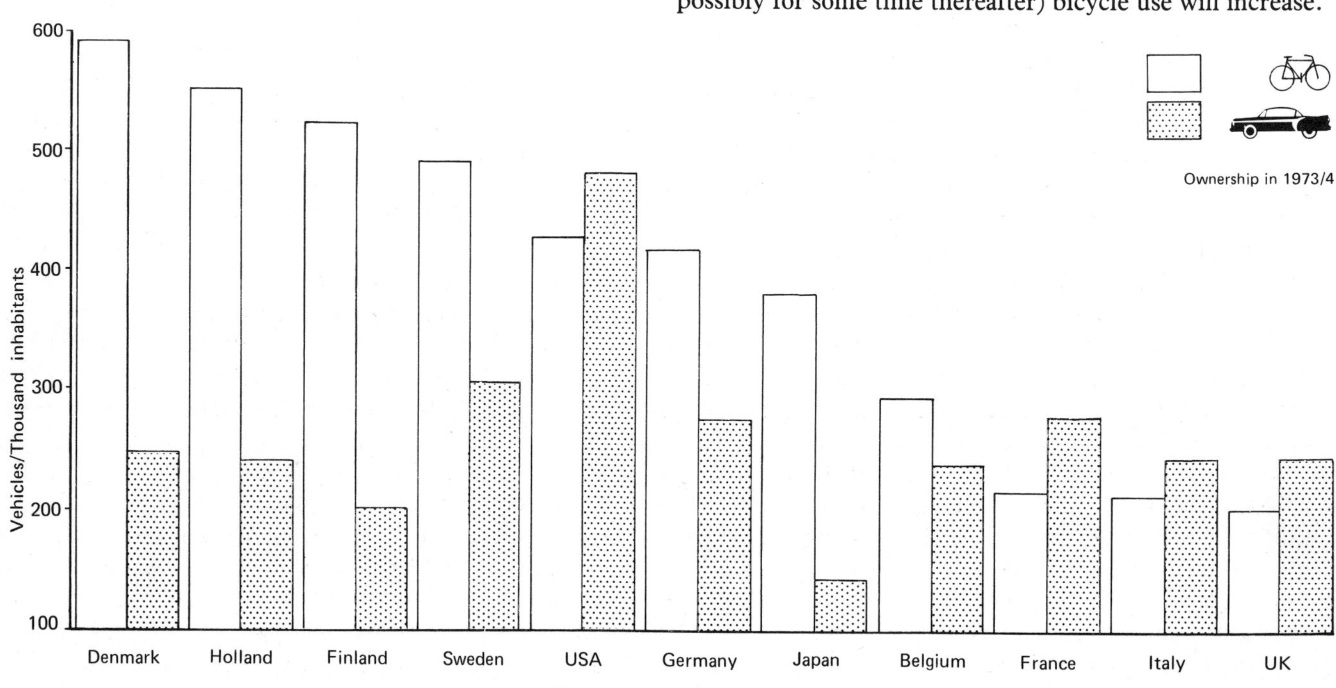

4.13 In many countries, bicycle ownership is higher than car ownership (Source: *Background Report No. 1.*)

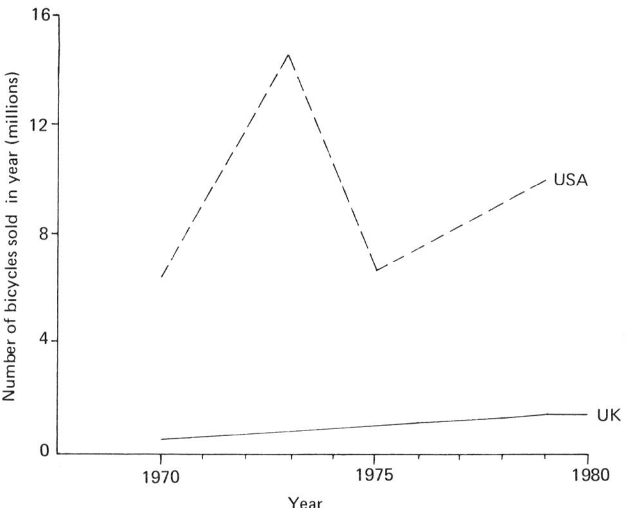

4.14 Sales of bicycles are now higher than ten years ago

4.3 PROSPECTS FOR BICYCLE USE

Among the factors affecting bicycle use discussed in the preceding sections there are a number which can, to some extent, change irrespective of the actions of planners; namely the design of bicycles, human performance, social attitudes, costs and ownership.

If these changes produce a significant increase in bicycle use, planners who have assumed that bicycle use will decline will be faced with a number of problems: bicycles strewn around shopping areas and public buildings, involved in more accidents, seen as a nuisance by other road users and residents, will all lead to pressure on local authorities to do something about the problems.

The economies of most Western countries are currently undergoing a period of restricted growth and both governments and individuals are having to make economies as the real costs of goods and services rise. It is unlikely that the rates of growth achieved until recently will be reached again in the near future.

The cheap forms of transport should therefore continue to gain popularity, with cycling and walking becoming more important. Bicycle ownership will almost certainly continue to rise as sales are maintained above those of cars, which have a shorter life. The versatility of the bicycles on the market should also continue to increase.

Sales of bicycles increased by an average of 0.1 million per annum in the UK in the 1970s and can be expected to increase further over the next twenty years. Ownership at the end of that twenty years could well be between two and three times present levels. There is every reason to believe that levels in the UK could double or treble since that would bring ownership rates up to those currently achieved in Holland. This in turn suggests a corresponding increase in usage over the next twenty years. Indeed, with an annual increase in usage of just 4%, bicycle use would double in twenty years and with an increase of 6%, it would treble. A three-fold increase would restore use to the levels of the 1950s and is therefore quite feasible. A 6% rise in bicycle use (current growth is as much as 10% per annum in the UK) would result from the transfer of just one in eighty trips under 5km currently made by car to the bicycle.

A three-fold increase in bicycle trips would almost certainly take place in the 1.5 to 5km range, despite improvements in the efficiency of bicycles and increases in the time which people are prepared to spend travelling. A more likely change will be in the nature of trips made, with group travel becoming more popular, particularly amongst families with young children, and with the more versatile design of bicycles permitting their use for a much wider range of trips. This type of use would contribute to the growing feeling that cycling can be the mode of choice, rather than necessity. It also suggests that increased usage will come substantially from adults, particularly women.

The sources of new bicycle trips will depend to a large extent on the purpose of the trip; the likely sources being as follows:

work – transfers from car and bus
education – transfers from bus and walk
shopping – transfers from walk, some generated
personal business – transfers from car and walk
social – transfers from car and walk, many generated.

4.4 THE EFFECT OF BICYCLE FACILITIES

A number of towns have introduced facilities for bicycles in various parts of the world. Since few of these have been in operation long, experience of their effects is limited. However, some measure of the effect of providing facilities can be gleaned from the results of limited studies in Sweden, Holland and the UK.

The increase in use on the routes improved was found to be as follows:

Sweden	15 to 30%
Holland	15 to 75%
UK	10 to 30%

Most of these increases are interim figures and all include both transferred and generated trips. The research suggests that about 10% of new trips are generated, the rest being transferred from other routes.

The other effects of providing new facilities are that the load on other transport facilities is eased and that more expensive investment in these other modes can be avoided.

4.5 COLLECTING LOCAL DATA ON BICYCLE USE

So far in this chapter, national data and data from selected towns have been used to illustrate the points. It is essential that any authority investigating bicycle use carries out its own surveys. These will reveal the pattern of cycling peculiar to that authority's area.

4.5.1 Assembling existing data

The assembly of all relevant available data should precede all other operations. Data may already exist on bicycle flows (from traffic surveys) or on ownership, attitudes and population structure (from private or Planning Department household or destination-based surveys). If initial research reveals little or no information on cycling in the area then the first step is to make sure that all relevant future surveys (interviews and traffic counts) include provision for the gathering of information on bicycle use on a regular basis.

4.5.2 Preliminary attitude survey

Authorities in areas where there is apparently little bicycle usage should nevertheless establish whether there are deterrents which are sufficiently serious to almost totally suppress cycling in their area but which could be easily overcome (For example an extremely busy, unavoidable ring road). This can be achieved by the wide distribution of a simple questionnaire containing, say, four open questions. For example:

Do you use a bicycle?
Have you considered using a bicycle?
What do you think your local authority could do which would encourage people to cycle (more)
(a) in general?
(b) in particular? (give problems or locations)

Would such measures make you cycle (more)?

The comments on possible measures to be taken by the local authority will give a guide to problems likely to arise as cycling becomes more popular over the years, or problems that could be rectified immediately to encourage cycling in the area. Widespread distribution of the questionnaire should be achieved so that most residents holding views on the subject have a chance of responding. The questionnaire could be sent out at little cost by including it in other council mailings, by leaving it in public buildings or distributing it in schools and places of work. Collection could be by means of boxes at public buildings.

4.5.3 Type of data needed

To design bicycle routes to accommodate existing flows, the planner needs only the following information:

existing flows
origins and destinations

Much more information is needed to predict change in use of the route over the twenty years of its design life, including:

current and expected structure of the area
current and expected structure of employment
current and expected structure of the population
(these are essential as they are unique to the area)
journey characteristics for modes other than bicycle
age and sex of cycling population
ownership of bicycles
attitudes towards cycling
(these are desirable as they will vary from area to area but where they are not available, national data can be used as a guide)

The data required falls into three categories according to the method by which it is obtained:

- Observation is used to discover vehicle flows and number of parked vehicles
- Questioning is used to discover the origins and destinations of journeys, journey purpose and bicycle ownership
- Assembly of existing data is used to assess population changes and proposed developments (see Section 4.5.1 above)

4.5.4 Observation

Observation is the most appropriate method of obtaining data on total flows. It can also be used to gauge the numbers of people cycling to given destinations by counting the number of bicycles parked there.

Some intuitive local knowledge must be used in selecting the sites for roadside counts. The general corridors in which there are bicycle movements should be found by observation, local knowledge or even talking to local bicycle clubs. Typical bicycle movements are: towards the town centre along radial routes; to schools or factories along district distributor roads or on existing bicycle facilities. It is important to realise that the main bicycle routes are often not the main motor vehicle routes.

Once the general direction of movement is established, the planner should look for barriers to this movement such as railways, ring roads, canals or rivers which have a limited number of possible crossing points. These are the natural locations for traffic counts as the limited number of survey points will provide information on all flows in a given direction (north to south, east to west, etc).

If such barriers do not exist, local knowledge must again be brought into play. Intuitive observation combined with informal questioning of local bicycle organisations can reveal where the most popular routes are and survey points can then be located on each type of road or path in the corridor. For example, a suitable 'screen-line', located to cut as few roads as possible, might cut the following roads in a corridor of movement:

two major radial routes
two district distributor roads
eight local distributor (access) roads.

An appropriate distribution of survey points would be:

one on each radial route
one on one of the district distributors
one on one of the local distributors.

The total flow across the screen-line is obtained by multiplying the flows for each type of road by the ratio of roads of that type crossing the screen-line to roads of that type on which counts were conducted.

The duration of counts will depend on the availability of personnel. The standard traffic count period is 16 hours

SAMPLE CALCULATION OF FLOW ACROSS A SCREEN-LINE

Observed flows **Survey points**	**Two-way flow (2 hr)**
Major radial 1	400
Major radial 2	250
District distributor	60
Local distributor	10

Total number of roads crossing screen-line

Type of road	**Number**
Major radial 1	1
Major radial 2	1
District distributors	2
Local distributors	8

Calculation of total flow

Flow = (major radials 1 & 2) + (2 × district distributor) + (8 × local distributor)
= 400 + 250 + (2 × 60) + (8 × 10)
= 850 bicycles in two hours

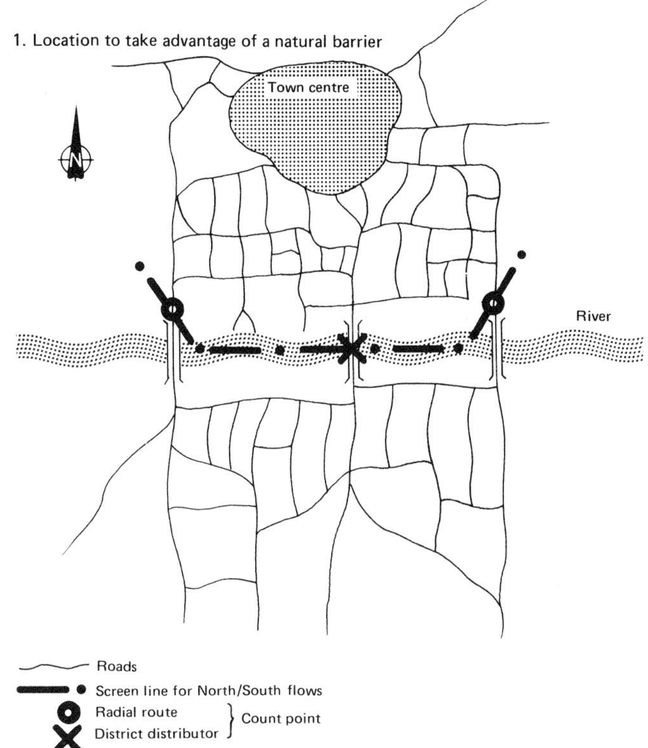

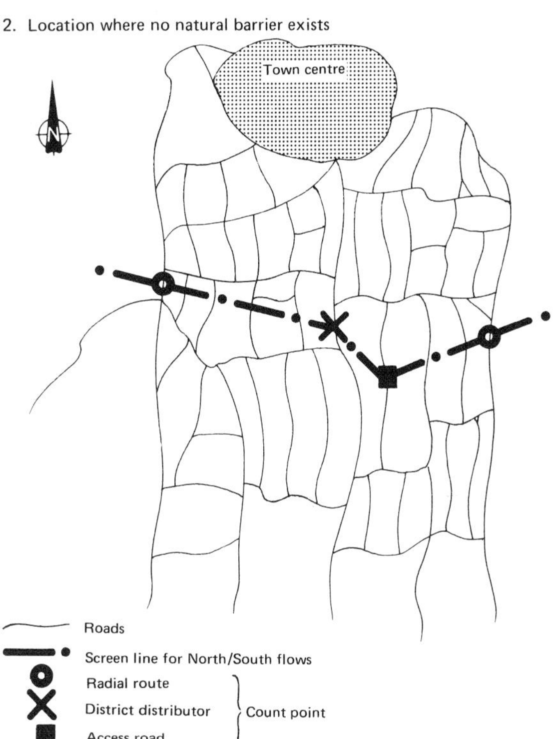

4.15 Traffic survey screen-lines should be located to cut as few roads as possible

(usually 0600 hours to 2200 hours) but this is far too expensive to be held on a regular basis by a local authority and too demanding for students or pressure groups. The minimum period covered should be the peak periods (about two hours each). These may not be the same for bicycles as for motor vehicles, especially if the flow is predominantly school children. Where possible, further counts should be added to peak counts on the following scale of priority:

off peak (two-hour period)
lunch time (two-hour period)

OBTAINING ORIGIN/DESTINATION DATA

Roadside surveys

- Approach cyclists as they stop at junctions near the normal traffic count sites
- Ask origin, destination and purpose of journey
- *Either* ask respondent to complete a written questionnaire at their leisure and return it by hand or post
  Or ask whether a home interview would be acceptable – this minimizes delay to the cyclist

Destination-based surveys

- Approach local schools, libraries, sports centres, theatres, employers and unions to obtain permission to administer questionnaire
- *Either* arrange for questionnaire to be administered by teachers at schools, left on desks in public places, mailed with theatre publicity or distributed in wage packets at places of work
  Or use a survey team to direct the filling in of the questionnaires
- The survey could be a simple origin and mode of travel survey or a far more complex one incorporating other information such as ownership and attitudes

If the intention is to observe variations over time, which can be locally quite pronounced, then frequent, short counts are of more use than infrequent, all-day counts. If resources are limited and the survey has to be spread over a number of days, then as many as possible of the counts should be held on the same day of the week, even if the counts are two weeks apart. Flows will vary from day to day because of factors such as early closing, market day and school games afternoon and the effect of these can be minimized by counting on the same day each week. For similar reasons it may be worth postponing a count if the weather is markedly bad for the time of year because casual bicycle use will be reduced and a false picture obtained. When trying to correlate total flow figures with origin/destination and journey purpose information, some breakdown of type of cyclist is useful. It is therefore worthwhile counting flows in four categories defined by the splits of male/female and child/adult. This latter category has to be somewhat arbitrary, especially outside school hours, but school-age/non school-age is the most useful division.

CITY OF WESTLAKE BICYCLE SURVEY – TRAFFIC COUNT FORM

Date: 25 FEBRUARY 1980 Location: HIGH ST.
Weather: FINE, DRY Enumerator: DB

¼ hour period starting	Adult		Child	
	M	F	M	F
0815	HHT HHT HHT HHT HHT HHT III 33	HHT HHT HHT HHT II 22	HHT HHT HHT II 17	HHT HHT II 12
0830	HHT HHT HHT	HHT HHT I	III	HHT HHT

4.16 Typical traffic count form

Information that can be obtained by questioning

Home based	**Roadside**	**Destination based**
Bicycle ownership Frequency of use Purpose of use Personal details of cyclists Attitudes towards cycling Vehicle ownership Household structure Travel diary	Origin Destination Address (if different) Purpose of journey Age } By observation Sex }	Origin Purpose of journey Mode of travel Whether cyclist Frequency of use Personal details of user Attitudes towards cycling Vehicle ownership Household structure Travel diary
Advantages		
Comprehensive Representative of population Contacts potential cyclists	Cheap and quick High cyclist response Relates to area of study	Comprehensive Concentration of respondents Contacts potential cyclists
Disadvantages		
Perhaps few cyclists Expensive Low response to written questionnaires	Covers existing cyclists only Hard to stop respondents Questionnaire must be short	Only a limited range of journey purposes are covered Low response to written questionnaire

4.17 There are advantages and disadvantages to all types of questioning

1. Home interview (administered verbally by interviewer) – extract

10. Please give the following information on bicycle ownership and use for members of your household:

Respondents:	1	2	3	4	5
Do you own a bicycle?	✓		✓	✓	
IF YES					
Do you use it daily?				✓	
once a week?			✓		
once a month?					
never?	✓				

IF NEVER

Why not? (indicate respondent number)

① Has car, cycle too dangerous

3. Destination-based questionnaire (completed by the respondent) – extract

6. How often do you travel to this destination?
(Please tick the most suitable answer)
☐ Every weekday ☐ Once a week
☐ Once a month ☐ Less than once a month
7. How did you travel here today?
(Please tick one box)
☐ Foot ☐ Bicycle ☐ Bus ☐ Train
☐ Car ☐ Motorcycle
Other (please describe method) ....
8. Is this your usual method of reaching this destination?
☐ Yes ☐ No
(Please tick one box)

2. Roadside interview (administered verbally by interviewer) – extract

CITY OF WESTLAKE BICYCLE SURVEY – ROADSIDE INTERVIEW FORM

Date: 3 MARCH 1980 **Location:** HIGH ST.
Weather: COLD, DAMP **Interviewer:** RH

¼ hour period starting	Adult M	Adult F	Child M	Child F	Origin	Destination	Purpose	Home interview arranged?
0815	✓				Alma Rd.	High St.	Work	✗
				✓	Green Lane.	Churchill School	School	✓

4.18 Typical questionnaires

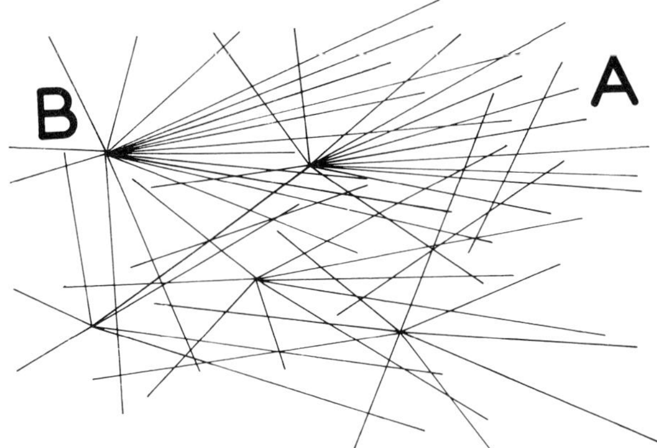

4.19 Diagramatic presentation of origin/destination data (desire-line diagram). Each line represents one journey plotted on, say, a 1:50 000 scale map. This diagram shows a large flow in the corridor **A** to **B**

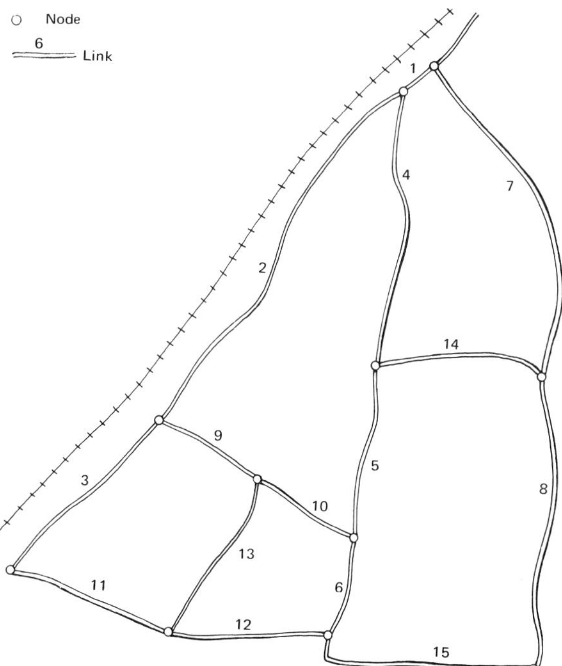

4.20 Typical link map for assigning flows to the road network

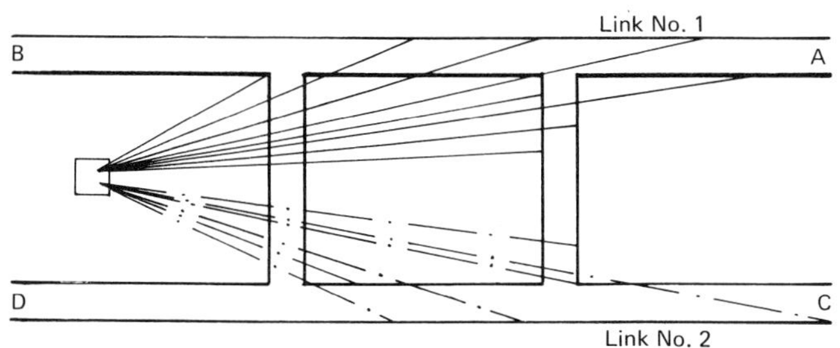

4.21 Assignment of present trips to the existing network using origin/destination data

Trips are assigned to routes to keep them as short as possible, ie:
Trips represented by desire lines drawn thus ——————
are assigned to route **AB** (link no 1)
Trips represented by desire lines drawn thus —— · ——
are assigned to route **CD** (link no 2)
The resulting flows should be consistent with traffic count data

HINTS ON SAMPLING FOR INTERVIEWS

Roadside surveys

At each site, carry out pre-survey traffic counts to establish the proportion of cyclists who fall into the four categories defined by the splits male/female and adult/child. Interviewers should stop as many cyclists as possible but try to maintain a balance of interviews which reflects the split in flows according to class of cyclist. The time period during which each interview is conducted should be recorded. It will generally be prohibitively expensive to conduct interviews throughout the day and the aim should be to obtain a representative sample of journeys during each period of markedly different type of use. This can be done by interviewing during the following periods:

- Peak period: throughout one of the peaks
- Lunch hour: throughout the period
- Off-peak daytime: one hour am and one hour pm
- Off-peak evening: one hour

The journey pattern obtained from each sample can be assumed to represent all journeys made during that period.

Home-based surveys (other than those following up a roadside interview)

Define the area considered to be within the catchment area for the facilities under study. Earlier roadside surveys may have given some indication of the area. Select the houses whose occupants are to be approached to give a cross-section of residents. For example, numbers 5, 10, 15, 20, 25, etc, in each street or block of flats.

Destination-based surveys

Select the destinations at which the interviews are to be carried out. Earlier roadside or home-based surveys may have given an indication of the main destinations likely to be served by the facilities under study. If not all the population at a given destination is to be interviewed, a simple but representative method of selection should be used. For example, all staff at a place of work whose family name begins with A or one form from each year at a school.

4.5.5 Questioning

Information on where cyclists are travelling to and from, or for what reason, which is particularly relevant in assessing the likely usage of a proposed facility, can only be obtained by asking the cyclists. This can be achieved by one of three methods of questioning:

home based
roadside
destination based.

Given economic and resource restrictions on most survey organisations, plus the need for rapid results, the best method is probably a combination of the roadside and destination-based surveys.

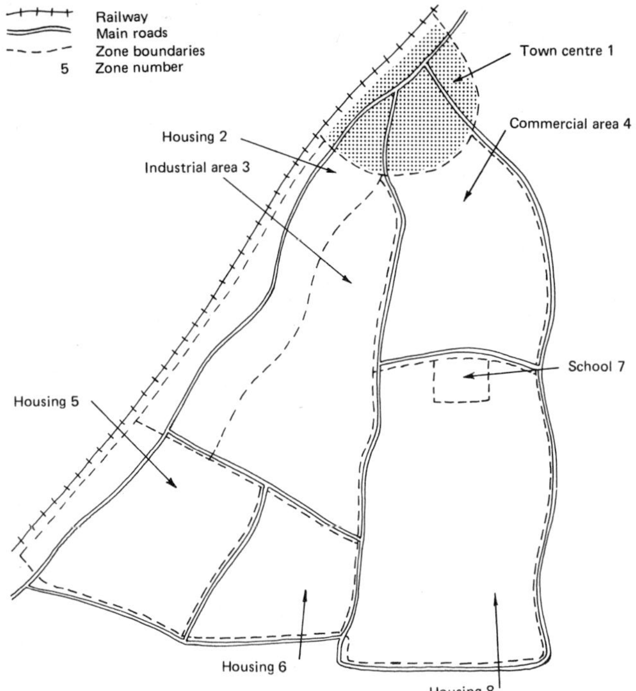

4.22 Origins and destinations should be found to fall into zones.

The particular advantage of destination-based surveys is that respondents whose journeys have been made by modes other than bicycle will also be approached and the potential for cycling can be assessed more easily.

The reliability of a questionnaire is always greater if the respondent is questioned verbally. If authorities use untrained interviewers, they must be carefully briefed and properly supervised if they are to produce reliable results. The size of sample that can be obtained will depend on the resources available. Details of sampling techniques should be read about elsewhere.

4.6 USING LOCAL DATA

The data obtained by the methods outlined in section 4.5 are suitable for any of the following purposes:

allocation of present flows to existing facilities
calculation of future use of existing facilities
calculation of future use of proposed facilities.

4.6.1 Allocation of present flows to existing facilities

Counts of total flows will have established where the main corridors of movement lie. These flows have to be correlated with the origin/destination (O.D.) data to provide a more detailed profile of bicycle movements. This can be done as follows:

For roadside surveys

- Establish O.D. pattern for the sample population interviewed
- Assume the same pattern for the population not interviewed
- Scale up the flows between pairs of origins and destinations using the ratio $\frac{\text{Total flow of bicycles passing interview site}}{\text{Number of cyclists interviewed}}$ and carry out separate calculations for each period and class of cyclist
- Check the resultant number of trips to a given destination that is implied against those measured (for example, by counts of parked bicycles or by trips claimed in interviews)
- implied usage should be less than or equal to the measured total.

For origin or destination based surveys

- Establish O.D. pattern for sample interviewed
- Assume the same pattern for the population not interviewed
- Scale up the flows for the sample interviewed using the ratio $\frac{\text{Total population of location where interviews conducted}}{\text{Number of people interviewed at the location}}$
- Allocate the flows to routes between the origins and destinations. These should generally be the shortest routes between two points with adjustments made to take account of the obviously popular routes as indicated by the counts of total flows
- Check the resultant flows implied on routes against the measured flows, making separate checks for each class of cyclist and the time at which a trip was likely to have been made. School trips, for example, are likely to have been made so that they finished in the half-hour before the start of the school day.
- Implied flows should generally be less than those observed

It is impossible to fully correlate O.D. data with measured flows but major discrepancies should not arise. For example, the number of school-age children observed cycling along a particular corridor may be fewer than the number claiming to ride along that corridor. A small error of this sort could be attributed to fewer children cycling on the day of the count than normal. A large error, however, would possibly indicate poor sampling techniques in the O.D. surveys or the omission of a counting site from one of the main cycling routes. Large errors should be investigated immediately and the cause removed before continuing with the analysis.

4.6.2 Calculation of future use of existing facilities

Changes in bicycle use over the period up to the design year (say twenty years) will come from two sources:

change in the structure of the study area
change in the popularity of cycling.

The effect of the change in structure can be assessed more easily if the area is divided into zones. If the O.D. data processed according to section 4.6.1 is plotted on maps of the area for each journey purpose, the origins and destinations should be found to fall into recognisable and different zones. Such zones might be shopping centres, school complexes, industrial areas, town centres or stations. The nature of bicycle journeys (short and flexibly routed) means that zones need to be smaller than those used in the analysis of motor vehicle trips. Having established a map of the zones for the area under study, the change in use can be calculated by obtaining the following information for each zone:

main function (employment, education, residence or other)
current size (work places, education places or population)
expected size in the design year.

The number of work or education trips to a zone depends primarily on the number of places available in that zone. The

5 The safety of cycling

5.1 The *feeling* that cycling is unsafe is undoubtedly a deterrent to potential cyclists

The feeling that cycling is unsafe is undoubtedly one of the greatest deterrents to both individuals and to local authorities considering whether to encourage cycling in their area. Unfortunately, the opinions of many decision-makers on the safety of cycling do not always fully correspond with objective measurements. Cycling is usually thought to be more dangerous than it actually is.

For the individual cyclist this belief may lead to a decision not to cycle. In the case of local authorities, the result has wider consequences. There is a tendency to believe that if nothing is done for cyclists, then cycling will disappear as a mode of transport and the accident problem will be removed. The evidence presented in Chapter 4 shows that bicycle use is likely to continue to increase, irrespective of the actions of planners. Bicycle accidents will therefore remain a problem.

This chapter examines objective measurements of bicycle safety and shows what countermeasures should be taken to make cycling safer.

5.1 MEASURING THE RISK OF CYCLING

5.1.1 Statistical basis

In many countries, the standard way of collecting accident data is from police reports of injury accidents. Dividing the number of such accidents by the total distance travelled by a particular mode determines the accident rate for that mode. Studies in both Great Britain and Denmark have shown that as few as 25% of accidents involving injury to cyclists are reported to the police. Over 90% of the reported accidents involved another vehicle and only 5% of the unreported accidents did so. Police accident reports can therefore provide a reasonable estimate of the number of accidents in which a bicycle and a motor vehicle are involved. These accidents are an adequate measure of the risk of cycling. Cyclists tend to accept occasional falls from their machines in the same way that pedestrians accept tripping on footways or

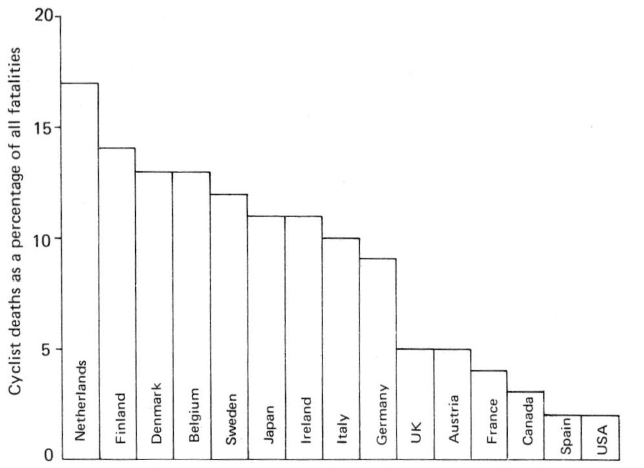

5.2 Cyclist deaths form a significant proportion of all road fatalities (Source: *Background Report No. 1*)

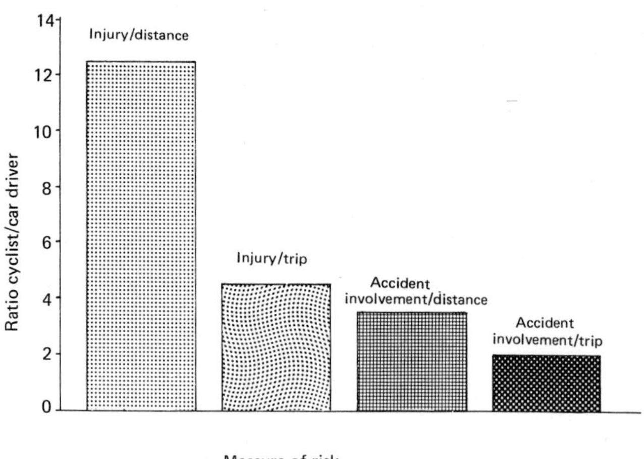

5.4 Relative risks of cycling and driving a car

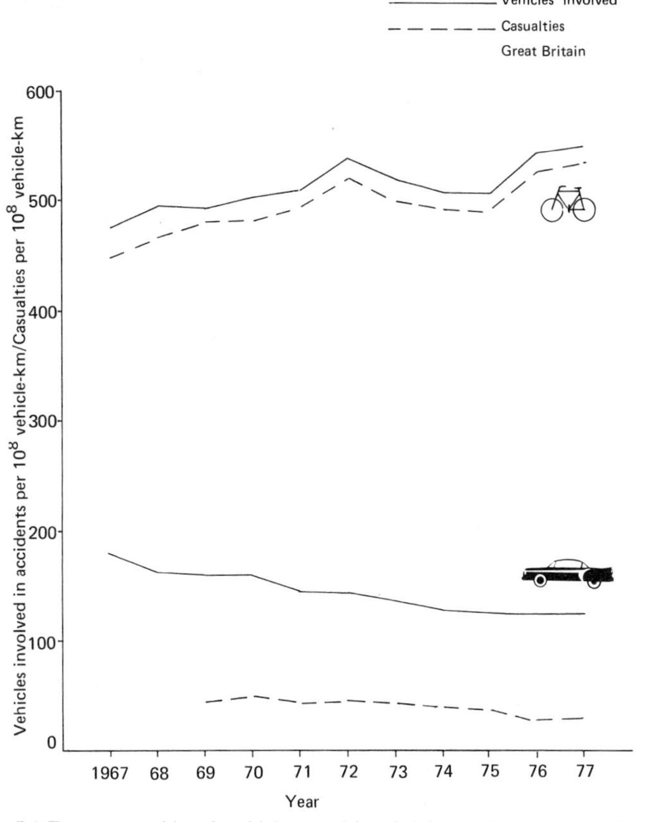

5.3 For every accident in which a car driver is injured, there are two others involving a car where someone else is injured (Source: *UK Annual Abstract of Statistics*)

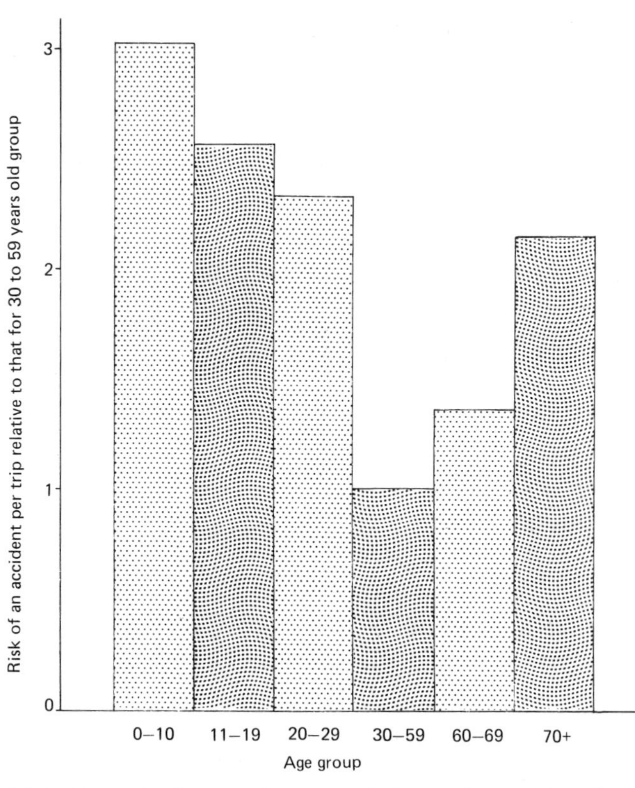

5.5 Cyclists under 10 years old are most likely to be involved in accidents

motorists accept damage-only accidents. None of these accidents is recorded in road accident statistics. It is collisions with motor vehicles which cause concern and fear among cyclists and it is these which are recorded in official statistics.

Information on the causes of single-vehicle accidents, however, provides a good indication of the standard of route required for comfortable cycling.

An alternative way of measuring the accident rate for a particular mode or user is by 'accidents per journey'. The average length of a journey is greater for a car than a bicycle because car owners use its greater range to extend their choice of destination or the location of their home. A car owner making a similar number and type of trips as a cyclist will therefore often cover a greater distance. On the 'accidents per journey' basis, cycling is therefore distinctly less dangerous than on the 'accidents per unit distance' basis when comparing modes.

Though the information needed to calculate accident rates on the basis of journeys completed is not as easily available as that for distance travelled, it is a better measure of the risk of injury to an individual.

5.1.2 Annual casualties

Every year in Great Britain, 20–24,000 cyclists are injured in road accidents, 300 of them fatally. This latter figure represents about 5% of all fatalities in road accidents, a lower proportion than in most European countries and on a par with North America. These figures say little about the relative risk of cycling in different countries because the proportion of trips made by bicycle will vary, but they do show that action to improve the safety of cycling could significantly reduce the total number of road accidents.

5.1.3 Age and sex of casualties

In Western countries, a substantial proportion of cyclist casualties are under 20 years of age. In Great Britain, 40% are less than 15 years old and the proportion of cyclist casualties under 10 years of age has increased over the past twenty years from 4 to 14% for fatal and serious casualties.

Younger cyclists do not have any alternative means of personal transport. They will therefore continue to be a likely source of bicycle accident victims and much effort will have to be expended to improve their safety.

In most countries where data is available, more cyclist casualties are male than female, especially in the younger groups. However, in the absence of data on the relative number of journeys made by each sex, it cannot be assumed that male cyclists are more at risk than females on a particular journey.

5.1.4 Accidents per unit distance

The casualty rate for cyclists in Great Britain, per kilometre travelled, has risen steadily as the distance covered annually by motor vehicles (excluding motorway use) has increased. The risk to users of motor vehicles has fallen steadily. It appears therefore that the measures successfully taken to improve motor vehicle safety have produced relatively few benefits for cyclists, who have found it increasingly dangerous to mix with larger flows of faster moving motor vehicles.

The casualty rate for a particular mode only measures how safe it is for users of that mode. It does not measure the risk to the whole community resulting from the use of that mode. This is determined from the 'casualty rate for accidents involving a particular mode' (ie, including accidents in which the user of the mode is not injured but someone else is). For example, in Great Britain in one year bicycles were involved in 24,000 injury accidents and in all but 50 of these the rider was injured. Cars and taxis were involved in 203,000 injury accidents and in 74,000 of these, the driver was injured. In other words, in most accidents in which a cyclist is involved the cyclist is injured, but for every accident in which a car driver is injured there are two others involving a car where someone else is injured. The casualty rate for accidents involving a car is therefore around 120 per hundred million kilometres travelled, compared with the cyclists' rate of around 500 per hundred million kilometres travelled.

5.1.5 Accidents per journey completed

The risk of a cyclist being involved in an accident in Great Britain is around twice that of a car driver per trip completed. The risk of being injured is about four-and-a-half times that of a car driver.

Cyclists under 10 years old are more likely than any other age group to be involved in an accident per trip made, with cyclists between 30 and 59 years old being the safest. This probably reflects the problem of training children to appreciate the dangers of using the roads and to behave in a way which minimizes danger.

5.1.6 Single-vehicle accidents

Single-vehicle accidents are primarily a cause of annoyance to cyclists and do not feature prominently in public discussion of the risks of cycling. Loss of control is almost always the cause and this loss is usually attributable to hitting an object in, or at the side of, the carriageway. Kerbs, drainage covers and mud are the common causes. Other causes include mechanical faults in the bicycle or the actions of the rider.

The causes of single-vehicle accidents are also often contributory factors to accidents with other vehicles. Data gathered on single-vehicle accidents may therefore provide local authorities with useful pointers to potential injury accident causes or locations.

5.1.7 Types of injury

In two-thirds of fatal bicycle accidents, head injuries contribute to death and in around half the fatal accidents it is the sole cause of death.

A hospital-based study of cyclist casualties (including accidents not reported to the police) found that among the 7% of those treated for severe to fatal injuries, the most common injury was to the upper or lower limbs. These figures support the classic picture of cyclist accidents. If struck by another vehicle, damage to the lower limbs will be sustained on impact and to the head on hitting the ground, unless this can be averted by sticking out the arms, in which case they will sustain injury. In the USA, 60% of injuries

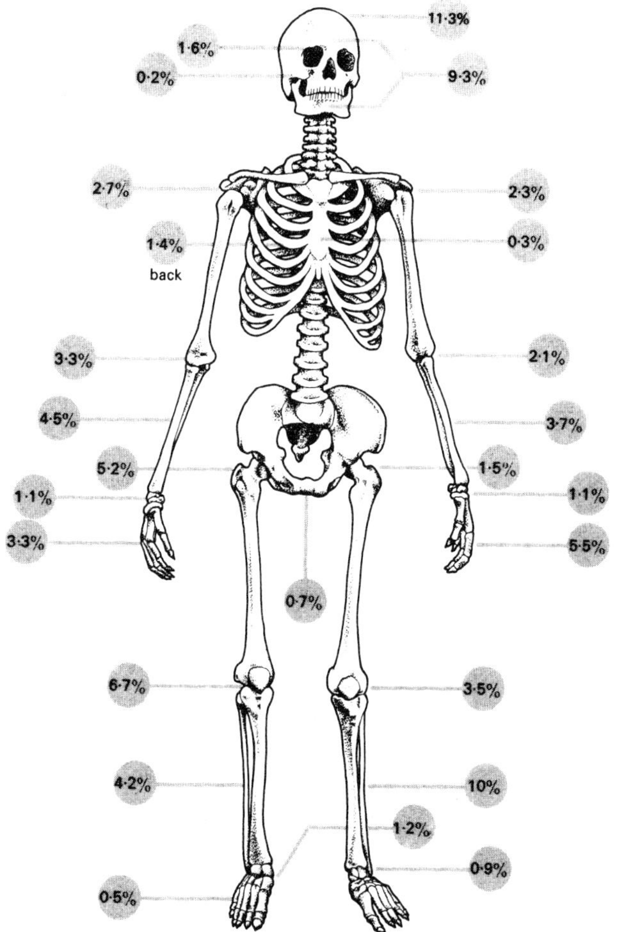

5.6 The most common injuries to cyclists are to the upper and lower limbs and the head (Source: *Pedal Cyclist Casualties in London*)

result from impact with the road and 42% from impact with a motor vehicle.

For single-vehicle accidents, injury to the lower limbs will be less common than injury to the head and arms. (About 25 cyclists die in single-vehicle accidents each year in Great Britain.)

5.2 CHARACTERISTICS OF ACCIDENTS

The factors which contribute to accidents can be split into four groups:

- The physical characteristics of the location (type of junction or road and its condition)
- The behaviour of the road users involved
- Variable factors beyond the control of the individual road user (traffic flow and speed, weather conditions and lighting conditions)
- The condition of the vehicles.

The problems associated with poor road surfaces and debris have already been mentioned in section 5.1.6. The other factors are discussed below.

5.2.1 Common locations and types

In Great Britain, about two-thirds of all cycling accidents occur at or within 20 metres of a junction. Even allowing for the fact that some accidents within 20 metres of a junction may not be attributable to the junction being there, junctions are clearly the major location of accidents involving cyclists. Five types of accident emerge as being common in three countries for which detailed information is available: Denmark, Great Britain and the USA:

- Cyclists turning across the traffic flow into a side road and colliding with a vehicle following or approaching
- Cyclists emerging from a side road into the path of a motor vehicle
- Motorist overtaking a cyclist
- Cyclist emerging from a footway or alleyway into the path of a motor vehicle
- Motorist emerging from a side road and hitting a cyclist.

An additional type of accident that is common in Great Britain is cyclists running into parked vehicles or open doors. These accidents are most common in heavily parked areas (arterial roads and roads in London).

The main movement involved in all of these accidents (except those involving overtaking or a motorist pulling out of a side road) is cyclists having to cross or join the path of a motor vehicle which has right of way. The frequency of this type of accident shows that this crossing movement is inherently difficult. Cyclists are slower than motor vehicles and less stable when moving away from a stationary position.

5.2.2 Behavioural factors

Immediately before an accident partially caused by a behavioural factor someone will probably have done one of the following:

- Failed to anticipate or perceive a potentially dangerous situation
- Anticipated or perceived the situation but failed to judge it correctly
- Perceived and judged the situation but deliberately taken a risk.

It is frequently difficult to determine objectively which way a road user has behaved and thus whether the user has been

TYPE OF ACCIDENT	PERCENTAGE OF ALL ACCIDENTS: UK children	Denmark	USA Fatal	USA Non-fatal
1. Cyclist turns into side road 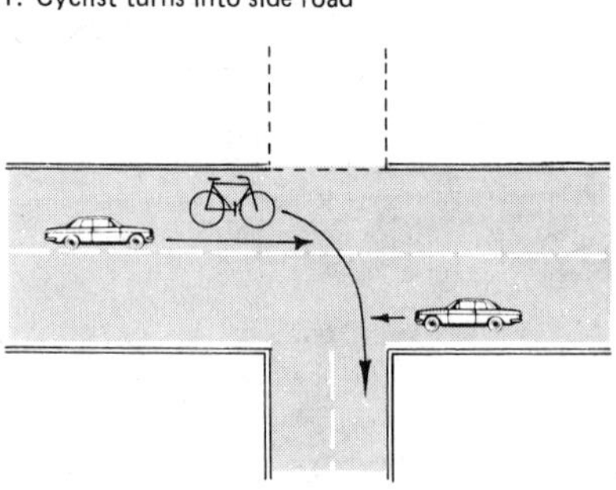	21.3	15.9	11.4*	11.6*
2. Cyclist emerges from side road 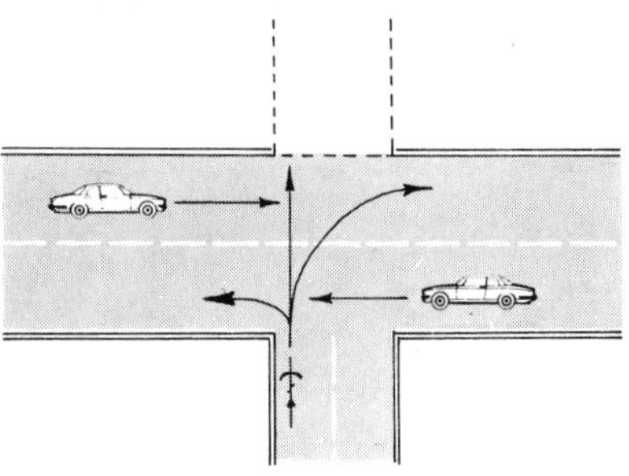	16.8	15.7	12.0	17.0
3. Motorist overtakes 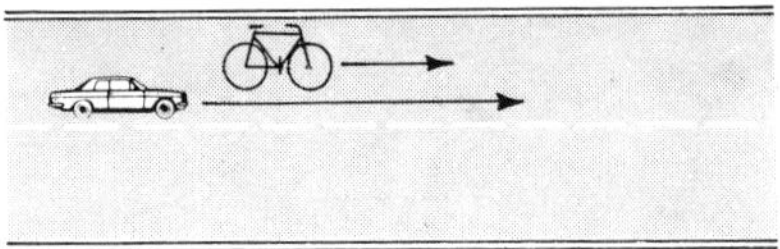	12.9	10.4	24.6	4.0
4. Cyclist rides off footway or drive 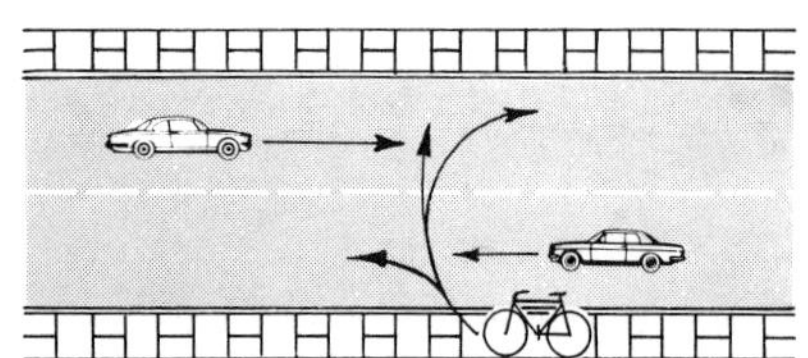	17.8	not recorded	15.1	13.9
5. Motorist emerges from side road 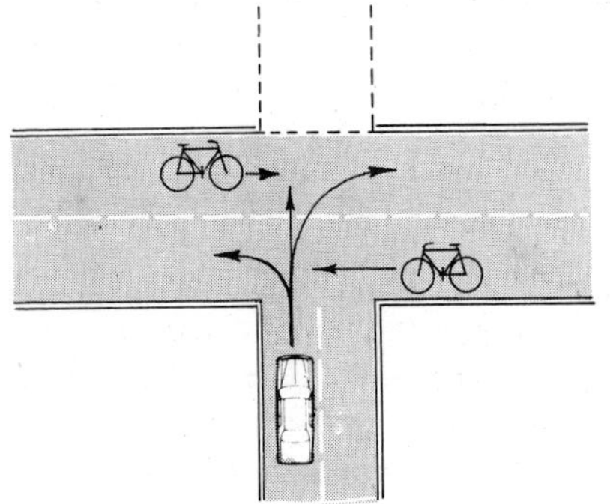	9.0	10.1	2.4*	18.7*

*Includes movements into or out of accesses

Figures for 'T' junctions and cross roads have been combined

5.7 Common types of bicycle accidents

simply inattentive or actually dangerous in their actions. The best available way of assessing who has caused an accident in which more than one vehicle is involved is to determine who has contravened a traffic law or code.

Cyclists' behaviour

A Metropolitan Police study in London judged adult cyclists to have contravened a law or code in one-third of accidents in which they were involved but cyclists under 15 to have contravened a law or code in two-thirds of their accidents. By comparison, an American study considered cyclists to be responsible for over two-thirds of all cycle accidents. This latter figure, however, includes accidents in which the cyclist was not necessarily contravening a law but was, for example, 'travelling too fast for conditions'. In the American bicycle accidents, the main reasons were found to be as follows:

faulty expectations and assumptions
operator distractions
faulty judgements
competing needs
loss of vehicle control.

Loss of control was assessed as the cause in 58% of child cyclist accidents in Great Britain. An Australian study highlighted the unpredictability of child cyclist behaviour and the poor quality of bicycle maintenance. Much of the unpredictability stems from their use of bicycles for play. In such circumstances they may not think of themselves as road users and therefore fail to recall road safety procedures.

Motorists' behaviour

Many bicycle accidents are caused by motorists contravening traffic laws. In the USA, these contraventions were found to be mainly attributable to:

faulty expectations and assumptions
operator distractions
faulty judgements
temporary driver impairment
degraded visibility.

In many of these accidents it was the failure of the motorist to see the cyclist which contributed to the accident. In some of these cases the lighting conditions were good and in others the bicycle was poorly lit or street lighting was poor. Temporary impairment of the motorist through alcohol was a significant contributor to error.

Overtaking behaviour

In overtaking accidents it is often difficult to determine which, if either, party contravened traffic laws or codes. Common factors contributing to such accidents are motorists giving cyclists too little clearance, often causing the cyclist to lose control and motorists failing to see the cyclist in time.

5.2.3 Type of road and traffic flows

In Great Britain, the risk of injury per unit distance travelled is greater for cyclists on urban roads than on rural roads. However, the risk of fatal injury is greater on rural roads in Great Britain and many Western countries. Rural roads do not have as many points of conflict and have lower traffic flows than urban roads but the traffic speeds are higher. Accidents are therefore less frequent but injuries more serious.

Within both rural and urban areas, the risk of injury is lower on minor roads than on major roads. Relative speeds of traffic again contribute significantly to this difference in rural areas. A more important reason on urban roads is probably that traffic is denser on the classified roads and they are used more by through traffic and strangers, who may be unfamiliar with the roads.

An investigation of the total numbers of cyclists injured according to class of road in Great Britain revealed that far more child cyclists were injured on minor roads than on major roads.

Three conclusions can be drawn from the above data:

- Accidents will be more likely where motor vehicle flows are high and junctions frequent
- The severity of accidents will be highest where traffic speeds are high
- Children are often injured on quieter roads where they are probably playing.

5.2.4 Weather and time

In most Western countries, between 70 and 80% of bicycle accidents occur during daylight. However, a Danish study indicates that it is more dangerous to cycle at night than during the day; furthermore, the risk of an injury being fatal is higher at night. In Great Britain, almost all accidents in darkness involve cyclists aged over 14. The risk of injury and death may therefore be greater to the individual after dark but the overall cost to the community of accidents during daylight is greater than that of accidents after dark.

The number of accidents involving adults varies little over the year but the number of accidents involving cyclists under 15 peaks in the summer, probably reflecting an increase in cycling by children in the summer holiday months.

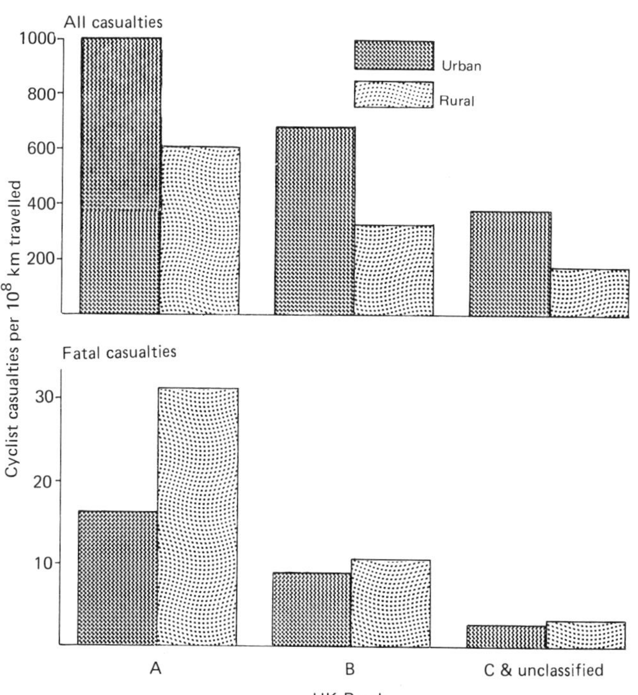

5.8 The risk of injury is higher on urban roads but the risk of death is higher on rural roads. Busy roads are more dangerous than quiet roads

Studies in London, America and Denmark have concluded that adverse weather conditions are not a major contributory factor to bicycle accidents.

5.3 THE COST OF BICYCLE ACCIDENTS

When a road accident occurs, costs are incurred by both those involved and the community as a whole. In Great Britain the costs are considered to be as follows:

police and administration
medical and ambulance services
damage to property
lost output
pain, grief and suffering.

The cost of an accident will therefore vary according to the people and vehicles involved. Current costs are around £2000 sterling for a bicycle accident (average cost) and £85,000 for a fatal accident (average cost, all road users).

If a local authority therefore prevents just one fatal bicycle accident by spending say £50,000 on improved routes or education, then the cost will have been recouped on the basis of improved safety alone. Any savings in travel costs or roads investment would be additional.
£50,000 might provide any of the following:

four signal controlled crossings
four kilometres of cycle track
road safety campaigns for five years.

There is a very good chance that any of these measures could save at least one cyclist's life and prevent a number of injuries. Funding for road safety measures is therefore actually a profitable investment for the community and not simply a socially desirable measure.

5.4 KEEPING LOCAL RECORDS

It is as important to obtain local data on the risks of cycling as it is on usage. National trends will give a guide to likely types of accident but will not serve to identify the particular factors in an area which contribute most to accidents. Local authority records have to be compiled from information gathered by the emergency services attending accidents or called on afterwards. This information should be collected in two forms:

standardised accident reports
police notes.

Information obtained from these sources should be all that is needed initially by the local authority. It will not, however, be in the most usable form for the local authority's purposes. An authority will therefore need to establish its own data storage system to suit its needs.

5.4.1 Standardized accident records

In order to establish centralized national accident records, some governments have arrangements with their police forces that each accident attended be reported on a standard form. The form will, typically, list the vehicles involved, the location, the conditions, the casualties and the manoeuvres of the vehicles prior to the accident. For simplicity, the various possibilities are usually coded, the alternative entries for each category being devised from experience of detailed reports. Copies of these forms may be sent to the local authority in whose area the accident occurred. If not, then the authority should arrange for this to be done. The standard forms are usually designed to cover all possible types of accident and cannot therefore give details of all aspects of the accident. If the local police force is agreeable, the local authority should arrange for a more detailed supplementary standard accident report to be made out. This could contain extra data on such items as conditions of the bicycle, apparent reasons for any loss of control or position of cyclist on the highway.

5.4.2 Police notes

If the police are not prepared to regularly forward standardised reports, or if the information recorded on the reports is inadequate, the police should be asked to allow an authorised member of the local authority staff to periodically examine the original notes of the police officers who attended the accidents. These notes will be the best of all sources of information as they will include:

sketches of the vehicle movements
uncoded notes on conditions
uncoded notes on casualties
statements of witnesses
notes on conditions of vehicles involved
descriptions of drivers' behaviour.

5.4.3 Local authority data banks

As each accident report is received, the information contained in it should be transferred to a data storage system. Many local authorities have access to computer storage facilities and each accident should be entered into such systems in a combination of coded and written information. In addition, all the information obtained should be transferred to a separate record sheet for each accident. These record sheets are best filed according to location.

5.5 PROCESSING LOCAL RECORDS

The data obtained by the methods described in section 5.4 will not immediately identify the main safety problems for

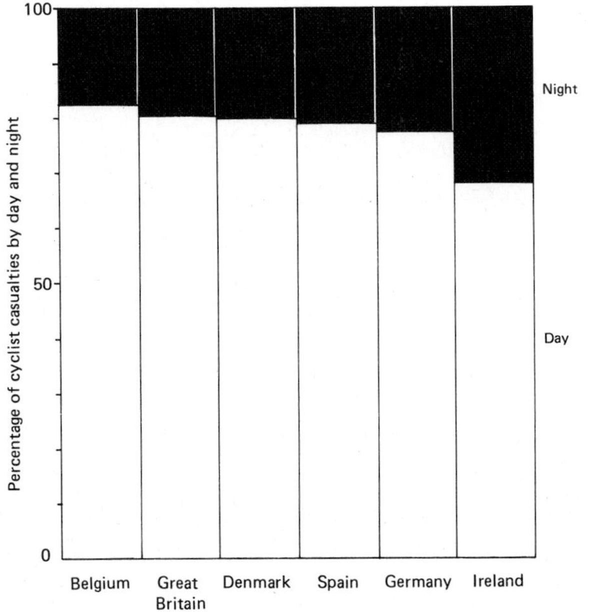

5.9 Between 70 and 80% of accidents occur during daylight (Souce: *Safety of Two-Wheelers*)

STATS 19 Coding Form - all fields must be completed

Exact Location

Map Reference (East) (North) Parish Local Authority

Description (In difficult cases attach sketch plan)

Record Type 1 | Accident Ret No. | Date | Time | Day | Speed 0 | 1st Rd Class & Num. * | 2nd Rd. Class & Num. *

Weather | Carriageway Type | Junction Detail | Junction Control | Pedestrian Crossing | Road Surface | Carriageway Hazards * | Parked veh. involved | Overtaking Pattern | Light | Special Conditions * | No of Casualties 0 | No. of Vehicles 0 ₦

Vehicle Reference | Suffix letter | Vehicle Type | No. of axles | Max. weight | Age of driver | Sex of driver | Parts damaged * | 1st point of impact | Breath Test | Towing | Vehicle Location | Manoeuvres | Compass point | Junction Location | Hit and Run | Hit objects off Carriageway * | Skidding | Hit objects in Carriageway * | Other vehicle hit | Vehicle leaving c/w | Sp. Proj. ₦

C | Casualty | Age | Sex | Severity | School Pupil | School Attended * | Vehicle Reference | Vehicle Type | Class | Pedestrian Location | Pedestrian Movement | Pedestrian Direction | Car Passenger | Seat Belts | P.S.V. Passenger | Sp. Proj. ₦ | School Attended

Pedestrian involved not hit - P

Q | Sel. | Contributary Factors * | Attended | D.T.P Sp. Proj. * | L.A Sp. Proj ₦

FOR COUNTY COUNCIL USE

Location L ₦

1st. Section No. | Grid Reference | Junction Node * | 1st Section * | 2nd Section * | 2nd Section No. *

Accident Type * | L.A. | Parish No. | Local Area Code * | Rec No of Cas. | Rec No of Veh. ₦

Description D ₦

5.10 Typical police accident report form

CITY OF WESTLAKE POLICE
BICYCLE ACCIDENT – SUPPLEMENTARY REPORT

Acc. ref. no. 76/032 Date 26/03/76 Time 09.25

Description of location
High St. jc. with West Rd.

Sketch of location at time of accident (show parked vehicles) and vehicle movements prior to accident

West Rd
SHOPS
CAR
SHOPS
VAN
P.C.
High St
N

Description of accident (include conditions and possible contributory factors)
Car pulled out of West Rd without stopping and hit cyclist. car had tried to brake at last minute but skidded on wet road. Driver had not seen P.C. until too late because of light van parked by jc. Cyclist had not altered course.

Source of description
Car driver and witness

Note of condition of vehicles prior to accident.
Car side windows misted. Cycle brakes defective.

Note of conditions of users prior to accident
No abnormal conditions

5.11 Typical supplementary accident report form

REF. NO	DAY DATE TIME	LOCATION SPEED LT. RD. TYPE	JC. TYPE MISC. CONDS.	LIGHT WEATHER SURFACE	VEH.	INJURIES CL VEH AGE DEG SEX	ACC. TYPE MOVES BEF. MARKINGS	DESCRIPTION
76/032	FRIDAY 26/03/76 09.25	730295 High St junc. West Rd 48 kph unclass	42 0	Day Dry Wet	1Car 2Cyc	Dri 2 10 Ser M	43 3 2	Car 1. travelling East pulled out West Rd hit cyc 2 travelling North on High St

CODED INFORMATION — BRIEF WRITTEN DESCRIPTION

5.12 Typical computer record entry

CITY OF WESTLAKE
BICYCLE ACCIDENT RECORDS **REF. NO.** 76/032

Date 26/03/76 Time 09.25 Location High St jc. with West Rd. N

L.A. Accident type 17

Sketch of accident

CAR
West Rd
VAN
P.C.
High St

Notes of accident
Car pulled out of West Rd. before looking and hit P.C.. Car disobeyed "Give Way" control. Driver's view obscured by van. Car skidded

Conditions
Road was busy and heavily parked. Road was wet but it was not raining at time of accident.

Vehicle users
Car driver – male, 35. Cyclist – male, 10.

Vehicle conditions
Car side windows misted. Cycle brakes defective.

Injuries
None to car driver. Cyclist – broken leg, internal injuries. Detained 10 days. No permanent disability

Legal action
Motorist convicted of careless driving.

5.13 Typical local authority accident record sheet

cyclists in an area. The data has to be processed to show whether accidents are common to a:

- specific location
- type of road
- type of junction
- type of manoeuvre
- particular environmental factor
- type of road user behaviour
- particular age group of cyclists.

The techniques that can be used are described in the following sections.

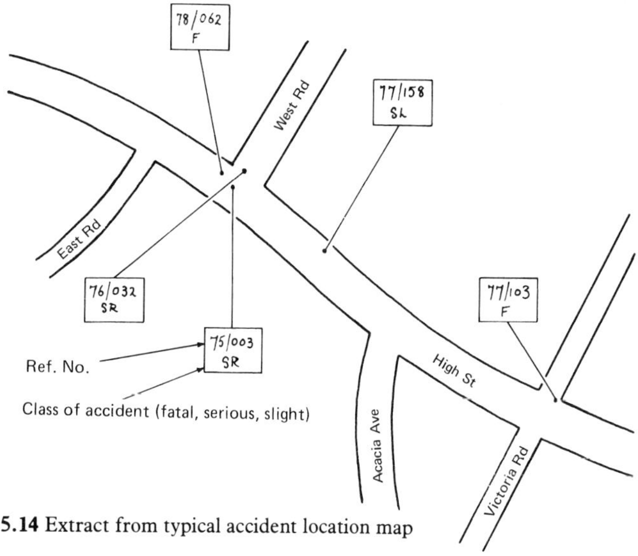

5.14 Extract from typical accident location map

5.5.1 Accident location

The first step in processing accident data should always be the production of an accident map for the area under study. Each accident that has occurred over, say, the five years preceding the study should be plotted on a scale map of the area (1 to 1250 or 2500 is suitable). Any locations representing a major hazard to cyclists will be evident from the map. Such locations might typically be a:

- roundabout
- section of major road
- school or park entrance
- major road junction
- shopping street.

Similarly, a particular type of location may be found to be dangerous to cyclists, although no one such location has a concentration of accidents. These might be any of the above, or others such as:

- residential streets
- major/minor junctions.

5.5.2 Accident type

Having identified a particular location or type of location as dangerous for cyclists, the next stage is to prepare a larger scale drawing (1 to 200 or 100) of the (type of) location, showing diagramatically the accidents which have occurred there.

These drawings will show whether a particular type of manoeuvre is putting cyclists at risk and enable remedial measures to be implemented, or they will provide the basis for more detailed field studies.

If a particular type of manoeuvre is identified as dangerous for one type of location, accidents at other types of location should be examined to see whether the same type of manoeuvre is causing problems elsewhere. For example, a turn across a following line of motor vehicles could feature at major/minor crossroads, at T-junctions or in a shopping area away from any junctions.

5.5.3 Causal factors

Comprehensive accident records should contain details of any factors which are considered to have contributed to each accident. These should relate to environment, behaviour and vehicular conditions.

Section 5.2 detailed some of the common factors contributing to bicycle accidents. Local authorities should establish the frequency with which various factors occur in accidents in their area. The best way of doing this is to tabulate the various causal factors against the accidents in which they occur. The nature of the original accident reports may to

1. Specific location

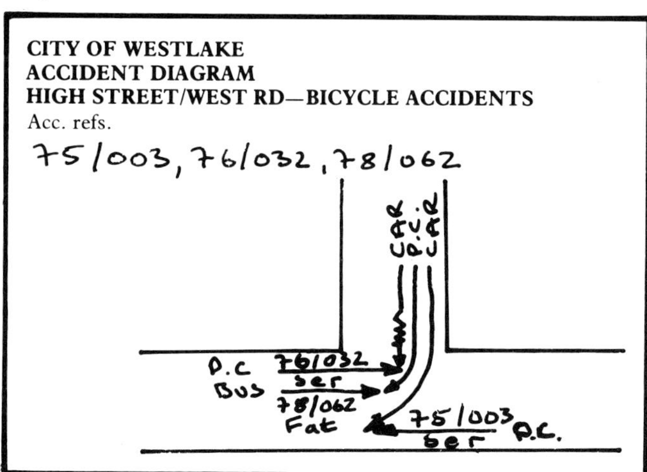

2. Type of location

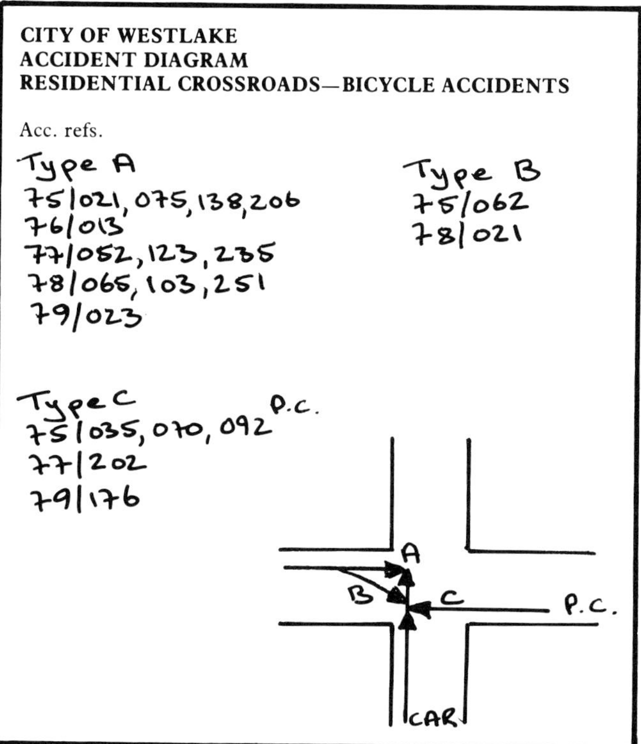

5.15 Accident diagrams will show whether a particular type of manoeuvre is putting cyclists at risk

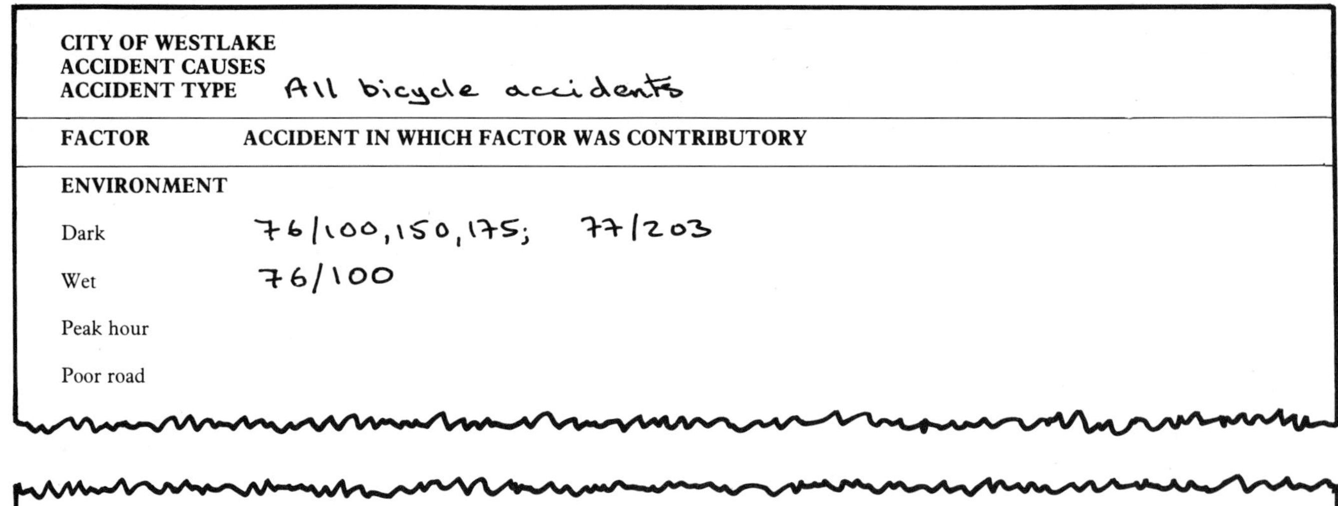

CITY OF WESTLAKE
ACCIDENT CAUSES
ACCIDENT TYPE All bicycle accidents

FACTOR	**ACCIDENT IN WHICH FACTOR WAS CONTRIBUTORY**
ENVIRONMENT	
Dark	76/100, 150, 175; 77/203
Wet	76/100
Peak hour	
Poor road	
Behaviour	
No signal	77/123; 78/032; 79/201
Disobeyed sign	
Vehicular condition	
Brakes faulty	
No lights	

5.16 Tabulations will identify causal factors for which countermeasures can be devised

some extent determine the categories of causes but local authorities should be able to devise their own categories by an in-depth study of, say, one year's accidents. Typical causes might include:

- Environment: darkness, rain, peak hour vehicle or pedestrian flows, obstructed vision, poor road surface, substandard lighting, bright sunlight or heavy shadow
- Cyclists' behaviour: talking to friend, bicycle overloaded, racing, riding no-handed, looking at shops, failing to signal, veering off line without warning, not seeing road sign, failing to stop, unsuitably clothed, drunk or under the influence of drugs
- Motorists' behaviour: speeding, failing to see road sign, disobeying road sign, failing to see cyclist, failing to signal, looking for unfamiliar destination, stopping suddenly, drunk or under the influence of drugs
- Vehicular conditions: lights, tyres or brakes in poor condition, lights not switched on, steering defective, bicycle the wrong size, motor vehicle windscreen dirty.

Tabulations of all accidents in the area should be made. The most common factors contributing to bicycle accidents will become apparent and countermeasures can be devised.

5.5.4 Characteristics of cyclists

The countermeasures devised for a particular accident problem may vary according to the age and sex of the user involved in the accidents. Separate analyses should therefore be carried out for the four groups defined by the splits male/female and under 16 years/16 years and above. Further subdivisions by age that prove practicable should be smaller for children than for adults; say five and ten year groups respectively.

A behavioural factor may be found to be common for a particular class of user (for example, failing to look before turning). Publicity and training measures can be devised to cope with the factor and schemes initiated at suitable locations such as schools, youth organisations, public buildings and work places.

5.6 LOCAL FIELD SURVEYS

When a local authority has processed the data obtained from local records, certain locations, types of location or causal factors will emerge as problems in their area. Before the introduction of countermeasures, further field studies may be needed to obtain information which is not contained in the original accident reports. There may, for example, be an obstruction to sight lines at a particular junction that has contributed to accidents but has not been specifically recorded in reports. Field surveys would detect its presence, identify its role and recommend its removal as a countermeasure. Field surveys fall into three categories:

studies of the cycling environment
(these are essential for all local authorities)
studies of the way the highway is used
interviews of users
(these are desirable if resources are available).

CITY OF WESTLAKE
CYCLING CONDITIONS SURVEY SHEET

Section Oxford Road	Date 25 FEBRUARY 1980	Surveyor LTC
Factor	**Location**	**Remarks**
Raised m/h	o/s No 28	Close to kerb, about 30mm up.
Flooding	o/s No 36	Gully blocked. Pond 50mm deep, 2m long, 1m wide

5.17 Area-wide studies will identify locations where a given problem affects cycling conditions

CITY OF WESTLAKE
CYCLING CONDITIONS SURVEY SHEET

Location Jc. OXFORD RD and HIGH ST.	Date 25 FEBROARY 1980	Surveyor LTC

N A B C

Factor	Position	Remarks
Raised m/h	A	25 mm upstand
Pothole	B	Road edge crumbling
Sunken reinstatement	C	Leads to ATS controller

5.18 Studies of a particular location will identify the problems at that location

5.6.1 Cycling environment

Studies of the cycling environment will fall into two categories:

- area-wide studies to find the locations where a given environmental factor affects cycling conditions
- studies at a particular location to find what adverse environmental factors affect cycling conditions at that location.

In both types of survey it is essential to be systematic. Suitable systems are described below.

Area-wide studies

Compile a standard field-survey sheet that can be used for any type of facility (path, street or track). Visit each facility in the area in turn, starting with those most used by cyclists. Record all the adverse factors that can be observed at that location. Accident reports will have revealed some likely problems and their severity. Intuition must be used to recognise others. It is important to realise that many features which are extremely hazardous to cyclists may not even be noticed in a motor vehicle and may therefore previously have escaped notice through ignorance rather than neglect. Typical factors to record are: raised manholes, high dropped-kerbs, poor reinstatements of trenches, blocked gullies, gully gratings with slots parallel to the kerb, ridges between areas of surfacing, accumulation of fallen leaves, litter or debris, run-off of water across the carriageway and potholes.

The notes obtained should then be transferred to a series of office record sheets, one for each factor. This will then enable all problems of the same type to be remedied together.

Studies of a particular location

The procedure is essentially the same as that for the area-wide study but its purpose is to identify the reasons for a particular location being dangerous rather than to anticipate causes of accidents as a whole. The field-survey sheet should therefore include a sketch of the location and the position of problem factors at that location. The factors identified can be transferred to the same office record sheets as those used for the area-wide surveys.

CITY OF WESTLAKE
MAINTENANCE RECORD SHEET
FACTOR Poor Reinstatement

Location	Authority responsible	Date recorded	Authority notified	Priority grading	Actioned
94 Oxford Rd.	Post Office	25/2/80	25/2/80	High	27/2/80
Jc. Oxford Rd. / High St.	County Council	25/2/80	25/2/80	Low	28/2/80

5.19 Record sheets should be kept showing all locations where a particular problem has arisen

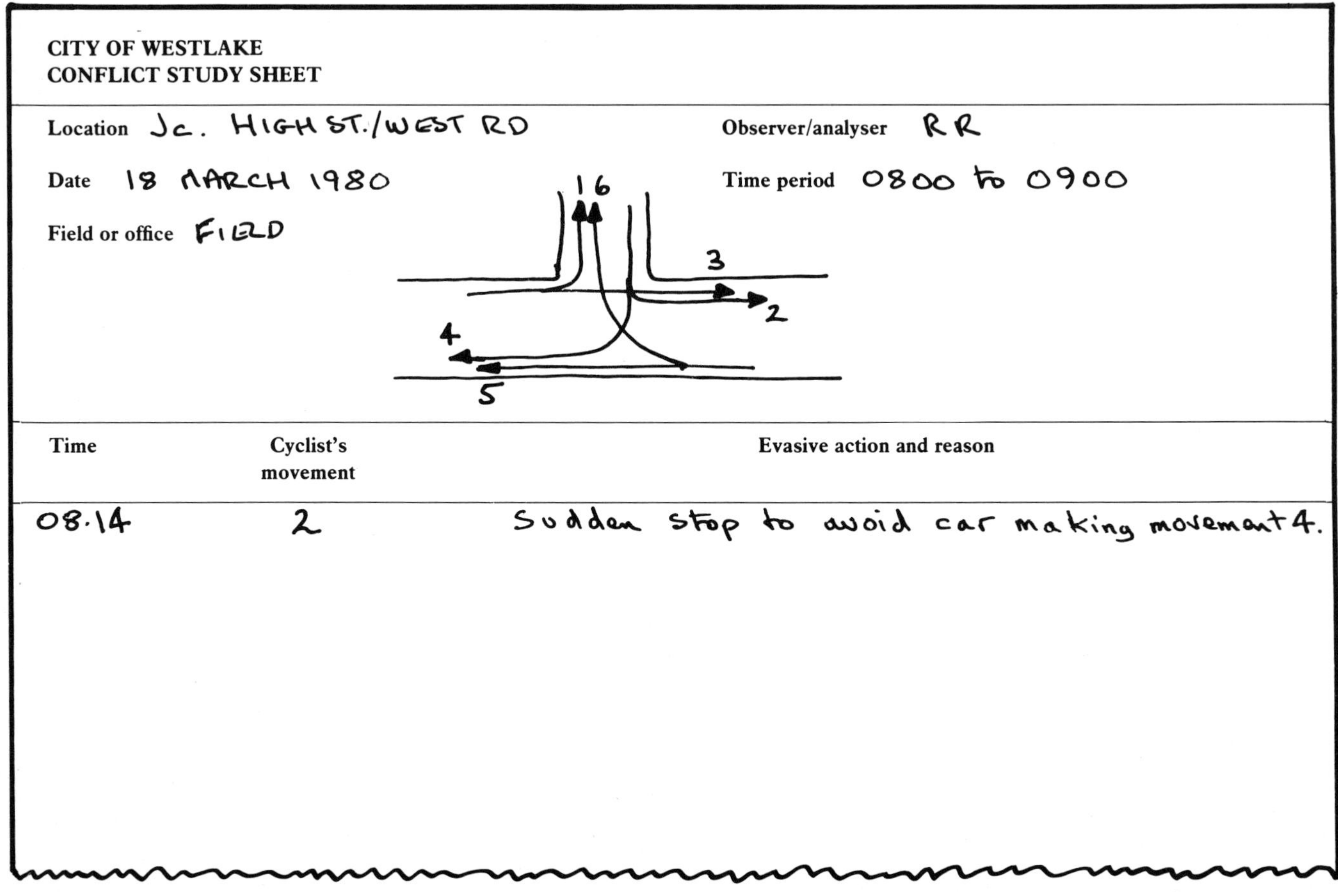

CITY OF WESTLAKE
CONFLICT STUDY SHEET

Location Jc. HIGH ST./WEST RD **Observer/analyser** RR

Date 18 MARCH 1980 **Time period** 0800 to 0900

Field or office FIELD

Time	Cyclist's movement	Evasive action and reason
08.14	2	Sudden stop to avoid car making movement 4.

5.20 A record of conflicts will indicate the dangerous manoeuvres through a junction. The form is suitable for on-site observation or film analysis

Once the survey procedure has been established for, say, a month, the extent to which a particular problem is prevalent in an area will have become evident.

The collection and processing of data on the cycling environment is essential to producing safer and more acceptable conditions for cycling. It can, however, consume a lot of time and resources. Much of the field-study work is not highly skilled once the surveyor has been trained to appreciate what is being sought. Local authorities would therefore be well advised to seek help from cycling organisations and interested members of the public in identifying problem locations.

5.6.2 The way the highway is used

Once particular locations have been identified as actual or potential sites for accidents and some indication of the (likely) causes obtained, further indication of the causes may be found through studying the features in use.

There is a relationship between the number and nature of conflicts observed at a junction and the number and nature of injury accidents. Thus although no accidents are observed in a period of study, a record of the conflicts observed will indicate the dangerous manoeuvres through a junction. A conflict occurs when a road user has to take some form of sudden action to avoid a collision.

CITY OF WESTLAKE
CYCLING SAFETY QUESTIONNAIRE

1. Have you had any cycling accidents or fallen off your bicycle while cycling in Westlake in the past 5 years? YES/NO*
2. If yes, please give details (dates, locations, what happened and what caused them)

3. Were these accidents or falls reported to the:
   police? YES/NO*
   council? YES/NO*
   hospital? YES/NO*

4. Please specify any locations in Westlake which you feel are particularly dangerous for cyclists (junctions, roads etc.)

5. Please say if there are any features of the roads in Westlake that are awkward for cyclists (gulleys, types of surface etc.)

How could these be improved?

*Delete as applicable

5.21 A one-off interview exercise may provide information on potential danger spots

5.23 An important area for action: repair poor road surfaces

CITY OF WESTLAKE
SCHEDULE OF MAJOR BICYCLE ACCIDENT PROBLEMS
1975–1979

	Slight	Serious	Fatal
Total number of accidents	295	61	4
Average annual number of accidents	59	12	1

Problem	Percentage of all accidents	Fatal and serious 1975–79
Victims under 15	37	25
Right-turn accidents	25	20
Loss of control	30	20
Accidents on High St./ London Road route	10	15

5.22 The first step towards formulating countermeasures is to list major bicycle accident problems

There are two methods of recording the use of a facility: manual recording and film recording. Film recording is generally the better method because it provides a permanent record of the events and avoids the problem of preconceptions about the use of a facility. Manual recording should be limited to locations where the cyclists' choice of movement is limited and each cyclist can be watched closely.

5.6.3 Interviews with cyclists

In addition to accidents which are reported to the police, there will be accidents in which the cyclist is uninjured or receives hospital treatment but does not report the accident. The causes of these accidents can provide local authorities with early warning of potential danger spots and of causes of annoyance to cyclists. Information on these unreported accidents can only be obtained from the cyclist involved in the accident. Authorities may consider a one-off interview exercise valid. Methods of interviewing cyclists were discussed in section 4.5.5 and these also apply to obtaining data on accidents. Destination-based or self-completion questionnaires are probably the best methods here.

5.7 PLANNING LOCAL COUNTERMEASURES

5.7.1 Identifying problems

Local accident studies will reveal several major types of accident prevalent in an area. As a first step to devising a programme of countermeasures, a local authority should identify, say, the six most common types of accident in their area. These will not be mutually exclusive and some accidents could feature in all the categories. A typical selection might prove to be:

- victims under 15 years old
- accidents on a particular arterial road
- turning accidents
- overtaking accidents
- accidents where the cyclist was not seen
- accidents where the cyclist lost control.

It is unlikely that an authority could introduce countermeasures for all these problems at the same time. Planners should assess which problems could be tackled by what method(s) with the funds available. This information and recommendations for action should be passed to those charged with determining priorities for expenditure.

5.7.2 Types of countermeasure

Most of the problems discussed in this chapter can be eased by one or more of the following:

education and training of road users
infrastructure changes
improved maintenance
legislation and enforcement.

Local authorities will be substantially responsible for the first three of the above measures and partially responsible for the fourth.

Data on the effects of measures introduced specifically to reduce cycling accidents are limited. What data there is, supplemented by qualitative information, leads to the following assessments:

Education

Education programmes have been found to have good short-term effects, especially on children. To maintain their effect, programmes must be prolonged and even then they can never be expected to be completely successful. Well established programmes, such as the 'Cycling Proficiency' scheme in the UK, are believed to have reduced accidents. Education is discussed in more detail in Chapter 10.

Action checklist

1. Locate all previous accident studies in the study area.
2. Establish regular accident reporting systems with the emergency services.
3. Establish thorough recording techniques for data obtained from the emergency services.
4. Establish well-referenced data storage systems for accident records.
5. Analyse data to identify major accident problems in the study area.
6. Carry out field studies to supplement the information obtained from the data banks.
7. Re-appraise major accident problems and identify the six most common causes in the area.
8. Draw up a programme of possible countermeasures for each major problem, indicating the advantages and disadvantages of each alternative, and recommending what action should be taken.
9. Submit the results of the studies, the recommendations and figures showing the cost-effectiveness of the measures to those charged with deciding priorities for expenditure. The submission should be made as part of the overall plan for improving conditions for cyclists.

CITY OF WESTLAKE
MAJOR BICYCLE ACCIDENT PROBLEM COUNTER-MEASURE PROPOSALS

Problem: Accident victims under 15 years old

Notes on problem
37% of bicycle accidents in Westlake involve children under 15. These accidents are distributed around the city and many are on residential roads. There is, however, a concentration on and around London Road. Many of these are during school travelling time and indicate accidents on trips between the Eastern residential areas and the schools complex to the West of London Road.

Possible countermeasures
1. Education programme to keep children from playing on roads. Organisation is already established and working well.
2. Ask police to clamp down on dangerous behaviour amongst child cyclists. Difficult at present because of police staff shortages.
3. Launch 'Look out for cyclists' campaign. Could be organised quickly and perhaps repeated later.
4. Erect cyclist crossing over London Road. This could be done by modifying the existing pedestrian crossing at Green Street which is already on the main desire line to the schools complex. It would also serve the industrial area.

Cost of countermeasures
1. About £1000 in current year
2. None to council
3. About £1000 in current year
4. About £5000 for signals and modifications

Proposal
A combination of countermeasures 1 and 4 is proposed. 1 is necessary to reach all children in the area and relieve problem as a whole. 4 will solve the specific problem of London Road for other users as well as children and will generate publicity for cycling in the area.

5.24 Proposals for countermeasures should be presented to those charged with deciding priorities for expenditure

Infrastructure

Recent schemes have yet to show whether they have a significant effect on accidents, as in most cases studies will have to be continued over several years to be statistically significant. Experience of a totally segregated system in Stevenage in the UK has shown that these are very safe for cyclists. Between 1972 and 1977 no fatal accidents occurred and there were only 40 accidents altogether involving cyclists on the cycleway system. The majority (24) of these accidents were with mopeds and only two involved pedestrians.

Signal-controlled crossings of major roads were rated higher by cyclists than any other measure introduced in the Peterborough scheme in the UK, except segregated cycle tracks. The rating dropped, however, when one of the legs of the crossing was shared with motor vehicles, reinforcing the view that mixing with motor vehicles is one of the main problems perceived by cyclists.

A Danish study produced three conclusions which must be carefully considered when proposing infrastructure changes:

- cyclists will detour only the minimum length from the shortest route for safety reasons
- such detours must be clearly signed and marked
- the detours must feel as safe as the original route.

Infrastructure changes are the most likely to make cyclists feel safer and will be those most welcomed by the cycling community. Their existence can, in itself, act as a method of creating awareness of bicycles amongst other road users.

Maintenance

No direct attempts have been made to measure the effect of improved road maintenance on bicycle accidents. High standards of maintenance will undoubtedly reduce accidents, increase comfort and make cyclists feel safer. They are also probably the best way for a local authority to demonstrate a constant awareness of, and concern for, cyclists.

Legislation

Changes in national legislation will be outside the role of local authorities. Stricter enforcement of legislation on behaviour in cooperation with the police can have short-term effects but, as with education programmes, long-term effects can only be achieved by prolonged enforcement. Local laws permitting the use of parks and other open spaces can reduce accidents and can be used to show a positive attitude on the part of the local authority towards bicycle safety.

5.7.3 Applicability of countermeasures

The type of countermeasures used for a particular problem will depend substantially on the nature of the problem. Typical applications of the measures are as follows:

- Education: problems associated with an age group or class of user, problems associated with a particular type of facility, area-wide problems
- Infrastructure: problems at a particular location
- Maintenance: problems at a particular location, problems associated with a type of road or facility, area-wide problems
- Legislation: area-wide problem(national and local legislation); localised problem (local legislation).

Opinions vary on the best type of countermeasure to employ where there is a choice and any advice must to some extent be subjective. Our view is that where a problem can be reduced by either infrastructure/maintenance changes or by education/legislation, then the more permanent infrastructure solution is preferable. If properly designed and implemented, these measures can be self-enforcing. The education/legislation measures need to be enforced or renewed and rely on human performance, which will always, on occasions, fall below safe standards.

MAIN ACCIDENT PROBLEMS AND POSSIBLE COUNTERMEASURES

Child accidents

EDUCATION
- Discourage playing on roads
- Encourage taking care when leaving play areas
- Encourage awareness of motor vehicles and rules of the road

INFRASTRUCTURE
- Provide recreational trails
- Provide segregated routes to schools
- Provide play areas

ENFORCEMENT
- Caution children seen contravening laws
- Report consistent offenders to parents

LEGISLATION
- Allow children to play in public open spaces

Motorists failing to see or take account of cyclists

EDUCATION
- Encourage motorists to look for bicycles
- Make motorists aware of instability of bicycles
- Encourage cyclists to use visibility aids

INFRASTRUCTURE
- Adopt high standards of lighting at crucial points

ENFORCEMENT
- Caution motorists seen endangering cyclists
- Caution cyclists not carrying statutory lights and reflectors
- Enforce drink/driving laws

LEGISLATION
- Introduce higher statutory standards for visibility aids

Injuries to head and limbs

EDUCATION
- Encourage the use of helmets and body padding

Loss of control or sudden swerve

EDUCATION
- Stress importance of correct sized bicycle, proper adjustment and maintenance of bicycle, not overloading bicycle, wearing appropriate clothing
- Encourage travelling at speeds to suit conditions

MAINTENANCE
- Adopt high standards for riding surfaces
- Adopt high standards for carriageway cleaning

ENFORCEMENT
- Caution bicycle riders whose machines are in dangerous condition

Turning accidents

EDUCATION
- Teach cyclists how to make turns onto and off roads and to look for motor vehicles when doing so

INFRASTRUCTURE
- Provide islands or refuges which break up turning movements into stages across each line of traffic
- Provide lanes for turning traffic
- Give priority to turning traffic by changing junction control

Cyclist or motorist contravenes junction control

INFRASTRUCTURE
- Improve signing and carriageway marking to reinforce existing control of junction
- Change method of junction control
- Change layout of junction

Accidents on busy roads

EDUCATION
- Encourage cyclists to use quiet roads

INFRASTRUCTURE
- Provide alternative routes to busy roads
- Reduce number of junctions on the busy road
- Improve facilities for crossing busy road

6 Routes for cyclists

The purpose of this chapter is to describe the different methods of creating and improving routes for cyclists. Any programme of improvements should consist of three components:

- Standards should be laid down to ensure that all new construction and improvement plans take account of the needs of cyclists
- Plans should be made to up-grade existing streets to make them more suitable for cyclists
- Proposals should be prepared for specific improvements which could circumvent or create a new alternative to an unsatisfactory route.

The first section of this chapter describes the range of measures which should be used to up-grade the whole of the street system, and in particular corridors used by cyclists. The rest of the chapter describes the specific improvements, including measures which are appropriate for local areas, measures which can be used to link different areas and top quality routes. The range of facilities shown should therefore be treated like a menu – once the specific problem to be overcome has been identified, the most appropriate solution can be chosen.

Before embarking on any plans to improve cycling conditions it is important to have a realistic perception of cyclists' size and their speed of travel. The size is shown in fig 6.1.

The speed of cyclists varies in different countries. Research in the UK, Germany and Japan shows that cyclists in these countries travel at 15kph on average. Since design speeds should accommodate the fastest cyclists, design speeds of 25kph have been used for cycle routes of zero gradient. In the USA more people have lightweight bikes suitable for faster travel, so average speeds are higher. The US Department of Transportation recommends a design speed of 32kph on flat sections of routes, increasing to 48kph when the slope exceeds 4%.

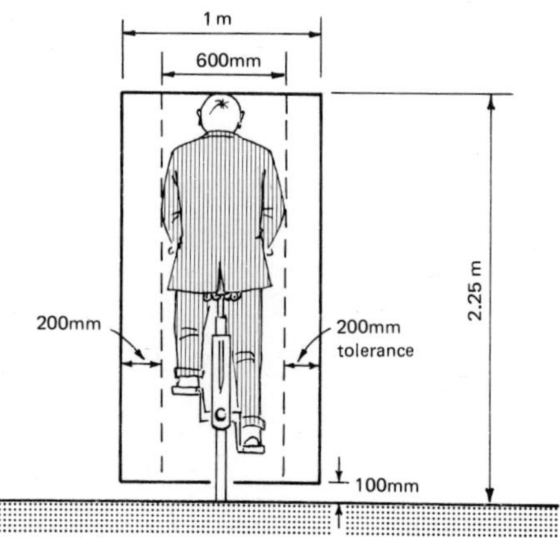

6.1 The dimensions of a cyclist, with tolerances

6.1 GENERAL IMPROVEMENTS TO THE ROAD SYSTEM

A methodology for evaluating the street system and ranking corridors used by cyclists according to the work required was set out in section 3.5. This section identifies the precise nature of the spot improvements which can be made.

Surface condition

One of the major problems facing cyclists on existing streets is the unevenness of the surface. Potholes, sunken and raised manholes, excessively thick carriageway markings and poor quality trench reinstatements combine to make many roads into a nerve-racking obstacle course. In recent times when many countries have been reducing public expenditure the

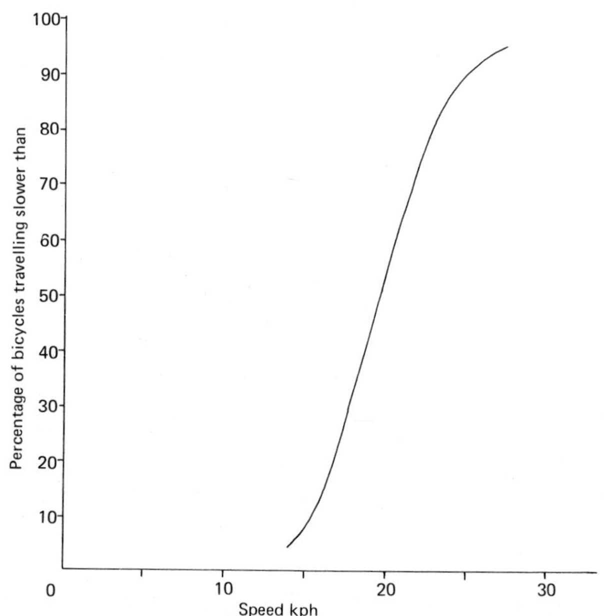

6.2 Profile of bicycle travel speeds on level ground (Source: *Safety and Location Criteria for Bicycle Facilities*, 1975)

situation has deteriorated to such an extent that loss of control and damage to bicycle wheels are both serious problems facing cyclists. The problem has to be tackled on a number of fronts. Firstly, public utilities and other organisations permitted to dig up the road should be made to restore the surface to its original condition. Secondly, local authority maintenance programmes should concentrate on those roads with the largest flows of cyclists and, when resurfacing is carried out, particular care should be taken to ensure that the surface is smooth across the whole width of the road. All too often resurfacing stops short of the edge and that is just where cyclists travel. Thirdly, when carriageway markings and in particular waiting restriction lines are replaced, textured thermoplastic should be used since ordinary thermoplastic is very slippery when wet. Particular care should be taken when new lines are laid or old lines replaced to ensure that the thickness of the line is less than 5mm since bicycle wheels cannot ride up onto a longitudinal lump in the surface.

Drainage gratings and manhole covers
All drainage gratings with bars parallel to the direction of travel should be turned or have straps put over them to stop bicycle wheels falling into the gaps. Manholes should not be placed at the edge of the road because they will always create an uneven surface.

Squeeze points
A squeeze point is a location on a busy street where the road suddenly narrows, forcing cyclists to move into the path of other traffic. In some places the road can be widened to remove the problem.

Gaps in road closures
Where roads are closed to through traffic, gaps should be left to allow cyclists through (unless it is unsafe, in which case cyclists should dismount and wheel through). Such streets form ideal cycle routes and no opportunities to take advantage of them should be lost.

Road widening and narrowing
The width of roads used by bicycles and other vehicles affects the perceived dangers of cycling (and may also affect actual dangers). Cyclists feel particularly vulnerable when motor vehicles, and more significantly trucks and buses, overtake and appear to leave only a few centimetres gap between the cyclist's elbow and the side of their vehicle. In practice the gap is usually between 1m and 2m, depending on the width of the road, the volume of traffic coming in the opposite direction and the visibility of the cyclists. Nevertheless, even at these distances considerable side thrusts are exerted on cyclists (fig 6.4).

There has been very little research into lane widths which cyclists find comfortable. Some work in Australia and the USA suggests that where parking is banned and the speed limit is 75kph, a lane width of 4.25m is adequate and 3.65m is inadequate. Where parking is allowed, 6.7m is described as adequate and 6.1m inadequate (fig 6.5). These figures may however be high for European countries where vehicles tend to be narrower. Where traffic speeds are higher, greater width will be required and, if flows are also high, cyclists should be physically segregated since a rear end collision at these speeds is likely to result in a fatality.

6.3 Bad road surfaces damage bicycles wheels

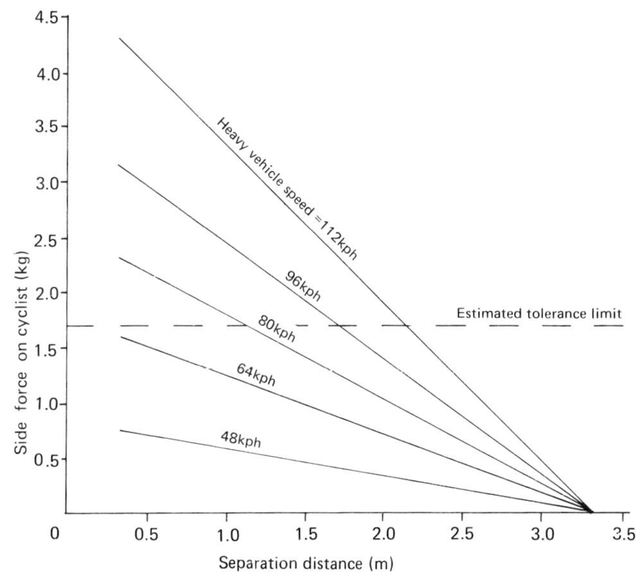

6.4 Estimate of side forces exerted on cyclists by passing heavy vehicles

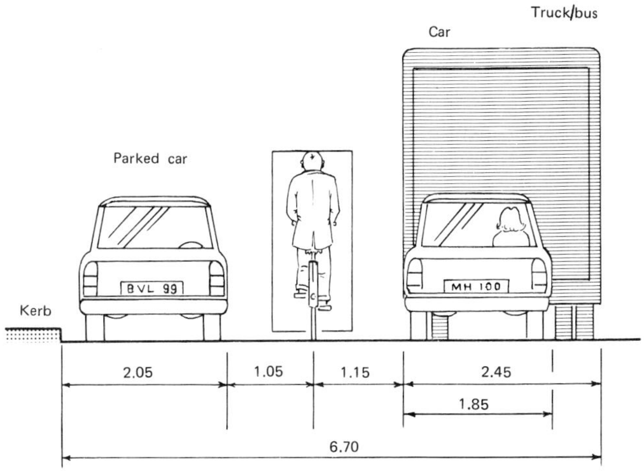

6.5 A suggested width for lanes shared by cyclists and motor vehicles on roads with a 75kph speed limit (Source: *Geelong Bike Plan*, 1977)

THE IDEAL CHARACTERISTICS OF CYCLE ROUTES

The ideal characteristics of cycle routes stem from an understanding of the vehicle and the rider. Bicycles in general have no suspension, are highly manoeuvrable and can be pushed or even carried. The riders dislike slowing down, making detours or going up steep hills because each requires extra energy. The ideal characteristics of cycle routes are that:

1. Routes should be as direct as possible
2. Routes should avoid heavily trafficked roads
3. Routes should have convenient access points which are clearly signed
4. Routes should not end at hazardous locations
5. Routes should have a smooth surface which is regularly maintained
6. Routes should be swept and vegetation cut back regularly
7. Routes should be as continuous as possible
8. The destination of routes should be clearly marked
9. Anyone else sharing the route (motor vehicles or pedestrians) should be alerted to the presence of cyclists
10. Routes should have good sight-lines throughout
11. Routes should avoid areas subject to extremes of climate such as wind or snow traps
12. Routes should be well lit
13. Routes should be attractive, running through parks and open spaces whenever possible.

There may also be maximum lane widths which are appropriate on roads used by cyclists. Where a lane is wide enough to allow cars to overtake without crossing the centre line, road narrowing may be justified to stop vehicles overtaking and pushing cyclists right into the edge of the road.

On four-lane highways the simplest way to improve cycling conditions is to make the two nearside lanes wider than the offside lanes. This is cheaper than creating cycle lanes since two new lines are required instead of four.

Railway level crossings

Cyclists can face four problems at railway level crossings: rails not flush with the road surface, road surfaces themselves of particularly poor quality, crossings forming squeeze points and approaches at acute angles which make it difficult to cross the rails in wet weather.

These can all be remedied by widening the road at the crossing point and improving the quality of the road surface. In addition, it has been suggested that since the problem is the gap between the rail and the road, this could be filled with rubber strong enough to support a bike but compressible under the weight of a train.

Dropped kerbs

Dropped kerbs are provided at points where cyclists leave the road to join a bicycle facility. They are invariably not flush with the road (fig 6.6). Where upstands for drainage are not required they should be re-set. Alternatively they could be replaced with one-piece units which lift the cyclist from one level to the other without a break.

Ramps on bridges and underpasses

Some cyclists may prefer to wheel their bicycles through an underpass or over a bridge to avoid a busy road junction. Steps are particularly difficult to negotiate but if a narrow ramp is provided beside the steps, the bike can easily be wheeled. Furthermore, where new bridges and underpasses are built they should have ramps rather than steps since this assists cyclists and any people pushing prams or shopping trolleys.

Regular maintenance

Debris tends to gather in the gutter of the road. Glass and thorns in particular cause cyclists to swerve to avoid getting a puncture. Regular sweeping of the gutter is therefore required. In addition vegetation such as shrubs and low limbs on trees which obstruct sight-lines should be cut back regularly.

Lighting

Cyclists prefer to use well lit routes because they feel safer and because it is easier to see poor quality road surfaces. Good lighting should therefore be provided on routes used by cyclists.

6.2 CREATING SPECIFIC ROUTES FROM EXISTING INFRASTRUCTURE

This section is about the creation of enhanced routes for bicycles on existing streets and paths. It should be stressed from the outset that measures to make cycling more pleasant by improving routes with low flows of motor vehicles and pedestrians must be integrated with measures to make junctions safer. Taking cyclists off the carriageway just after a junction and returning them to the carriageway before the next junction is likely to cause an increase in accidents. Furthermore if such a route is the traditional unmaintained and unenforced cycle track, it just will not be used.

6.6 A dropped kerb which is not flush with the road surface

6.7 Closing half the road reduces traffic flows on an advisory cycle route

6.2.1 Advisory cycle routes

Within the existing street system there are many opportunities for providing enhanced routes for cyclists. In particular, residential roads with low vehicle flows can be linked together to provide routes which avoid the dangers and unpleasantness of busy main roads.

The area in which this type of route is most appropriate will usually consist of a network of backstreets, so keeping traffic out of one will only put increased pressure on another. Thus, advisory cycle routes will sometimes have to be considered as part of an overall traffic and environmental management plan. However, it is increasingly accepted that residential streets should be designed for community use giving priority to walking, playing and the creation of an attractive environment. These conditions ideally suit the cyclist.

A number of factors need to be taken into account when determining which combination of streets should be used to create a bicycle route:

- The peak vehicle flows should be less than 100 vehicles per hour. If there are more than this, measures will be required to reduce the flow.
- The type of traffic using the street should be mainly residential. If much of the traffic is non-residential measures are more likely to be accepted by residents.
- The route should link the origins and destinations of cyclists' journeys as directly as possible (a 10% detour being the maximum acceptable unless the route enables cyclists to avoid a particularly nasty road or junction).
- The route will undoubtedly have to cross main roads. The opportunities for creating safe junctions will often be a significant factor in route choice.

The major problem associated with the creation of an advisory cycle route is how to keep all unnecessary traffic off the street. Various measures can be adopted to solve this problem, the choice of approach depending primarily on the pressure from motor traffic. In quiet residential areas, with streets which are not used by motor vehicle drivers as short cuts, the provision of route definition signs and warning signs for motorists is all that will be required. If necessary these can be supplemented by putting weight restrictions on the street, or by creating an access only street. This last measure will, however, often require physical constructions to discourage motor vehicle drivers from violating the signs. Narrow mouths, ramps, surface texturing and bollards can all be used depending on the severity of the pressure.

If such an advisory route crosses a large number of side roads with flows of less than 250 vehicles/hour, the priorities of junctions can be altered to give cyclists right of way. This will avoid cyclists having to stop and start frequently and will also give them a greater sense of security. These must, however, be monitored to check that motor vehicle drivers respect the road markings and that a new 'rat-run' for motor vehicles has not been created.

Another method of reducing traffic flows is to construct speed control humps in the road. In the UK the height, shape and frequency of the humps must conform to the government standard if they are used on public roads. The standard width is 3.7m and the height is 100mm. Humps have been shown to reduce traffic flows significantly. However, they are not particularly comfortable for cyclists but can be used to stop traffic entering a cycle route without being used on the route itself.

Banning left and right turns at junctions and exempting cyclists is another method of restricting traffic flows. Alternatively, motor vehicles can be made to turn off a proposed advisory cycle route. However, this is likely to require some form of physical deterrent. An alternative option is to stop traffic entering the street at one end (fig 6.7).

The most effective and most popular control is to close the street completely at one end or in the centre. A variety of designs of street closures have been used, some of which allow access for emergency and maintenance vehicles.

The measures which are used to create advisory cycle

6.8 Residential precincts are designed to discourage motor traffic

DUTCH DESIGN STANDARDS FOR RESIDENTIAL PRECINCTS

Since the early 1970s the Dutch government has been pursuing a policy of making traffic more compatible with housing in residential areas. In 1976, new legislation governing residential precincts was passed and since then over 800 have been introduced. The main feature of a residential precinct is that design and layout should express the fact that motor vehicles are subordinate to residential, pedestrian and cycling requirements. A number of minimum design standards for *woonerven* were published in 1976. The main points are as follows:

Article 1. A *woonerf* must be primarily a residential area.
Article 2. Roads, or the road network, within the *woonerf* must only carry vehicular traffic with an origin or destination within that particular *woonerf*.
Article 3. No road within a *woonerf* should carry a flow of traffic which will affect the character of that road as part of a *woonerf*.
Article 4. The impression that the highway is divided into a separate motorway for motor vehicles and a footpath must be avoided.
Article 6. The entrances and exits of a *woonerf* must be so designed that they can be clearly recognised and it must be obvious that those used by motor vehicles are access roads. In the case of vehicular entrances and exists which cross footpaths, the footpath should be continued right across the highway.
Article 7. The boundaries of parts of the highway intended for parking should be clearly shown.
Article 8. There must be adequate parking facilities for the residents of a *woonerf*.
Article 9. On those parts of the highway intended for use by motor vehicles, features must be introduced which will restrict the use of all types of vehicles.

routes have, in some countries, been combined together to create whole areas where traffic is restrained, called residential precincts. When this is done, the surface of the street can be treated to make it clear that the residential purpose of the street predominates. This can be achieved by providing one surface for pedestrians, cyclists and motor vehicles, and by placing street furniture such as flower beds and cycle parking facilities in different positions across the street to reduce the speed of the traffic which requires access.

The concept of residential precincts is most advanced in Holland (where they are called '*woonerven*'). Following a great deal of carefully monitored experimental work a series of fourteen design standards have been drawn up (see box). The precincts are introduced on a street by street basis, the lessons from the first being applied to the second. Considerable effort is put into thorough community consultation. The Dutch believe that the introduction of residential precincts is the beginning of a significant new development in urban planning and traffic engineering. Providing cyclists' requirements are incorporated, they could prove to be a boon for cyclists as well (fig 6.8).

The design standards for advisory cycle routes will depend on the other functions of the street, the traffic flow and the numbers of cyclists expected to use the route. Where vehicle or cycle flows are small, or where a street does not have other functions, lower tolerances are acceptable.

The following points are a guide to the standards which the street should meet. It should:

have a smooth surface
be regularly swept and maintained
not have obstacles which obscure cyclists sight-lines
be well lit
have good drainage
direct cyclists in relatively straight lines
be well signed.

The cost of creating an advisory cycle route will vary according to the work undertaken. An initial treatment (signs and road closures) might cost approximately £1,000 per km. Creating residential precincts will be considerably more expensive. The Dutch have found that a minimal standard precinct (removal of kerbs and modification of drainage patterns) costs at least 50% more than re-surfacing. Where flower beds, seats and other street furniture are installed, costs are considerably higher.

6.2.2 Cycle tracks

The term cycle track encompasses any route used only by cyclists. However, they are commonly conceptualised as tracks running beside major roads which in the UK were often built beside dual carriageways in the 1930s. This type of cycle track has always been unpopular with cyclists because it is seldom swept and maintained, often has cars parked on it, and, most significantly, puts cyclists back onto the main roads at the most dangerous points, just before junctions. However, there are situations where this type of track is appropriate provided certain criteria are satisfied (see box). There are also a variety of routes not beside roads where a cycle track is an appropriate provision, such as across parks or along disused railway lines. Such routes will often be shared with pedestrians. The additional considerations for cycle-pedestrian tracks are set out in the next section. This section sets out the basic criteria which should be used to determine whether a path can be converted for use by bicycles. Since the criteria are similar to those for all types of cycle route, other sections will generally refer to the standards set out here.

Width

The first consideration in determining how wide a path needs to be to accommodate a flow of cyclists is the width of cyclists themselves (see fig 6.1). To determine the width required for a proposed cycle track, the expected peak flow of bicycles is also required. Often this will be in the morning or evening peak period.

There is a remarkable shortage of data on the capacities of cycle tracks of different width and although a variety of theoretical calculations and graphs have been published, no firm conclusions can be drawn from them. The maximum capacity figures which have been suggested in different countries vary widely. This may be partially due to the definition of width since there is a difference between the width of the track and the width required by cyclists, the latter being larger because almost half of a bike can be extended over the edge of the track. However, given that no other data is available these figures will have to be used to calculate the width of track required to handle the predicted usage of a track. Broadly speaking, if the peak flow of bicycles does not exceed 1000/hour then a 2.5m wide path will accommodate the flow. Where the path cannot be widened, 2m is adequate but not comfortable. If the flow exceeds 1000 bicycles/hour, then the path will have to be wider.

The next consideration is the boundary conditions. If there is no obstruction beside the track, then cyclists can position the wheels of their bicycles nearer the edge of the track than if there is, say, a solid wall at the edge. Various additional widths have been suggested to take account of lateral obstructions, ranging from 0.3m for an intermittent obstruction to 0.6m for a continuous obstruction.

Bringing these considerations together will give the minimum width for the track. Since there is such a paucity of information, these figures should be used with considerable flexibility. For example, the UK Department of Transport recommends a standard of 3.6m which could be relaxed to 3.0m and further relaxed to 1.5m in certain qualified situations. The US Department of Transportion recommends a minimum paved width of 2.4m.

In general, it is always better to use a path with a width which will cope with a capacity that will not be exceeded during the life span of the track, rather than having to widen it after only a few years.

Sight-lines

A criteria for the conversion of a path to a cycle track is that cyclists must be able to see and react to a variety of hazards including other vehicles, junctions and obstructions such as a maintenance vehicle round a bend or over a hump. The most quoted formula for calculating sight stopping distances (the distance cyclists require to perceive a problem, react to it and bring the bicycle to a halt) is based on a standard highway engineering formula used in the USA. This gives the sight stopping distances shown in fig 6.9.

These figures may appear to be particularly high but it should be noted that most bicycle brakes are particularly ineffective in wet weather, and that the distances shown are the maximum a cyclist will require to stop and not the average, which will be considerably less.

In many urban situations such long sight-lines will be unrealistic. These figures should therefore be treated as an ideal to be aimed at.

The sight stopping distances should be used to determine the sight-line required in three basic situations: junctions, bends and humps. Figures 6.10 and 6.11 show examples of these calculations.

It should be noted however, that different countries use different figures. In the UK, cyclists in the middle of a side road should, from a point 2.4m back from the junction edge, be able to see 90m along the roadside edge of the major roads with a 48kph speed limit. (Details of these calculations are given in *Residential Roads and Footpaths, 1977*.)

Turning radii

Various formulae have been suggested for calculating the radius of curvature required on cycle tracks, some depending on the design speed and some on surface conditions as well. Recent draft guidelines from the US Department of Transportation suggested the following figures, which provide a reasonable guide for determining whether the radii on an

---

CYCLE TRACKS

Since there has been considerable controversy over cycle tracks beside main roads, they deserve special consideration. The critical question to ask when new or rejuvenated cycle tracks are considered is: are the tracks and associated junction treatments sufficiently beneficial to cyclists to be used instead of the roads?

To answer this question, certain criteria have been drawn up which, when adhered to, should create a desirable facility.

- Junctions with major roads should be grade separated or have traffic signal control.
- At junctions with minor roads, the cycle track should continue across the mouth of the road and priority should be given to cyclists. Raising the cycle track 5cm, marking it with a red surface and white edge lines and putting 'give way' lines behind the track would clearly indicate its presence to motorists.
- If the cycle track rejoins the road, it should do so at an angle of less than 15° to the road kerb and should be followed by a short section of cycle lane. Motor vehicle drivers should be warned of emerging cyclists.
- At T-junctions entering the road on the opposite side to the track, protected junctions should be provided for cyclists (see Chapter 7).
- Motor vehicles should be physically prevented from using tracks by raised kerbs and bollards.
- Cycle tracks should pass behind lay-bys and bus stops.
- Regular maintenance and sweeping schedules must be adopted and arrangements should be made for salting and clearing snow in winter.
- Clear signing should be provided in positions easily read by cyclists.

existing path make it suitable for conversion to a cycle track:

Design speed (kph)	Radii (m)
24	10
32	21
40	27
48	38

Clearly, paths with smaller radii can be negotiated at lower speeds. The UK Department of Transport recommends a minimum of 6m, though curves with radii down to 2m have been provided.

Gradients

The gradients which cyclists can reasonably expect to climb (or fall) safely and comfortably will depend on a number of factors including:

general topography
length of the gradient
proficiency of the cyclist
characteristics of the bicycle
surface conditions
wind and temperature.

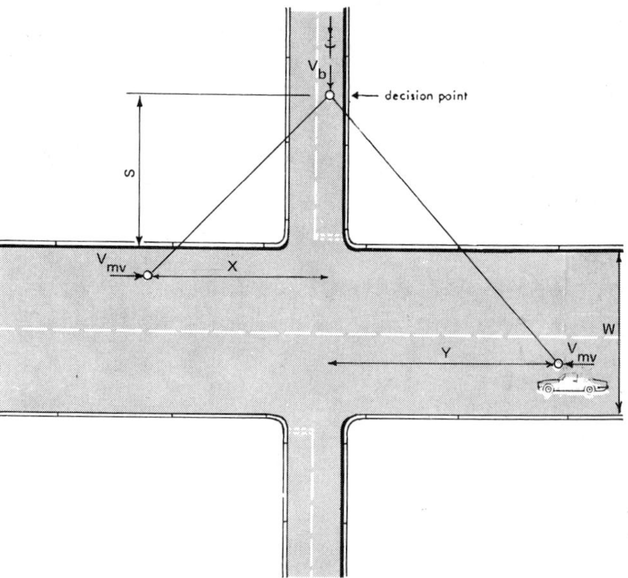

6.10 Calculation of intersection sight clearances (Source: *Safety and Location Criteria for Bicycle Facilities*, 1975)

Time for full intersection clearance from the 'stop-go' decision point is given by:

$$\frac{S + W + 6}{Vb} = t_1$$

Where S = Stopping Distance (including perception and reaction time) at design
W = Width of crossing
Vb = Actual bikeway typical approach speed (rather than design speed)

Time for near side lane(s) clearance is given by:

$$\frac{S + W/2 + 6}{Vb} = t_2$$

A crossing cyclist at the 'decision point' must be able to see any vehicle which would threaten conflict in the crossing within time t_1 to t_2. Thus, the cyclist at the decision point must be able to see approaching vehicles at the following distances:

$$\text{near side } x = t_2 V_{mv} = \frac{V_{mv}(S + W/2 + 6)}{Vb}$$

$$\text{far side } y = t_1 V_{mv} = \frac{V_{mv}(S + W + 6)}{Vb}$$

Projections between the 'stop-go' decision points and the points given by x and y define the sight clearance areas

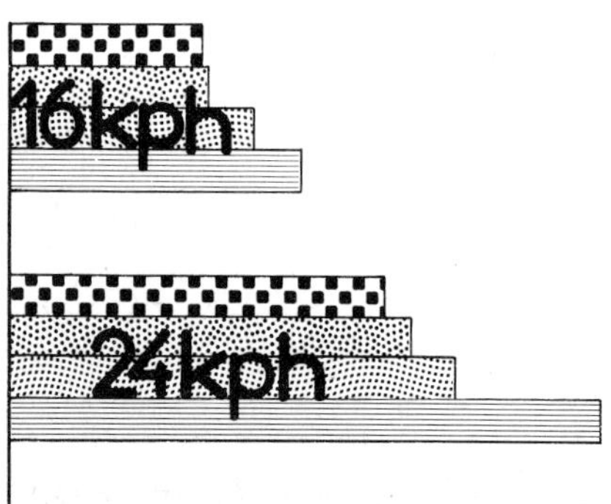

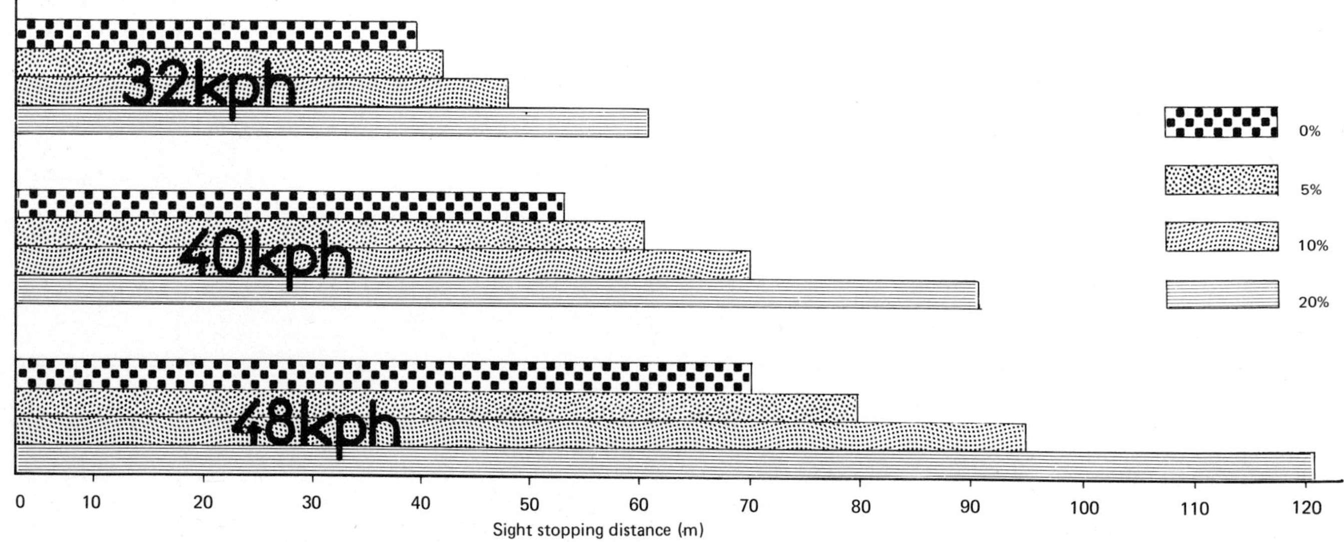

6.9 Maximum sight stopping distances for various downhill gradients (Source: *Design and Construction Criteria for Bikeway Construction Projects*, 1980)

Sight distance (S) measured along centre-line inside lane

m

R

Object

Obstruction

Cyclist's eye

Line of sight is 0.6m above centre-line inside lane at point of obstruction
S = Sight distance
R = Radius of centre-line inside lane
m = Distance from centre- line inside lane

Should the obstuction be removed?

1. Knowing cyclists' speeds and the gradient of the path, the sight stopping distance(S) can be calculated.

2. Knowing S and the radius of the path R, read the lateral clearance to the object (m) from the chart. If m is not large enough to allow cyclists to stop the obstruction should be removed.

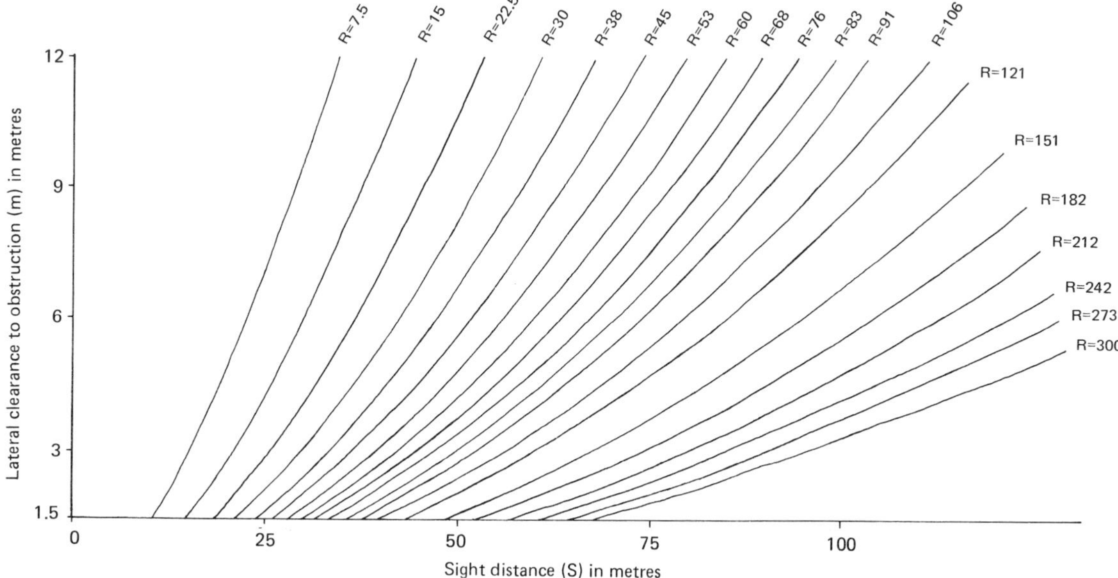

6.11 Lateral clearances on horizontal curves (Source: *Design and Construction Criteria for Bikeway Construction Projects*, 1980)

The engineer's goal will be to choose paths with the shallowest slopes. Where slopes have to be climbed a widely accepted guideline is a maximum slope of 5% over not more than 30m. An ideal standard would be 2.5% over not more than 200m (fig 6.12). Where steeper slopes have to be negotiated, most people can cycle up 15% over no more than 20m. Above that many people will have to dismount, but it should be noted that a short steep slope on a cycle track is often better than no track at all.

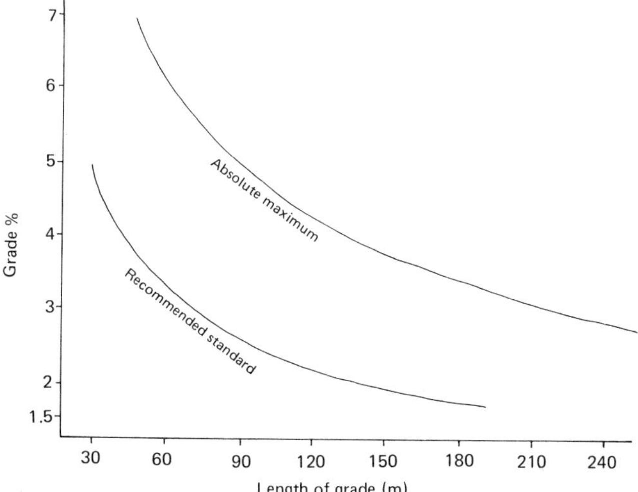

6.12 A suggested relationship between grade and length of grade (Source: *Bikeway Planning and Design Manual*, 1979)

Drainage

It is preferable that paths converted to cycle tracks should drain well, since water makes most bicycle brakes very ineffective. Where the soil on which the path has been constructed is relatively porous, a crossfall of 2–4% will allow surface water to run off the track and drain naturally. Where the soil is not porous, there should be a small drainage channel on the downfall edge with gullies at 40m intervals. Where a path is on the side of a hill there should be a channel or French drain on the uphill side of the path to collect hillside water. Mud banks on the uphill side should be seeded. If there are drainage gratings, the bars must be perpendicular to the line of the path and should not be easily removable. If a path does not meet these requirements, drainage facilities could be installed as part of the process of up-grading the path.

Construction and surfacing

The basic criterion for the structural section of a track which is to be converted for use by cyclists is that it must support the weight of maintenance vehicles, or where alternative

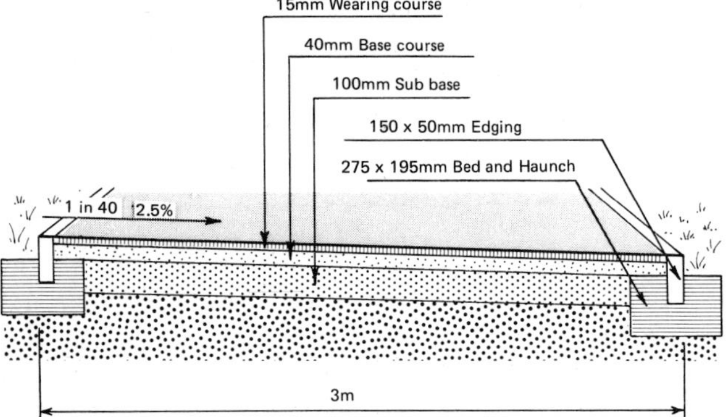

6.13 A flexible footpath standard for UK cycle tracks

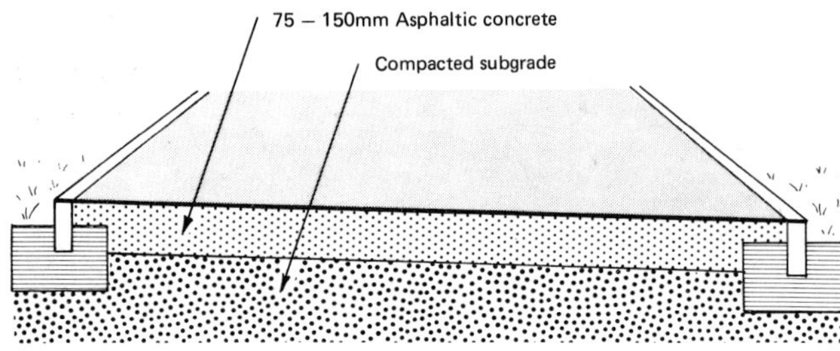

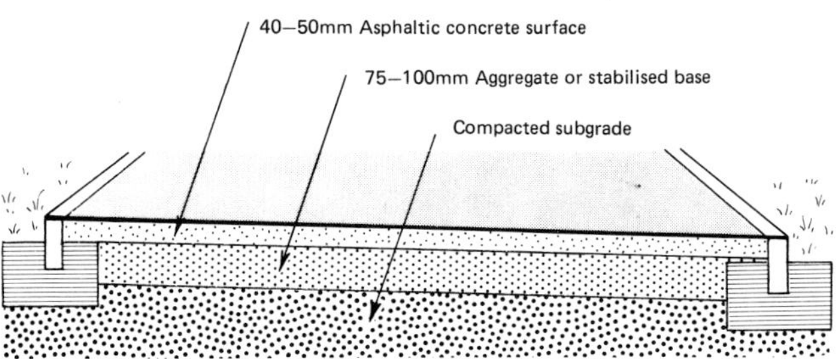

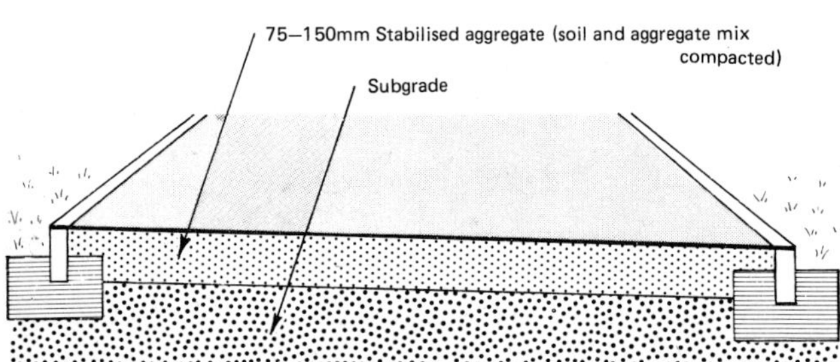

6.14 Flexible cycle track designs (USA)

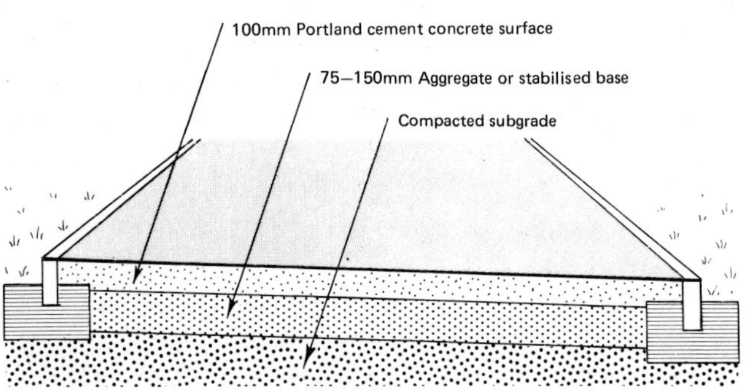

6.15 Rigid cycle track design (USA)

6.16 'On tracks away from the highway special lighting will be required' (Bedford, UK)

maintenance arrangements have been made, the weight of cyclists and their bicycles. In the UK the standard set for cycle tracks is that of a flexible footpath (fig 6.13). Clearly, the application of this standard depends on the type of soil on which the track has been built, but in the majority of cases a standard such as this will be adequate.

In the USA, standards have been set for flexible pavements (fig 6.14) and for a rigid pavement (fig 6.15).

The UK standard includes edging, which helps to prevent crumbling and makes surface laying easier. However, it is not a necessary prerequisite for conversions in recreational areas, parks and on riversides, where the grass should be allowed to grow onto the track so that it blends in with the surroundings.

The surfacing of the track should provide a way which is safe and comfortable to ride along. The surface should also have a good coefficient of friction. In the UK and other countries the standard 'wearing course' for cycle tracks is fine cold asphalt. Alternatives such as concrete, hot rolled asphalt or even compressed stone chippings are adequate. Broadly speaking almost any material which is used for surfacing footpaths is adequate, the only exception being concrete paving slabs which tend to shift if vehicles drive over them. This makes an uneven surface for cycling, and should only be used if the surface is regularly maintained.

Lighting

On paths which are within the highway boundary additional lighting will generally not be required because the road lights will illuminate the track. However, where paths are not beside the highway, special lighting will be required. Lighting should be to the standard specified for footpaths. In the

6.17 Line segregation of a cycle-pedestrian track (Peterborough, UK)

UK, standard Group B lighting should be used. The columns should be spaced at 30 to 40m intervals, the lights 5m high, giving off 3400 lux from mercury lamps, and 4500 from sodium lamps (fig 6.16). The cost of providing such lighting will be in the region of £250 per column.

Maintenance

Any path which is converted to a cycle track will require a regular schedule of maintenance. Unlike motor vehicle tyres, bicycles tyres are too narrow to have an effective self-cleansing action which moves debris to the edge of the road. Maintenance vehicles will therefore have to sweep the whole of the track.

The layout of the track and ancillary facilities must enable maintenance vehicles to enter and travel along the complete length of the track. Other maintenance work may include cutting back trees and shrubs to preserve good sight-lines.

The regularity of such maintenance work will depend on the location of the track, tracks in urban areas generally requiring more frequent attention than others. This should be determined by regular inspections.

If the path meets the standards set out above, then structural maintenance should not be required. Again, regular inspections will be required to determine need.

Vehicle control devices

In some situations, cars, or more often motor cycles, will be tempted to try and use cycle tracks. Measures may therefore be required to physically stop them entering the route. Concrete bollards and steel posts have in some places been erected in the centre of the path to stop cars entering the route. However, they must be lit or reflectorised unless used on well lit paths. Collapsible posts will be required where maintenance vehicles need access.

The problem is more complicated for motor cycles. The entrance gap could be narrowed to 0.7m allowing bicycles and not motor cycles to pass, but this will restrict the capacity of the path. In the end, a period of intense police enforcement may be the only solution.

Rigidity of standards

If a path meets all the standards set out above, it will make an ideal cycle track. In practice, many paths will not meet them all, so decisions will have to be made about which standards should be applied rigidly and which more flexibly. The only standards which should never be relaxed are those for the riding surface and maintenance. If the surface is uneven, the route is unlikely to be heavily used.

The application of the other standards and the work required to bring the path up to standard ultimately depends on the finance available for the work. Unless the work can be set against other budgets, for example where the road beside a path is being up-graded, trade-offs will have to be made against other elements of the bicycle plan.

Cost of conversions

Since costs will depend heavily on the quantity of work required, the following figures are only approximations. On paths which require repair, trimming of vegetation and dropped kerbs, but no widening, the cost is likely to be in the region of £2,000/km. Where widening is required £10–13/sqm of new path should be added to this figure.

6.2.3 Cycle-pedestrian tracks

These are widely used in many European countries but not nearly so often in the USA. This may be partly because American cyclists travel faster than their European counterparts and are therefore less suited to sharing with pedestrians. In Europe, this type of facility is considered to be second best after cycle-only tracks. In the USA cycle lanes are ranked second and 'sidewalk paths' third.

The major fear in countries which have not provided shared cycle-pedestrian tracks is that they are dangerous. This fear sometimes manifests itself in political opposition to the conversion of footpaths and footways to shared cycle-pedestrian tracks.

It should be made clear from the start that there are situations where shared paths are appropriate and some where they are not. Paths which have high pedestrian flow-rates, which are used as play areas or which are frequently intersected by drive ways are not suitable for conversion. Furthermore, the conversion of paths should not be considered where they just take cyclists off roads which are adequate in the first place. However, there are situations where wide paths can be used to avoid busy roads and awkward junctions. In particular paths in parks, across open spaces or through residential estates, disused railway lines, canal tow paths and riverside paths are all routes which have the potential for providing cyclists with high quality routes in pleasant surroundings.

Where a suitable path is being considered for conversion, the needs of pedestrians, in particular the blind and the disabled, must be taken into account and their organisations consulted to identify potential problems.

In addition to helping utilitarian cyclists through busy urban areas, some cycle-pedestrian tracks can be justified on

6.18 Barriers have been used to segregate cyclists and pedestrians, but they may present safety problems at night

6.19 A riverside path which is suitable for cyclists and pedestrians

recreational grounds and therefore funded from different budgets.

This section looks at the design and construction standards which paths should meet if they are to be converted into cycle-pedestrian tracks.

Width

A major consideration in the conversion of a path will be whether there is sufficient width to accommodate cyclists and pedestrians, or whether the path should be widened. The UK Department of Transport recommends a minimum width of 2.5m for segregated paths (1m for pedestrians and 1.5m for cyclists). However, narrower paths have been converted. One in Peterborough is only 1.8m wide; average peak hour flows were in the region of 50 bicycles and 100 pedestrians (fig 6.17) and time lapse photography showed no evidence that either cyclists or pedestrians found difficulty using the path.

Segregation

The width will depend to some extent on whether bicycles and pedestrians are segregated, and if so, on what type of segregation is chosen. Where the track is less than 2.0m wide, segregation is not possible. Where it is wider than this, segregation is advisable because it helps to provide better protection for pedestrians and to calm their legitimate fears about sharing the path with cyclists. Three basic types of segregration are available:

1. *Spatial segregation:* Raising the level of the footpath or providing a verge between cyclists and pedestrians are methods of giving both groups a feeling of security. However, this is the most expensive type of segregation because the tracks have to be wider than those using other means of segregation and, more importantly, because the conversion of an existing path in effect requires that another is built parallel to it.

2. *Colour or line segregation:* These types of segregation are useful where space is limited. In European countries the most common colours are red for cyclists and black for pedestrians. The colour difference can be provided by applying a 'slurry seal' or 'paint' to the bicycle section of the surface.

3. *Barriers:* On tracks which have few access points, barriers or low rustic fences (fig 6.18) can be used to provide segregation. Although the minimum width of the track will have to be increased by 0.4m, the cost of this type of segregation is considerably less than spatial segregation. Gaps will have to be left in the barrier at every point where cyclists join or leave the track and lighting will have to be particularly good to avoid collisions with the barrier.

Other design standards

Not all paths will be suitable for conversion, for example, gradients may be too steep, sight-lines poor, curves too tight. The standards set out in section 6.2.2 for the conversion of paths to a cycle-only track should be used to determine the suitability of the paths and the extent of the work required to convert them. These standards should also be used to determine lighting and maintenance requirements.

The following additional points should also be noted:

- generosity with sight-lines at junctions on cycle-pedestrian tracks will minimise the risk of bicycle/pedestrian conflicts
- lane widening may be required when a minimum width cycle track has to negotiate tight bends
- particularly good lighting should be provided at all junctions to minimise bicycle/pedestrian conflicts.

The conversion of some types of paths raises special problems for planners and engineers. The next few sections discuss these in detail.

Canal towpaths and riverside paths

Most European countries have comprehensive systems of canals, parts of which are no longer heavily used for transporting goods. The towpath beside canals can, in most cases, be easily converted to utilitarian or recreational cycle routes. Their great advantage is that they can provide an alternative to busy radial roads. The most common objection to the use of canal and riverside paths is that cyclists will fall into the water. There is however little evidence to support this myth, and riverside paths (and some canal towpaths) often have a grass verge between the path and the water. Furthermore, cyclists will tend only to ride near the water when overtaking.

In the UK most canals towpaths are owned by the British Waterways Board and riverside paths by local authorities. Approaches will therefore have to be made to gain permission to use, lease or buy the land. Where a public right of way has already been established, this should be relatively easy.

On paths which will be primarily used for utilitarian trips,

6.20 (above) An example of a floating cycle-pedestrian track used to create a link underneath a bridge (Bedford, UK)

6.21 (below) A disused railway bridge used to cross the Grand Union Canal (Great Lingford, UK)

the design standards given in section 6.2.2 for width, sight-lines, turning radii and maintenance should be used. For recreational routes these standards can be relaxed. Given that both types of path are flat and relatively straight the work required will often be limited to upgrading the route (and possibly widening the surface) and avoiding obstructions, particularly bridges. Solutions to this obstacle include the provision of a floating section of cycle track (fig 6.20) or, where a low bridge is unavoidable, clear warning signs. If the path under the bridge is less than 1.5m wide, a railing should be erected adjacent to the waterway under the bridge and for 2m either side.

Disused railway lines

Throughout Europe and the USA there are thousands of miles of disused railway lines. Since railway lines do not have steep gradients or tight bends, they are a ready-made opportunity to provide recreational routes out of town centres and to link other elements of a bicycle network within those areas.

The critical factors in the use of disused railway lines are:

leasing the land
providing access points
re-constructing and maintaining bridges
lighting tunnels.

The majority of disused railway lines are still owned by the railway company who created the line. However, parts have been sold on a piecemeal basis, and these gaps in the route will present problems, since buyers' main motivation appears to be the restriction of public access. In the UK, where a whole route is available, the local authority can lease or purchase land from the British Rail Property Board. Where parts have been sold off, it may be possible to lease these back from the owner, or if the route is important, and the owner unwilling, to compulsorily purchase the land.

Since railway lines are often in cuttings or on embankments, the provision of access points will be an immediate consideration. Access points should be as close as possible to the origins and destinations of people's journeys. If necessary, ramps will have to be built, though since most routes will be primarily for recreation they could be quite steep, say up to 20% over a short distance.

On many lines, bridges over roads have been dismantled because they became expensive to maintain. The most expensive item in providing the route will therefore be the provision of a new bridge. However, these need be no more than 1.5m wide (if bicycle flows are low) and of a lightweight construction. Such a bridge might cost £10,000 to £15,000.

The two problems in tunnels are lighting and drainage. On recreational routes lighting will only be required in tunnels over 10m long and this will only be required in daylight hours, since the route is unlikely to be used at night. On routes used for other purposes, particularly where usage is expected to be heavy, good lighting will be required since fear of danger will deter people from using the route.

Drainage in tunnels should be provided by a 2% crossfall on the surface and channelling the water out of one end of the tunnel.

The design standards set out in section 6.2.2 should be used for other aspects of the design. Where a sub-base of ballast already exists, this can be compacted to provide an adequate surface for recreational use. Care must be taken, however, to remove ridges made by sleepers, particularly in tunnels.

6.2.4 Pedestrianized streets

The pedestrianization of a street provides an excellent opportunity to improve conditions for cyclists. However, many such opportunities have been missed and cyclists have often been forced to take circuitous detours on busy roads.

Cycle routes in pedestrianized streets should be conceived of as a miniature road system, with the routes segregated from pedestrian areas by colour, or if the flow of bicycles exceeds 150/hour, by lowering the level of the cycle route. In many streets, the availability of width should not cause a problem, unless they are less than 10m wide or carry particularly high pedestrian flows. Since delivery vehicles are allowed into many precincts, the surface which has been provided for them will be adequate for bicycles.

The design standards for width, sight-lines, radii, gradients and maintenance given in section 6.2.2 should be applied to any conversion. In a large pedestrianized area a number of cycle routes may cross. Here miniature junctions should be marked out giving priority to the route with the highest flow of bicycles.

6.2.5 Cycle lanes

The purpose of providing cycle lanes is to give cyclists some protection and a sense of security on the road. On roads with one lane in each direction, cycle lanes have been shown to make cyclists follow a straighter route, to reduce the number of hazardous close passes and to reduce motorists' wide avoidance swerves. However, they also imply to drivers that cyclists will stay in their lane and that may not be possible if the surface is uneven or if debris has to be avoided. A further shortcoming of lanes is that they have to be stopped at either side of junctions. However, there are situations where it is desirable to create more predictable movements by cyclists and motorists, and where it is important to increase cyclists' confidence that motor vehicle drivers will not stray into their paths. Three types of lanes can be provided: with flow, contra-flow and cycle/car parking lanes. The following sections outline design and construction guidelines for these. It should be stressed, however, that cycle lanes are particularly sensitive to the different behavioural customs found in different countries, so that a particular design may be appropriate in one country but inappropriate in another.

With-flow lanes

In the UK two types of with-flow lanes can be provided: an advisory lane which has no legal backing, and a mandatory lane which is backed by a Traffic Regulation Order. Advisory lanes are delineated by a dashed white line (fig 6.22) which does not ban motor vehicles from entering the lane. Mandatory lanes provide the cyclist with better protection because motor traffic is banned from the lane (see section 8.7 'Carriageway markings'). The minimum width for a with-flow lane recommended by the UK Department of Transport is 1.5m.

Contra-flow lanes

Contra-flow cycle lanes have been used in the UK and other European countries. In the USA, contra-flow lanes are thought to be undesirable, because they could encourage

6.22 An advisory cycle lane (right) and a mandatory lane (left). (Peterborough, UK). An attitude survey discovered that cyclists thought these lanes (1.2m) were too narrow

6.23 A contra-flow cycle lane with line segregation (Cambridge, UK)

6.24 A cycle and parking lane (USA), with sufficient space for car doors to open without forcing cyclists out of the lane

wrong-way riding, an American habit which results in significant numbers of accidents.

Contra-flow lanes are a useful way of exempting cyclists from one-way traffic systems when the alternative is a busy or lengthy detour. In some urban situations, the only opportunity for creating a link in a route may be to use a contra-flow lane.

In the UK, the suggested minimum width of a contra-flow lane is 2.0m and the absolute minimum recommended is 1.5m. Where space permits, physical segregation, such as a paved strip, should be used as this gives both motorists and cyclists a greater feeling of security and will ensure that vehicles do not park in the lane. Parking and waiting must not be allowed at any time and the regulations should be strictly enforced to ensure that cyclists are never forced to move into the lane of on-coming traffic. In the UK, traffic islands must be constructed at either end of the lane because traffic regulations do not allow authorities to put exemption plates under no entry signs, so a separate entrance has to be constructed. Other European countries have less stringent stipulations.

Position of lanes

The type of lane chosen and its position in the highway will depend on a number of factors:

- the width of the highway
- motor vehicle flows
- bicycle flows
- the number of access points
- the usage of access points
- car parking requirements
- delivery vehicle waiting requirements
- drivers' and cyclists' behavioural habits.

Cycle lanes will be safer if all waiting and parking is banned. Where streets are currently used for parking, this is likely to raise opposition from the (often vociferous) group of people who feel that they have a right to park there. It should be noted, however, that highways are provided for traffic, and their use for other purposes is a privilege which is granted where it does not conflict with traffic flow. Nevertheless, in some situations the provision of parking will be an important criterion to be considered.

6.25 This cycle lane is surfaced in red tarmac (The Hague, Holland)

6.26 A bus and cycle lane (London, UK)

6.27 A contra-flow bus and cycle lane (Sheffield, UK)

6.28 A bus and cycle only street (Leighton Linslade, UK)

Shared parking and cycle lanes, with the cyclists on the roadside, have been provided in the USA and Australia. They are said to work successfully provided the turnover of parked cars is not too high and the lane is wide enough to allow cyclists to pass cars with their doors open (ie, 4m). The positions of the parked cars can be controlled by marking out bays. This also encourages drivers not to park in the bicycle section of the lane. A particular use of with-flow cycle and cycle-parking lanes is to reduce the width of road available for motor vehicles in situations where two vehicles can only just pass and will force cyclists into the gutter.

Lane delineation

The most popular method of marking a lane is to paint a line on the surface of the road (see section 8.7 'Carriageway markings'). In some places this has been supplemented by colouring the surface of the lane differently from the highway to provide a stronger deterrent to motor vehicle drivers. Physical barriers have been used, but these present considerable hazards to cyclists and are not generally recommended.

Side roads

Although junction treatment is the subject of a separate chapter (Chapter 7), the problem of side roads and with-flow cycle lanes merits attention here because it is one of the major problems associated with the use of cycle lanes. Where cycle lanes cross private entrances, the cycle lane should be continued across the entrance. On public roads, junction treatments should be considered. From the safety point of view the best solution will be to close the road. Where this is not possible all turns into the road could be banned. Where side-road flows exceed 100 vehicles per hour and the installation of traffic signals is not justified, then the benefits of introducing a cycle lane should be re-considered.

Width

The width of a cycle lane will depend more on the width of the road than the number of cyclists using the road. In general with-flow lanes should be 2m wide. The minimum width in the UK and the USA is 1.5m. Below that the

Action checklist for improving routes used by cyclists

1. Determine the origin and destination of the route under consideration. (See Chapters 3 and 4 for identification of routes and determination of priorities.)
2. Use a set of standards (see section 6.1) to decide which roads and junctions are adequate, which require improvement and which are so unsuitable for cyclists that alternative routes are required.
3. On routes which are inadequate determine precisely what improvements are required.
4. Check whether any of the improvements can be incorporated into existing plans for the road.
5. Where alternatives are required, identify what routes are available, whether they increase journey length by more than 10% and how attractive they would be as cycle routes.
6. If an existing route is to be converted into a cycle route:
- check widths, sight-lines, turning radii, gradients, constructions, surfacing, drainage, lighting and maintenance requirements against a set of standards (see section 6.2)
- determine what work is required to make the route suitable for cyclists
- calculate the cost of the work.

7. If a new construction is required:
- determine ownership of the land
- produce alternative designs for the route (width, sight-lines, etc)
- calculate the costs of the alternatives.

8. Decide how junctions should be treated (see Chapter 7).
9. Design the sign layout (see Chapter 8).
10. Discuss the proposed improvement plan with other people involved in the bike plan (cycling organisations, the police, road safety officials, etc) and with anyone who may be affected by the proposals (ie, the blind, local residents, etc).
11. Use safety and political considerations to determine the priorities for the improvements.
12. Use budgetary considerations to prepare a programme for the improvement work.
13. Obtain agreement for the proposed programme through the normal decision-making channels, ensuring that cycling organisations muster the necessary support.
14. Formulate work programme.
15. When necessary carry out a land survey.
16. Check the location of services.
17. Assess and order materials.
18. Prepare any publicity material which may be required (see Chapter 10).
19. Set dates for the completion of different aspects of the project.
20. Carry out any monitoring required for before and after studies (see Chapter 12).
21. Mark out site.
22. Excavate where necessary.
23. Carry out physical construction.
24. Issue publicity materials.
25. Erect traffic signs.
26. Agree maintenance schedules.
27. Monitor each facility after its introduction (see Chapter 12).

benefits of providing the lane are dubious. Where the edge of the carriageway forms a drainage gutter, this area should not be included in the width of the lane.

Surface quality
The most frequent criticism of cycle lanes is that they force cyclists into the edge of the road where the surface is most uneven. On narrow lanes and on contra-flow lanes this can be particularly dangerous, because motorists are not expecting cyclists to swerve to avoid potholes. It is therefore essential that a top quality surface is provided across the whole width of the lane, and that particular attention is paid to the gutter area.

Sight-lines
Sight-line calculations are particularly important at junctions and on bends of cycle parking lanes. At junctions parking should be banned at least 20m before the junction to ensure that vehicles turning into the road can see approaching cyclists. On bends, parking should only be allowed where drivers opening car doors can see cyclists.

Turning radii and gradients
Although these will usually be determined by the existing highway, where cycle lanes are provided on tight bends or steep hills, the lanes should be widened to allow space for cyclists leaning on the bend or pushing up the hill. Furthermore, since motor vehicle drivers tend to cut across or swerve out at bends, physical segregation could be provided to give cyclists extra protection.

Drainage
Drainage gratings should, wherever possible, be outside the lane.

Maintenance
The maintenance of lanes will usually be part of a highway maintenance schedule. Site checks should be made to ensure that these are sufficiently frequent and systematic to account for the higher surface quality required by cyclists. Where physical segregation has been provided, special maintenance procedures may be required since road vehicles will throw debris into the lane and mechanical maintenance vehicles will not be able to clear it.

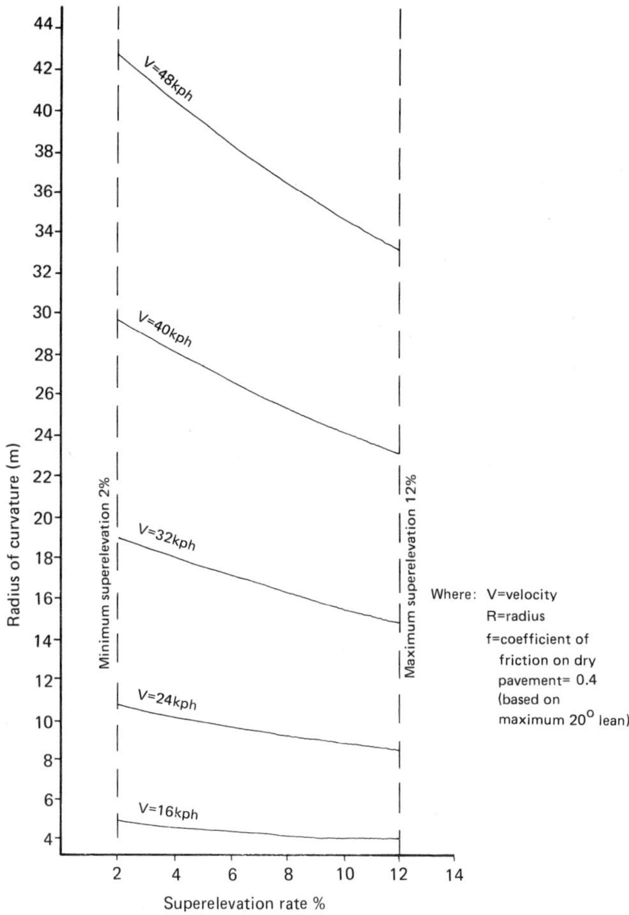

6.29 The effect of superelevation on minimum radii for various design speeds

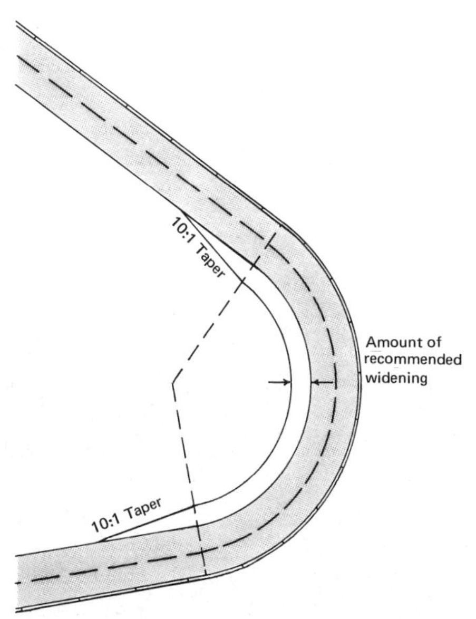

Design speeds kph	Curve widening for given radius					
	4.5m	6	8	10	20	27
16	1.1	.8	.6	.5	.25	.18
24		1.2	1.1	.7	.33	.27
32			1.2	1.0	.45	.36
40				1.2	.57	.45
48					.66	.51

6.30 Curve widening for various radii and design speeds (Source: *Bikeway Planning and Design Manual*, 1979)

6.2.6 Bus and cycle routes

During the last decade, towns and cities in a number of countries have introduced bus lanes to speed public transport through congested areas. In the UK, the government has encouraged local authorities to allow cyclists to share these lanes with buses.

The major problem is keeping other motor vehicles out of the lanes. In the UK, periodic policing appears to significantly improve the behaviour of motorists who are tempted to encroach into the lane. In addition, coloured surfacing has been used to further deter motorists from this temptation.

Since with-flow bus lanes are relatively cheap to implement, they are a good way of giving cyclists a feeling of greater security on busy urban streets, However, bus lanes usually end before junctions. They are therefore unlikely to significantly affect accident rates. Furthermore, many only operate during the peak period, so the protection given is limited to commuter cyclists. Contra-flow bus and cycle lanes are more difficult to implement because they ought to be at least 5m wide to allow buses and cyclists to overtake without encroaching into the on-coming traffic (1.4m for cyclists and 3.6m for buses). However, there are situations where the advantages of allowing cyclists to use a contra-flow lane outweigh the disadvantages of the alternative, for example where it would allow cyclists to avoid continuous flow intersections in a one-way system.

Bus and cycle only routes can be created by closing streets to all traffic except buses, cycles and in some situations, taxis. The measure is designed to reduce traffic flows in a street without restricting access to those modes of transport which an authority wishes to encourage (fig 6.28). Such streets can be closed to traffic travelling in one or both directions. Other traffic is excluded by using a combination of signs and carriageway markings, and, where a stronger deterrent is required, by constructing a low ramp.

Where the flow of buses is over 60/hour (for example near to a bus station), or where there is a high volume of turning buses, it may be inappropriate to allow bicycles to use the route. In practically all other situations, bus and cycle routes are preferable to bus and cycle lanes because total traffic flows are lower and the routes therefore more pleasant.

6.3 CONSTRUCTING NEW ROUTES

In some situations the most appropriate way of creating a link in a bicycle network will be to construct a new facility.

6.3.1 Cycle tracks

The design and construction guidelines which were set out for determining whether a path is suitable for conversion to a cycle track (section 6.2.2) should be used as standards for the construction of new tracks. The following additional points should also be incorporated in the design:

- Curves can be superelevated up to a maximum of 12% (fig 6.29) to enable cyclists to travel round tighter bends at the design speed.
- Bends can be widened to take account of the extra space required by cyclists (fig 6.30)
- Tracks on slopes with gradients over 5% can be widened by 1m to enable faster cyclists to overtake slower cyclists or people pushing their bikes.

The cost of constructing a new cycle track will depend on

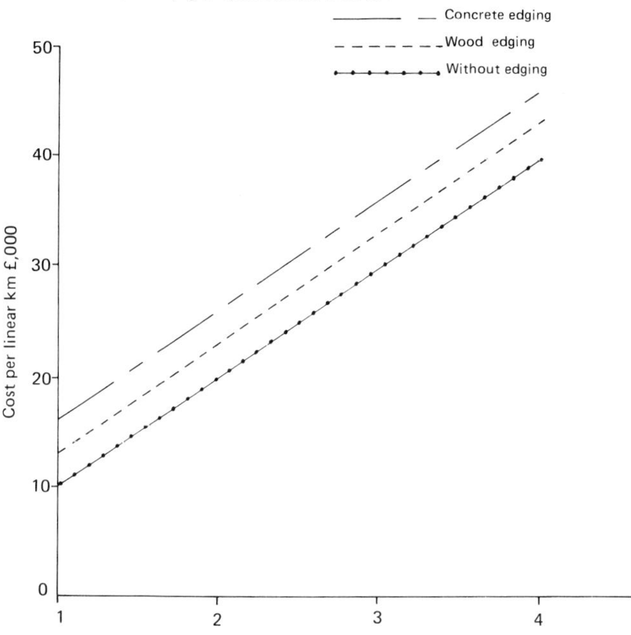

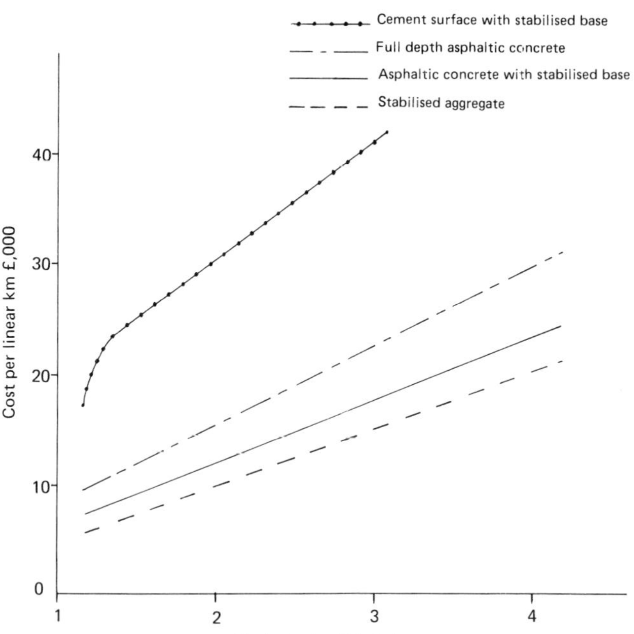

6.31 Construction costs of cycle tracks, based on an average of maximum and minimum costs

the type of construction and the width of the track. Accurate calculation of the width required will therefore be an important factor in the design process. If it is too wide, money will be wasted, and if it is too narrow, it may have to be widened in a few years' time. Some approximate estimates of the cost of building a cycle track are given in fig 6.31.

6.3.2 Cycle-pedestrian tracks

Where space and finance permit, new cycle-pedestrian tracks should be built with spatial segregation to ensure that the benefits of mixing the two groups are not affected by an increased risk of accidents. The design of a suitable path is shown in fig 6.32.

The standards set out in section 6.2.2 and 6.2.3 should be used for all other aspects of the design.

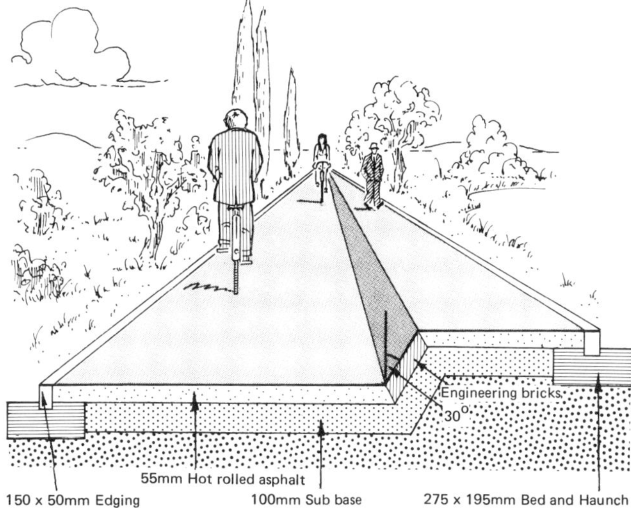

6.32 Design of a segregated cycle-pedestrian track

6.33 The segregated cycle-pedestrian network at Stevenage (UK)

7 Designing, constructing and altering junctions

Treatment of junctions is undoubtedly one of the most difficult problems facing anyone preparing proposals to make cycling safer and more attractive. These difficulties arise because of the combination of constraints present in most situations: space is limited, there is pressure to keep motor vehicles moving and there may already be conflict between motor vehicles and pedestrians. Furthermore, improvements which are really effective will often be expensive compared to other parts of a plan for enhancing cycling.

Nevertheless, improvements are important because the majority of accidents involving cyclists occur at or within 20m of junctions. Furthermore, junction improvements may have considerable effect on the perceived dangers of cycling, since they are often given as reasons for not cycling. From the analysis of accident types (see section 5.2.1, 'Common locations and types') eight design principles can be identified. These should be observed in the design or alteration of any junction.

- Wherever possible bicycles should be segregated from motor vehicles by space or time
- Where segregation is impossible, adequate space must be provided to allow bicycles and motor vehicles to move together
- The time that cyclists are exposed to danger should be minimised
- Where cyclists have to pause during a manoeuvre physical protection should, if space permits, be provided
- The points where bicycles have to cross vehicle flows should be as far apart as possible
- Cyclists and motor vehicle drivers must be able to see each other clearly whilst waiting or manoeuvering through a junction
- Cyclists must be able to wait in a secure position before entering the junction
- Clear signing should indicate destinations and, where necessary, how cyclists should manoeuvre through the junction to get to those destinations.

From the cyclists' perspective, all intersections are a necessary evil. They make cyclists slow down and lose momentum, turning and emerging vehicles present additional risks and, when cyclists themselves turn across a traffic flow, they are put in vulnerable positions. These problems are compounded by the lack of consideration given to cyclists' needs in the design and layout of the majority of junctions in existence today. All too often so-called improvements are introduced to junctions in urban areas which speed the flow of traffic at the expense of cyclists' safety. In recent years, the situation has deteriorated with the introduction of more one-way systems and free flow interchanges.

One of the first priorities is therefore to ensure that all road 'improvements' and new constructions are not sanctioned until they have been viewed from a cyclist's perspective. The next task is to identify existing junctions which are dangerous or which put cyclists in a vulnerable position and to take steps to implement a programme of improvements.

The first part of this chapter explains how to identify junctions requiring attention. The second part gives details of the different types of improvements which are available and where they are appropriate. They are described in order of ascending cost. In practice, the best solution will be to completely segregate traffic (by space or time). However, this type of facility is at the more expensive end of the range. Trade-offs will therefore have to be made between the introduction of a large number of minor improvements and the creation of a few much improved junctions.

7.1 IDENTIFYING JUNCTIONS REQUIRING ATTENTION

There are four ways of identifying junctions where cyclists are put in highly vulnerable positions or where their safety is threatened. The first is to identify the flows of bicycles and other vehicles making different manoeuvres at a junction. This will determine the potential for accidents at that site. For example, if there is a large flow of vehicles turning off the road across a flow of cyclists, the potential will be much higher than if most vehicles and bicycles travel straight across the junction (see fig 7.1).

Clearly, the actual potential for accidents will also depend on the layout of the junction and the methods employed to control the traffic. There has been little research into the relationship between the potential for conflict and the actual occurrence of accidents. However, an investigation into the potential for accidents will help to determine the scale of the problem (observant investigators are likely to see a number of near misses or risky manoeuvres at a busy junction) and the priorities for action (see also section 5.6.2).

The second indicator of junction problems is the location

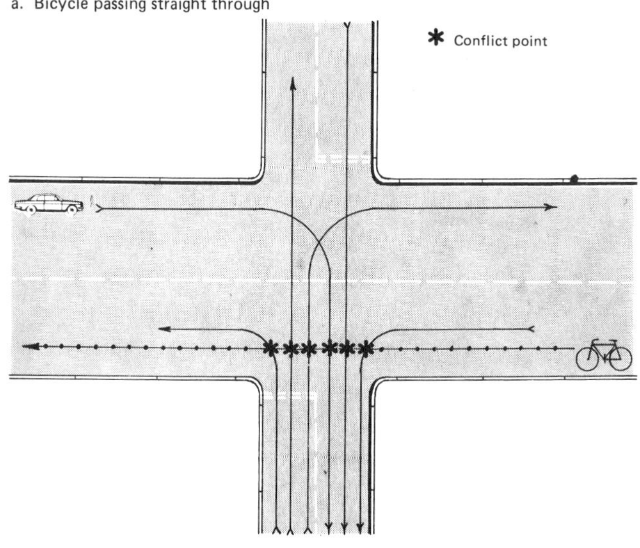

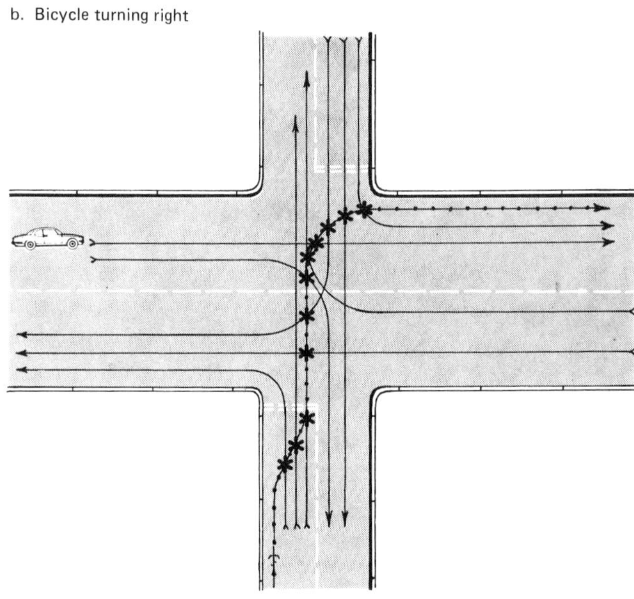

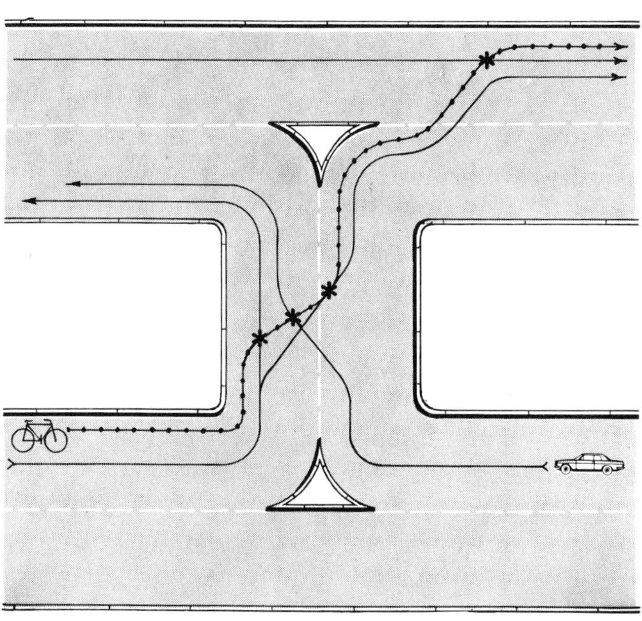

7.1 Potential conflict points between bicycles and other vehicles

RULES FOR IDENTIFYING JUNCTION PROBLEMS

1. Count the number of bicycles and vehicles making different manoeuvres
2. Check the location and details of reported accidents
3. Check that loop detectors at signalised junctions register bicycles
4. Check that signal phasing allows cyclists time to get across the junction before traffic from another direction gets a green signal.
5. Check that entrances and exits do not narrow suddenly and create squeeze points which force cyclists into traffic streams
6. Check that vehicles are not regularly parking or waiting within a specified distance from the junction mouth (15m is suggested as a minimum)
7. Check that vehicles do actually come to a halt at junctions controlled by stop signals
8. Check that surfaces are scrupulously maintained, because cyclists cannot concentrate on turning vehicles and the road surface simultaneously
9. Check that there is sufficient waiting space for cyclists turning across traffic flows
10. Talk to cyclists to obtain their views on the problem.

of reported accidents, and if further studies have been undertaken, the detailed drawings of the incidents.

The third way of discovering problems is to check junctions against a set of basic rules (see box). This will help to identify junctions which are awkward for cyclists. The final method of identifying problems is to ask a sample of cyclists where they have had minor accidents, near misses, and, where they cannot avoid being put in vulnerable positions (see section 5.6.3).

In practice a combination of all four methods of identification is likely to yield the best results. Junctions should be chosen for detailed analysis by picking those with the highest flows of bicycles, the accident data and survey of cyclists being used to identify less-used junctions which nevertheless have problems.

All the data gathered can be listed by junction and plotted on a map to determine the priorities for action.

Roundabouts and gyratory systems

Roundabouts and gyratory systems deserve a particular note because they present special problems for cyclists. Roundabouts are provided to maximize the traffic-carrying capacity of a junction. Multiple-lane entry and wide weaving sections are an essential part of maximizing capacity, but they are also the very factors which make cyclists vulnerable. Four factors in particular contribute to this vulnerability:

- vehicles overtake on both sides of cyclists
- vehicles leaving the junction cut across in front of cyclists
- streams of vehicles send cyclists in undesired directions
- vehicle movements are often very unpredictable.

If the capacity of the roundabout is not to be sacrificed, then there is little that can be done to help cyclists short of

CHECKLIST OF MINOR IMPROVEMENTS TO JUNCTIONS

Some of the problems identified at junctions can be dealt with quickly and easily.

1. Tune loop detectors which are not sensitive to bicycles.
2. Move loop detectors which are sited in positions not ridden over by cyclists.
3. Increase the inter-green period of signals which do not allow cyclists time to cross.
4. Introduce or enforce waiting restrictions if cars wait or park within 15m of a junction.
5. Enlarge the mouths of junctions which form squeeze points.
6. Resurface junctions with potholes, raised or sunken manholes or poor edges.
7. Introduce traffic islands on junctions at which motorists cut across the lanes of emerging traffic.

providing complete grade separation. However, in some situations roundabouts have more capacity than necessary, and this exaggerates the problems facing cyclists. Four measures can be considered as ways of reducing cyclists' vulnerability:

- vehicle movements can be made more predictable if lane striping is provided at the entrances and exits, and, where possible, on the roundabout itself
- lane marking at entrances should clearly identify the lane which drivers taking different exits should use
- approach lanes, exit lanes and lanes on the roundabout should all be at least 4.25m wide to allow cyclists to share the space with motorists
- unnecessary manoeuvering space should not be provided.

7.2 ROAD MARKINGS

Having identified the junctions where layout or other more significant changes are required, decisions should be made on the most appropriate solutions. Providing or altering road markings is one of the cheapest ways of giving cyclists a little protection. Clearly the markings which are applicable to ordinary roads (eg, lane, give way and stop markings) are equally applicable on cycle tracks. In addition to these uses, road markings can be provided to segregate motor vehicles and bicycles, and to warn motor vehicle drivers of the presence of cyclists.

7.2.1 Lane segregation

One of the simplest ways of giving cyclists protection at the entrance of a junction is to move the 'centre-line' off centre, to give a greater share of the road width to those legs of the junction which carry larger volumes of bicycles.

The new space created can be more clearly allocated to bicycles by providing a lane up to the edge of the junction. The lane can be in one of three positions depending on the flows of straight over and turning traffic (fig 7.2). When positioned in the middle of the road this type of lane increases the length of road in which cyclists can cross the motor vehicle flows and therefore increases the number of crossing

a. Main bicycle flow turning left

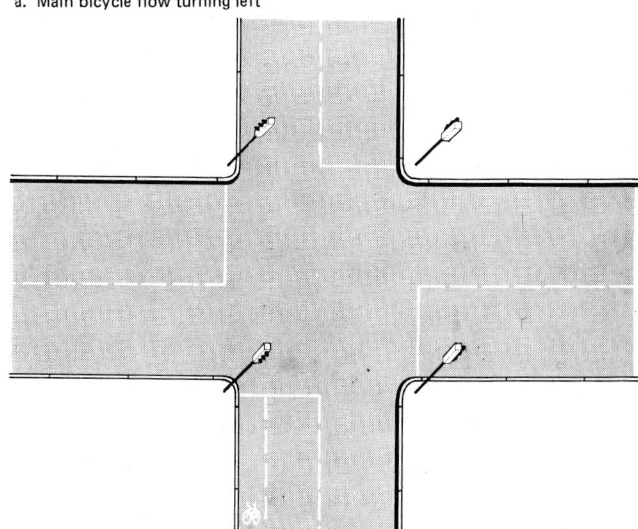

b. Main bicycle flow going straight over

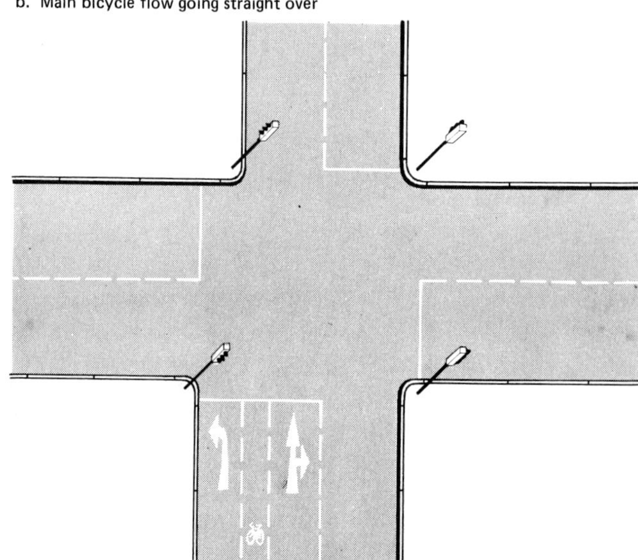

c. Main bicycle flow turning right

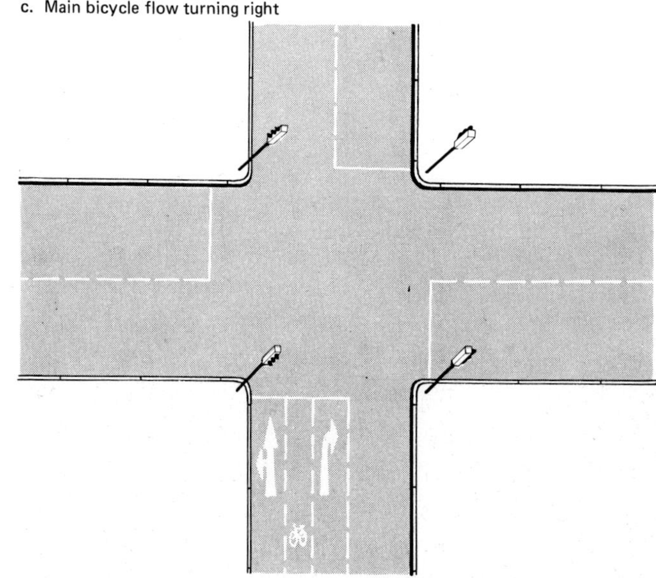

7.2 Three positions for a cycle lane protecting the predominant movement of cyclists at junctions

7.3 A bike lane in the central position, for cyclists going straight ahead (USA)

7.6 An advisory crossing guiding cyclists across the road (Leiden, Holland)

opportunities for the cyclists. In addition it warns motorists to look out for crossing cyclists.

When positioned at the kerb-side, the lane allows cyclists to travel to the front of the queue and pull away ahead of other vehicles. This type of lane is particularly useful it it widens out into a so-called 'fat cycle lane' at the front of the queue, encouraging cyclists to pull up in front of othe vehicles (fig 7.4). Such an arrangement can be further refined by giving cyclists a separate traffic signal which goes green, say, 5 seconds before the signal controlling the rest of the traffic, thus allowing cyclists to clear the junction whilst it is free of traffic.

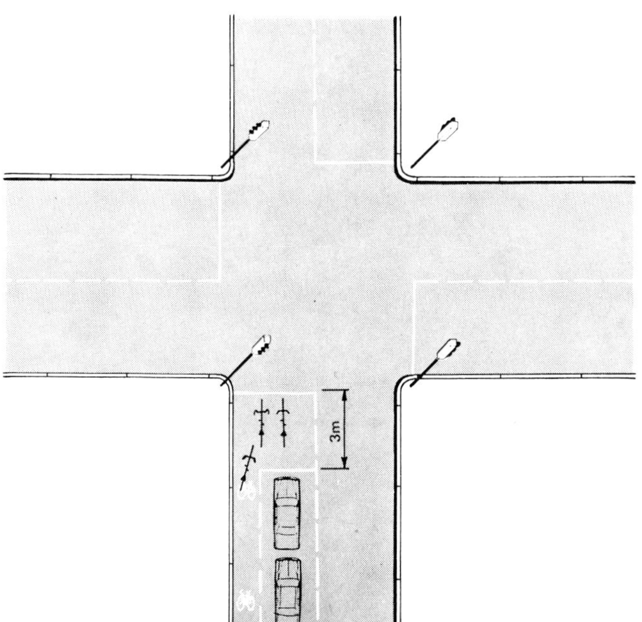

7.4 A 'fat cycle lane' allows cyclists to stop in front of the vehicle queue and pull away first

7.2.2 Advisory crossings

This type of junction is created by marking a row of squares across the road. Its primary purpose is to alert motor vehicle drivers to the presence of cyclists. It has been widely used in Europe in two types of situations:

- where a cycle track with a peak flow of less than 50 bicycles/hour crosses a road with a peak flow of less than 300 vehicles/hour (fig 7.7)
- where a cycle track crosses the mouth of a T-junction.

The markings do not give cyclists priority over other vehicles. Where the road being crossed is wider than 10m, and the traffic flow on the road is not controlled anywhere nearby, a refuge can be provided in the centre of the road to give protection to cyclists waiting in the centre of the road. Where there are bicycle flows in both directions, the markings should be between 2 and 3m apart, each square should be 400mm by 400mm and spaced 400mm apart.

7.3 LAYOUT ALTERATIONS

The purpose of altering the layout of a junction is to:

provide more space (for cyclists but not for motor vehicles)
provide physical segregation (if possible)
improve sight-lines
reduce unnecessary waiting time.

7.5 A cycle lane approach to a junction (Amsterdam, Holland)

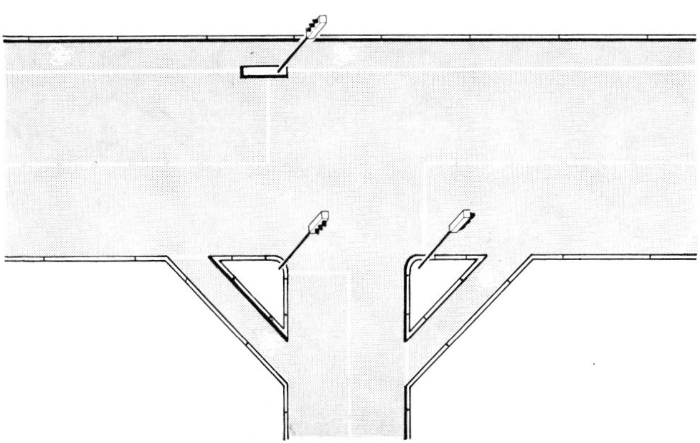

7.7 Provisions for left-turning cyclists

7.8 Traffic is held to allow cyclists to turn off the main road. Those carrying straight on are not delayed (Leiden, Holland)

7.10 A staggered refuge protects cyclists crossing this dual carriageway (Bedford, UK)

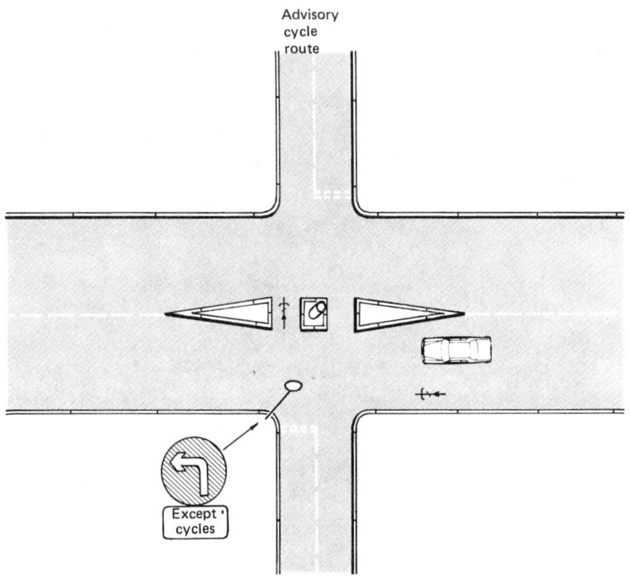

7.9 An island refuge to protect cyclists crossing a road

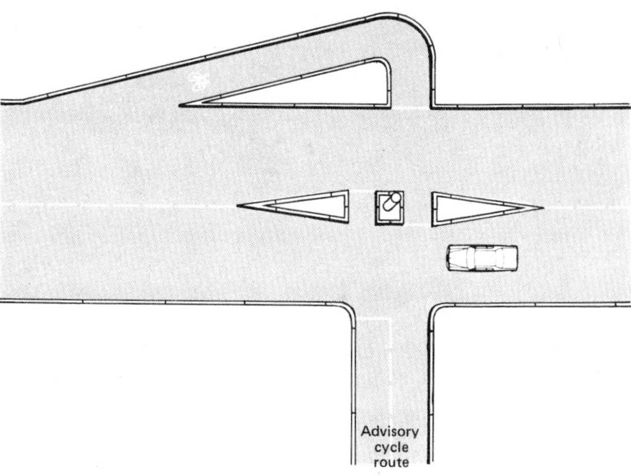

7.11 A protective lane and a central island to help cyclists crossing both lanes of traffic

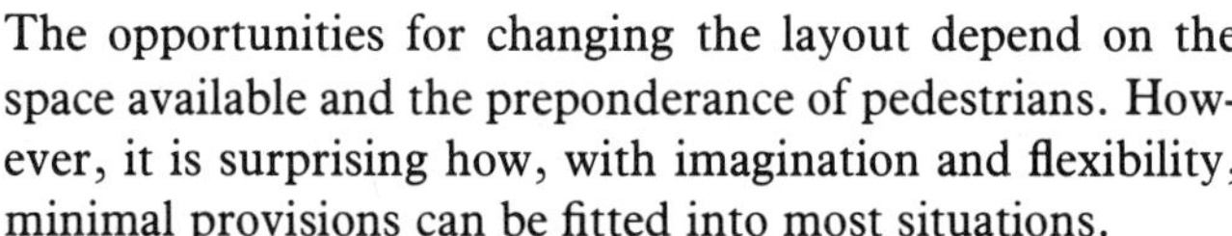

The opportunities for changing the layout depend on the space available and the preponderance of pedestrians. However, it is surprising how, with imagination and flexibility, minimal provisions can be fitted into most situations.

The first method of improving a layout is to eliminate squeeze points. They are particularly awkward at junctions because cyclists have to concentrate on the movement of other vehicles as well as the layout of the road.

Where there are many turning cyclists, a filter lane which enables cyclists to avoid waiting unnecessarily at red lights can be provided. (fig 7.7). This facility is particularly appropriate in circumstances where there is a cycle lane leading up to and away from a junction. (In countries which allow traffic to turn against a red light this provision is obviously less necessary.) Another layout improvement is to allow cyclists through T-junctions on an inside lane (fig 7.8). Again this is most appropriate where bicycle flows are high and pedestrian flows are low. A more sophisticated version of this facility would be to give cyclists a separate signal which only goes red when pedestrians wish to cross.

7.4 ISLAND REFUGES

The purpose of creating island refuges is to break the problem of crossing roads into two sections. They can also be used to protect cyclists turning off main roads. They should not be used on roads less than 10m wide because the islands would create a squeeze point for cyclists travelling on the main road. However, where the road is wider they are a useful device for stopping vehicles overtaking at junctions and slowing traffic speeds. They also block some motor vehicle turning manoeuvres into and out of the side road, thus reducing traffic flows on the route used by cyclists.

Island refuges are an appropriate measure on routes where the flow of bicycles does not justify the provision of traffic signals. In practice, peak flows on the cycle route should be less than 100 bicycles/hour and flows on the main road should be between 300 and 500 vehicles/hour.

The entrance and exit of the refuge should be approximately 4m wide to allow 2 bicycles to pull up alongside each other in both directions, and the refuge should be 2m wide (fig 7.9). Where the two ends of the cycle route are not opposite each other a staggered refuge can be provided (fig 7.10). This should be a minimum of 2m wide. The entrance and exit points should be 3m wide. Since there has been little evaluation of such facilities, these measurements should be treated as provisional guidelines.

At a T-junction on a busy road, further protection could be given to cyclists by providing a lay-by at the edge of the road (fig 7.11).

DEFINITION OF TERMS CONNECTED WITH TRAFFIC SIGNALS

Phase
The sequence of conditions applied to one or more streams of traffic which, during the cycle, receive identical signal light indications.

Minimum green time
The duration of a green signal following the extinction of a red-amber signal during which no change of signal lights can occur.

Vehicle extension period
The duration of a green signal which can be secured by the operation of a detector by a vehicle having right of way.

Maximum green time
The time that a green signal can continue after a demand has been made by traffic on another phase.

Inter-green period
The period of time between the termination of the green signals for one phase and the beginning of the green signal for the next phase to receive right of way.

Demand
A request for right of way for traffic on a phase which has no right of way when the request is made.

7.5 CYCLISTS' ROUNDABOUTS

It was noted earlier that conventional roundabouts present particular problems for cyclists. However, where an advisory cycle route crosses a road with flows in the 100–400 vehicles-/hour range, it is often necessary to increase the priority given to cyclists, increase the visual presence of the junction and reduce motor vehicle speeds. A roundabout similar to a small or mini-roundabout would perform these functions well.

The important factors in the design of such a junction are manoeuvring space and the island size. The area between the island and the inscribed circle needs to be large enough to allow delivery vehicles to turn, but small enough to stop motor vehicles overtaking cyclists on the roundabout. The potential for providing such a roundabout will therefore depend on the space available at the junction and the layout of the approach roads. The central island should be large enough to present a visual obstacle and to provide sufficient deflection to make vehicles reduce their speed to 15 kph (fig 7.12).

Such a design takes advantage of cyclists' greater manoeuvrability (they can pass through the junction a 12 kph if it is clear) and provides a layout which controls motor vehicle movements without unduly hindering their progress.

7.6 AUTOMATIC TRAFFIC SIGNALS

Short of complete physical segregation, traffic signals are the best way of getting cyclists onto, off and across busy roads. However, they are expensive and there is a direct trade-off with other traffic flows; the more time allowed for cyclists, the longer other traffic has to wait to get through the junction. The major advantage of traffic signals is that they completely clear the junction for short periods of time, allowing cyclists to enter, leave or cross without having to compete with other motor vehicles for space. Various attempts have been made to define criteria which can be used to determine when the installation of traffic signals is justified, but none have produced conclusive results. In general, if the peak flow of vehicles through the junction is in the region of 500 vehicles/hour and the peak flow of bicycles reaches 100/hour then signals should be considered.

7.6.1 Methods of detection

There are three ways of detecting cyclists approaching a junction. The most versatile and convenient method is to place loop detectors in the surface of the road. These detect a passing bicycle (or vehicle) and register a demand. Three

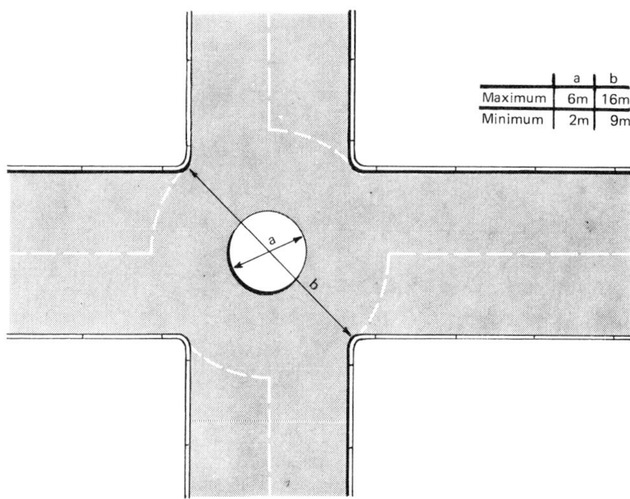

7.12 Possible measurements for a cyclists' roundabout suitable for low flow roads

7.13 A push button to trigger the bicycle phase of traffic signals (Holland)

7.14 A cycle track turned through 90° to cross a main road. Note the loop detectors in the foreground (Peterborough, UK)

7.15 A cycle track meets the road system at an existing junction (Bedford, UK)

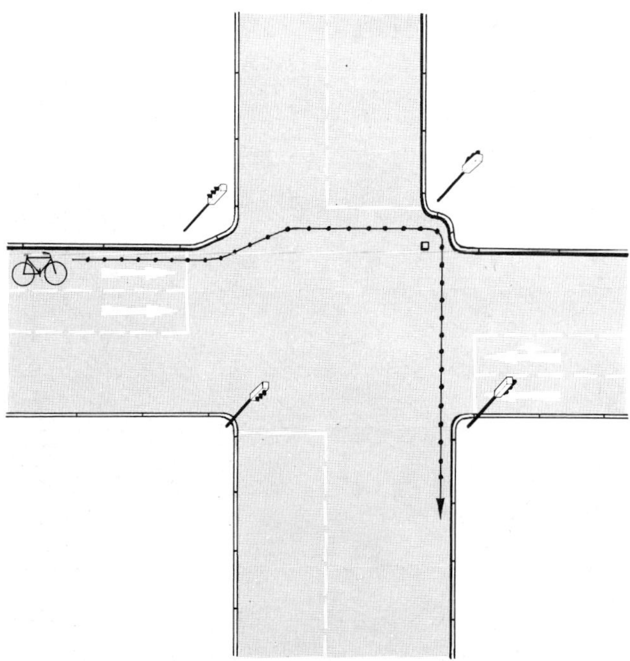

7.16 A two-stage crossing for cyclists at a signal controlled junction

loops are normally used, and should be placed 1m, 10m, and 20m back from the stop line. If it is possible for cyclists travelling in the opposite direction to pass over a loop, then uni-directional loops (three sets of double loops) should be used.

The second type of detection is a mounted push button (fig 7.13). These are cheaper and easier to install, but less convenient for cyclists who have to stop to register a demand. The third type is radar detection, which is less expensive and easier both to install and to maintain.

7.6.2 Different layouts

The simplest use of automatic traffic signals is where a cycle track crosses a main road. Where the track approaches the road at an angle between 45° and 90°, it can be continued straight across the road. Where the angle of approach is smaller, the track should be turned to approach the road at 90° (fig 7.14).

In urban areas the two ends of a cycle route may not be opposite each other. If the stagger is less than 25m, the junction can be controlled with one set of lights. If they are further than 100m apart, two sets of lights and suitable treatment of the main road will be required. At intermediate distances the design of the junction will depend on the layout of the particular location.

Traffic signals are also an appropriate measure where a cycle track is designed to enter or leave the main road system at an existing junction (fig 7.15). They have also been used where the layout allowed cyclists to make a turn across the traffic in two stages (fig 7.16). Although this is a more time-consuming manoeuvre, it does avoid cyclists having to wait in a vulnerable position in the centre of the road. This measure is also an appropriate way of exempting cyclists from bans on turns across the traffic. Such bans often require cyclists to take unnecessary detours through a number of other junctions. It has been used in France and is reported to be popular with cyclists and motorists.

7.6.3 Pedestrian facilities

Pedestrians add one more dimension to the problems at junctions, and where the flows are significant their legitimate needs will put further constraints on the junction designer. There are two immediate considerations. Firstly, pedestrians are encouraged to cross the road at 90°, so cycle-pedestrian tracks which meet the road at other angles should be turned to make a perpendicular approach. Secondly, where an unsegregated cycle-pedestrian track crosses a road, it is advisable to segregate cyclists and pedestrians to minimise the risk of conflict on the junction. To do this, counts or estimates of the number of cyclists making turning movements will have to be made to determine whether the cycle track should be on the left or the right of the pedestrian track. This segregation should start 30m back from the junction and the width of the path should preferably provide 2.25m for cyclists and 1.5m for pedestrians. Loop detectors should be used to register cyclists and a push button should be provided for pedestrians.

Where flows of pedestrians are high, it may be necessary to ban cyclists from turning across the pedestrian section of the crossing. The UK Department of Transport requires that such turns are banned whatever the pedestrian flow (fig 7.17); other European countries have less strict stipulations.

7.17 A cycle-pedestrian signal crossing (Middlesbrough, UK)

7.19 In the UK, the Department of Transport will at present only authorize a bicycle silhouette on the green aspect of signals

7.18 Sweden has a flexible attitude towards mixing cyclists and pedestrians at junctions

7.20 A cycle track crossing of a major road. Note the repeater signal at cyclists' eye height (Grenoble, France)

7.6.4 Signal timings

Although standard highway formulae are available for the calculation of optimum signal timings for different vehicles and cycle flows, in the majority of cases the bicycle flow will not be sufficiently large to require a green period greater than the minimum time taken to cross the road.

In the UK the Department of Transport recommends a minimum green time of 7 seconds. This will enable a cyclist to cross a 16m wide carriageway. Where loop detectors are provided, extensions can be called. The extension period will depend on the time it takes a cyclist to travel from the loop detector to the edge of the road being crossed. It will usually be in the 2 second to 4 second range. The number of extensions will depend on the bicycle flow rate, higher flows requiring more extensions.

7.6.5 Bicycle aspects

In a number of European countries, all the aspects of cycle signals have a bicycle silhouette displayed on a black background. In the UK, the Department of Transport will at present only authorise such silhouettes on the green aspect of the signals (fig 7.19).

7.7 BRIDGES

Bridges are a convenient way of getting cyclists across rivers, canals, railways and busy roads. More often than not an existing bridge will be converted for use by bicycles, since the construction of new bridges is expensive and unlikely to be justified unless it is expected to carry a large number of cyclists. Conversions will include the use of pedestrian bridges, the use of footways beside the road and the narrowing of the carriageway to make space for the provision of a bicycle facility.

The two critical factors which determine whether a bridge is suitable for conversion are the width and the approach gradient. Broadly speaking, the widths set out in section 6.2.3 for cycle-pedestrian tracks provide an appropriate standard. Whenever possible, the width of a cycle track on a bridge should be 0.5m wider than the width of the approach routes. Therefore, the minimum width for a bridge which is expected to carry moderate flows of pedestrians and cyclists is 3.0m.

On existing highways consideration may be given to using part of the footway for cyclists. Such a measure could usefully link cycle routes at either end of the bridge, and would

7.21 A segregated cycle-pedestrian underpass (Peterborough, UK)

be particularly appropriate where lane widths on the bridge were narrow and traffic speeds or volumes high. These one way cycle tracks should be a minimum of 1m wide and, if space permits, should be set back 30–50cm from the edge of the carriageway. The approach gradients on such a track should be no more than 5% over 30m or 15% over 20m.

Pedestrians and cyclists should always be segregated on bridges. Either colour segregation or a combination of colour and special segregation can be used to make the route absolutely clear. Guard railings on the side of a bridge should be 1.5m high to ensure that a cyclist involved in an accident could not be tossed over the edge.

New bridges will generally only be constructed to cross canals, rivers or railways and roads which are set in cuttings. The height which cyclists would have to pedal up to cross a railway or road not in a cutting makes a bridge an unattractive solution to the problem.

A low cost bridge 3m wide over an 8m road would require a budget in the region of £30,000–£50,000.

7.8 UNDERPASSES

The major advantage of using underpasses to cross roads is that cyclists are completely segregated from other vehicles.

Since the construction of underpasses under existing roads is difficult and expensive, the key question will again be whether existing underpasses can be converted for shared cycle-pedestrian use. In this case there are four critical considerations: width, gradient, height and sight-lines. The UK Department of Transport has produced a set of guidelines for the construction of new cycle-pedestrian underpasses (*Combined Pedestrian and Cycle Subways*, 1979). This provides a useful reference for authorities considering conversions.

Dimensions of cycle-pedestrian underpasses

Width	= 5.0m
Height	= 2.4m (for subways less than 23m long) or 2.7m (for subways more than 25m long)
Approach gradient	= 3% (desirable maximum) or 5% (absolute maximum)
Stopping sight distance	= 16m (where gradients are 2% or less) or 26m (where gradients are greater than 2%)
Height for the line of sight	= 1.45m

Action checklist for junction improvements

1. Draw up a set of criteria which junctions should meet to be safe and convenient for cyclists, and discuss them with local cycling organisations.

2. Instigate procedures to ensure that junction improvements introduced for reasons other than assisting cyclists meet these criteria.

3. Using knowledge of corridors heavily used by cyclists, visit junctions on each route and check them against the agreed criteria.

4. Separate the list of work required into two: a list of minor works required to bring some junctions up to standard and a list of junctions which require traffic control measures, major changes in layout or a complete change in the type of control measure employed.

5. Use the guidelines given in this chapter to determine which of the available control techniques is appropriate for junctions requiring major work, and cost the whole programme.

6. Use safety considerations to determine an order of priorities. Produce a rolling programme of improvements and discuss them with cycling organisations.

7. Issue work orders for the minor improvements.

8. Design the layout, control mechanisms and sign arrangements for junctions requiring major improvements. Carry out a land survey and check the location of services. Prepare any publicity material required to inform people of the changes. Formulate a work programme and assess and order materials. Mark out the sites, carry out physical construction and erect traffic signs. Open the new arrangements and ensure that the reasons for making the change are well covered in the press.

9. Monitor use of the junction immediately after introduction of the changes to see how it is being used, and whether any problems are encountered. Monitor again formally 6 months later, and, if possible, informally at different times of the day and on different days of the week.

10. Once a year draw up a list of all the work done on junctions and use this to get publicity for the programme of work being undertaken to help cyclists.

Good lighting and drainage and regular maintenance are essential if an underpass or subway is to be well used. Poor lighting could be dangerous and standing water is annoying to both cyclists and pedestrians. Regular maintenance is particularly important in underpasses because debris and detritus tend to gather at the bottom. Regular site visits will be the best way of determining suitable maintenance schedules. Experience in the UK suggests that these inspections should take place approximately once a month.

Where subways are being constructed under a new road, the same standards should be used. The advantage of working on a new site is that the road can be raised (by say 2m) and the cycle route dropped (by 1m) thus minimising the gradients of the approaches.

8 Signs and carriageway markings

The success of any route for cyclists depends both on the design of the route itself and on the correct use of signs. The purpose of signing bicycle facilities is to tell cyclists, motorists and pedestrians what has been provided, so that each can react accordingly. The choice of which signs to use, their location and their size depends on the information which has to be presented and the group of users it is aimed at. The signs and carriageway markings used on facilities for cyclists fall into four groups:

- route definition signs
- signs giving orders
- warning signs
- direction signs.

A wide variety of signs is used in different countries. It is therefore essential that the general guidance given in this chapter is used in conjunction with government, state and local regulations and advice.

In some countries the signs available to mark bicycle facilities are in a considerable state of disarray, probably as a result of piecemeal development. However, a clear and uniform approach is a prerequisite for understanding and obedience. One country, Australia, has drawn up a set of proposals for such a system of signs, and although they have yet to be incorporated in the road traffic regulations, some examples have been included in this chapter.

In the UK, the only bicycle signs which have been prescribed for unrestricted use are those shown in figs 8.1(a), 8.1(b), 8.3 and 8.16, and a sign to identify the destination of a cycle route. All the rest are at present treated as experimental and are not catalogued in Traffic Signs Regulations 1981 or in the Highway Code. They are therefore generally unfamiliar to the public.

As for the USA, the signs shown in figs 8.1(c), 8.13 and 8.24 are the main signs relevant to bicycles included in the Manual on Uniform Traffic Control Devices. A variety of other signs are used by individual states.

8.1 ROUTE DEFINITION SIGNS

Route definition signs are erected on a cycle route to tell cyclists, pedestrians and motor vehicle drivers what type of route they are approaching. In addition to showing who can use a facility, some signs show how and when it can be used.

Route definition signs differ according to the type of cycle route they define. The following sections therefore correlate with the sections on different types of route described in section 6.2.

In the majority of countries one sign is used to mark the different types of cycle routes (fig 8.1). In the UK there are two, one series being circular and the other rectangular. The circular signs are 'mandatory' and are erected on cycle routes which have been created by Traffic Regulation Orders (TROs). These signs mean that cyclists have sole legal right to use that route. The rectangular signs are 'advisory' and are used mainly on cycle routes which have been implemented without the use of TROs. The mandatory signs should be used wherever possible because the TROs create a set of offences for misuse of the facility (for example by motor vehicles) which assist enforcement of the proper use of the route.

(a) The UK 'route available for pedal cycles only' sign (white on blue background)

(b) The UK advisory cycle route sign (white on blue background)

(c) The American standard route sign for bicycles (white on interstate green background)

(d) The type of bike route used in many countries (white on a blue background)

8.1 Signs used to identify cycle routes

8.2 Signs and carriageway markings for a road closure (London, UK)

8.3 (left) No through road except for cycles
8.4 (right) In Australia, there is a special sign for cycle tracks though it is not yet legally prescribed (white on blue background with black lettering)

8.5 Signs used to mark the end of a cycle track. The sign with a slash through could be confused with the no-cycling sign in other countries
(**a**) France (white on blue background with red slash)
(**b**) Australia (white on blue background with black lettering)

8.1.1 Advisory cycle routes

Since advisory cycle routes are used by other vehicles, the purpose of signs used to mark them is both to identify the route for cyclists and alert motor vehicle drivers to the presence of cyclists. Advisory cycle routes can therefore be marked with the basic cycle route sign (fig 8.1), carriageway symbols (see section 8.7 'Carriageway markings') or a combination of the two. They should be placed at both ends of the route and at every point where a significant number of pedestrians and cyclists join the route. It is not however necessary to erect a large number of such signs. Strategically positioned signs at all junctions will often be all that is required.

Advisory routes will often pass through road closures. Bicycle signs should be placed on the road closure itself (fig 8.2), and an exemption plate should be added to the sign informing motor vehicle drivers that it is a 'no through road' (fig 8.3). In the UK the wording 'except cycles' should be used where bicycles and tricycles can pass through the road closure, and 'except bicycles' where only the former will fit through.

8.1.2 Cycle tracks

The main purpose of marking a cycle track is to identify its presence to cyclists. The width of the entrance to the track will normally indicate to motorists that a track is not suitable for them, but signs can be used to reinforce the message. Signs are also available in some countries to identify the end of a cycle track. In most countries the basic cycle route sign is used to identify cycle tracks (fig 8.1). In the USA and Australia there are special signs for cycle tracks (fig 8.4), though neither of these are yet legally prescribed. These signs should be erected at the beginning of any track to show what the track is and where it begins. On the reverse side of this sign there should be one saying that the track is ending (fig 8.5). If an end of cycle route sign is not available, then a carriageway marking can be used to show that the track is

8.9 A 'no motor vehicles' sign. Note also the direction sign to Toulon

8.6 Unobtrusive location of a sign

8.7 UK signs for segregated cycle-pedestrian tracks (white on blue background) (a) **(left)** A 'mandatory' track (b) **(right)** An 'advisory' track

8.8 UK signs for unsegregated cycle-pedestrian tracks (white on blue background) (a) **(left)** A 'mandatory' track (b) **(right)** An 'advisory' track

ending. In the UK, the Department of Transport recommends that repeater signs are erected at all locations along a cycle track where permitted users can join it. In the absence of any joining places these repeater signs should be placed at 200m intervals.

Signs for cylists and pedestrians can be smaller than those for motor vehicle drivers because cyclists and pedestrians travel at much slower speeds. Signs at the beginning of a track should however be no less than 450mm in diameter and repeater signs should be no less than 200mm in diameter. Where cycle tracks pass through parks or recreation areas it is undesirable to clutter the environment with repeater signs. A tidier solution is to alternate between signs and carriageway markings at 200m intervals.

The height of a sign depends on its location and the proximity of pedestrians. Where signs cannot be erected at least 0.5m from the track, they should have a minimum vertical clearance of 2.0m. Where there is space, signs can be 1.0m to 1.5m high and they can be set into concrete bollards or wooden posts (fig 8.6).

8.1.3 Cycle-pedestrian tracks

Some countries have prescribed signs for cycle-pedestrian tracks; some just mark the cycle part of the track with the general cycle route sign and some put cycle and pedestrian signs on top of one another. The countries which have prescribed such signs have based it on the general cycle route sign. Two types of sign have been produced, one to mark segregated cycle-pedestrian tracks (fig 8.7) and one to mark unsegregated tracks (fig 8.8). The sign for segregated tracks can be reversed, thus identifying which side of the track is for pedestrians and which for cyclists.

Where special cycle-pedestrian track signs have not been prescribed, the 'no motor vehicle' sign can be used (fig 8.9).

8.10 Signing a pedestrianized street. The addition of a cycle route sign would make it clearer that the route is available for cyclists

8.11 (below) Signs used to mark cycle lanes in the UK (all white on blue background except (d) which is black on white background)

(a) Cycle lane ahead

(b) Cycle lane

(c) Pedestrian's warning sign

(d) Side road sign

(e) Contra-flow cycle lane

8.12 A sign used to mark bike lanes in the USA

8.1.4 Pedestrianized streets

Where a street has been closed to through traffic but not to vehicles requiring access, the 'no motor vehicle except for access' sign is appropriate (fig 8.10). The advisory cycle route sign (fig 8.1) can be added to this to inform cyclists positively that it is a cycle route.

Where segregated cycle tracks are provided in pedestrianized streets, the mandatory cycle route sign (fig 8.1) should be mounted at both ends of the track and at any junctions within the pedestrianized streets. These signs need only be 200mm in diameter and can be mounted on street furniture provided checks have been made to ensure that parked cars or growing vegetation do not obscure them from view.

8.1.5 Cycle lanes

The purpose of marking a cycle lane is to define the route itself to make it clear to motorists and cyclists where each should be in the road. A combination of signs and carriageway markings will be required to achieve this objective.

In the UK five signs are used to mark with-flow and contra-flow cycle lanes and to warn motor vehicle drivers and pedestrians of the lane (fig 8.11). In the USA, the bike route sign (fig 8.1) and the bike lane sign have both been used to mark cycle lanes (fig 8.12). In addition a number of signs have been prescribed to control the use of cycle lanes (fig 8.13). These signs should be erected at the extremities of cycle lanes and at every point where they are intersected by

8.13 Despite the sign and road marking, some Americans insist on riding the wrong way in bike lanes (black bike on white background, red circle and slash)

8.14 (above, left and right) Signs for a UK bus and cycle lane (white on blue background)

8.15 Signs for a UK bus and cycle street
(a) Right turn is for buses, bicycles and taxis
(b) Bus and cycle street (white on blue background)

8.16 No cycling signs
(a) The UK sign (black on white background, red circle)
(b) The American sign (black on white background, red circle and slash)

other highways. In addition a sign warning motor vehicle drivers and cyclists that they are approaching a cycle lane should be erected 20m before the start of the lane. On contra-flow cycle lanes repeater signs should be erected at approximately 100–200m intervals depending on the visibility of the route.

Since the majority of signs have to give information to motor vehicle drivers as well as cyclists, they should be of similar dimensions and erected at the same height as normal traffic signs.

8.1.6 Bus and cycle routes

In the UK the signs for bus and cycle lanes are similar to the cycle lane signs, though many have plates attached making the signs applicable only during the morning or evening peak traffic period (fig 8.14).

Bus and cycle-only streets can either be marked positively with a sign saying bus and cycle-only street (fig 8.15) or negatively, with a sign saying no motor vehicles and an exemption plate for buses. There is no clear evidence to indicate which is the most effective sign. Where there are strong physical deterrents, only carriageway markings will be required.

8.2 SIGNS GIVING ORDERS

The sign giving orders that is most used in many countries is the 'no cycling' sign (fig 8.16). This sign is not popular with cyclists because it has often been erected as a matter of course with little forethought being given to the relative dangers of cycling on the alternative route. Examples abound of banned routes which are considerably less dangerous than busy main routes.

8.17 The sign arrangement used to force cyclists to use a cycle track. This is likely to generate opposition from cyclists unless it is very carefully justified (Peterborough, UK)

8.18 In some countries, signs giving instructions have been supplemented with a bicycle plate to make it clear that the sign applies to cyclists

Where it is legitimately required (for example on single-lane flyovers), this sign should be placed at the extremities of paths or highways which cyclists are banned from using. In the UK, this sign can also be used to ban cyclists from highways where alternative cycle tracks have been provided (fig 8.17). However, this may generate political opposition because cyclists will see it as the thin end of a wedge which could lead to bans on the use of many other roads. Moreover,

8.19 (left) This sign should be a cycle-pedestrian sign, but the plate does indicate one way of persuading cyclists to give way to pedestrians
8.20 (right) Exemption plates can be added to some signs giving orders to enable cyclists to avoid circuitous detours

8.21 A sign which should only be used where there is no alternative

it is argued that if the cycle route is safe and convenient, cyclists will use it, and if it is not used there is a problem with the design of the route itself.

In the USA, it is currently mandatory for cyclists to use a cycle track if one is provided. This has generated considerable political opposition and although attempts to change the regulation have not succeded it is likely that they will at the next meeting of the National Committee on the Uniform Vehicle Code, in 1983.

Other signs giving orders do not cause such problems. Since clarity is of the utmost importance, they are generally based on the commonly known highway signs. These signs are most frequently used to tell cyclists to give way or stop at road junctions (fig 8.18) and can also be used to tell cyclists to give way to pedestrians (fig 8.19).

Clearly, all the usual signs which give orders to vehicles also apply to cyclists. However, there are often situations where they need not apply to cyclists. Exemption plates (fig 8.20) are therefore used to inform cyclists that the sign does not apply to them.

In some situations it may be necessary to tell cyclists to dismount (for example across a narrow bridge shared with pedestrians). Where signs are displayed to this effect (fig 8.21) it should be remembered that this takes away the advantages of cycling over walking and that the rest of the route will have to bring considerable benefit to cyclists if it is to be used.

8.3 WARNING SIGNS

The correct use of warning signs is as important as the accurate use of route definition and instruction signs. The most common requirement is for a sign to warn motor vehicle drivers to look out for cyclists (fig 8.22). These should be erected 50m before a cycle route crosses or joins a highway.

8.22 (above left) The UK sign to warn motor vehicle drivers to watch out for cyclists (black on white background with red surround)

8.23 (above right) In some countries, direction plates can be added to the warning sign to inform motorists of cyclists' direction of travel.

8.25 Sign directing cyclists to a cycle route (blue bicycle symbol; Le Pradet, France)

8.24 Sign used in the USA to warn motor vehicle drivers of crossing bicycles (black on yellow background)

8.26 Small signs are appropriate on bicycle and pedestrian facilities

8.4 DIRECTION SIGNS

Direction signs are used to give cyclists:

- guidance in finding a cycle route (fig 8.25)
- warning of and instructions for junctions (fig 8.26)
- information about where a route starts or continues
- information about where a route goes to and how far away the destination is.

Advanced direction signs should be used where cycle routes meet or cross other routes. On routes not used by motor vehicles small signs can be located on posts 1.0–1.5m high. Where the route is shared with motor vehicles, standard size signs will be required. Finger posts indicating the start or continuation of a cycle route should, wherever possible, include the destination of the route and the distance to the destination.

In the USA, signs showing the direction and destination of a route are attached below the standard cycle route sign.

8.5 SIGNS FOR OTHER FACILITIES

Wherever bicycle parking facilities are provided they should be marked with a sign which can be identified from a distance of at least 50m. Likewise, where facilities for the carriage of bicycles on other modes of transport are provided (for example at particular bus stops along a bus route), then signs will also be required.

8.6 LIGHTING AND MAINTENANCE OF SIGNS

National or local regulations will usually stipulate where and when signs should be lit. In the UK most signs should be lit when placed within 50m of a street lamp. This includes the mandatory cycle route signs. The main consideration with

8.27 Clear identification of bicycle parking facilities (Nice, France)

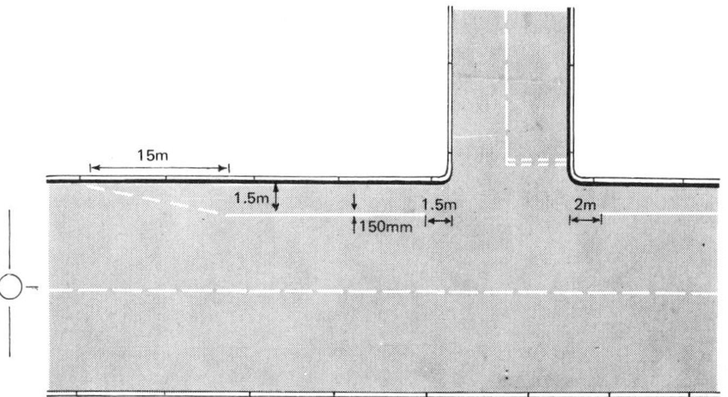

8.28 Dimensions for cycle lane carriageway markings

signs which are not required to be lit is whether the cost of providing lighting can be justified. In making this judgement, it should be remembered that cyclists' own lights are of no assistance because they are not powerful enough and do not point towards signs.

Most authorities will have procedures for the inspection and maintenance of signs, so signs on cycle routes can be incorporated into the existing schedules. In some instances, people responsible for checking signs may not accord cycle signs the priority they deserve. Periodic informal checks should therefore be used to back up the existing procedure.

8.7 CARRIAGEWAY MARKINGS

Carriageway markings will be required on practically every cycle route. They can be used singly or in combination for the following purposes:

8.29 (above and opposite) Carriageway markings used in the USA to identify cycle lanes

8.30 Markings for the end of a cycle track

8.31 Advisory junction markings assist cyclists across a T-junction (Bremen, W. Germany). This is only suitable for low flow roads. Note the cycle track continuing *behind* the bus layby

To segregate cyclists from vehicles and pedestrians
Cycle lanes and segregated cycle-pedestrian paths are defined by a line painted on the ground. In the UK a continuous 150mm wide white line is used to indicate a mandatory lane (which other vehicles are not allowed to use) and a 100mm dashed line is used to indicate an advisory lane (which vehicles can encroach on, for example to pass drivers waiting to turn across the traffic flow).

8.32 Carriageway markings create a shared cycle-pedestrian crossing of a low flow road. Note that the dropped kerbs are nowhere near flush

A dashed line should be used at the start of a mandatory lane. Both types should stop short of the mouth of a junction (fig 8.28).

In the USA the line is yellow and its width varies from 50–250mm in different states. There is controversy over the type of lane delineation which should be used where a lane is provided for cycling and for parked cars. Since vehicles in the USA are allowed to cross a solid line, a lane containing few parked cars has the appearance of another traffic lane. Some jurisdictions have therefore used coloured lines (Seattle uses a strong yellow green) to identify cycle lanes and others have used a double white line.

The line dividing pedestrians and cyclists on a segregated path should be continuous, 50mm wide and extend over the whole length of the track.

To identify cycle routes
Bicycle symbols should be located at the beginning of cycle tracks and lanes and repeated at all intersections. If the track or lane is intersected at intervals of less than 200m, then further symbols should not be required. Where there are no intersections, bicycle symbols should be repeated at this interval, or alternated with with route definition signs at the same interval. In the USA, the use of the words 'ONLY BIKE' is preferred because it is more visible from low angle at which drivers approach it (fig 8.29).

In the UK, the end of a cycle route is often marked with a symbol supplemented with the word 'END' (fig 8.30).

To mark a bicycle junction
In addition to their normal function of marking stopping positions at junctions, carriageway markings can be extended right across a junction. This concept is used in many European countries to create 'advisory' cycle crossings (fig 8.31). These do not give cyclists priority, but they do warn motorists of the presence of cyclists. They can also be used to supplement a controlled bicycle crossing.

Carriageway markings have also been used in some countries to create joint cycle-pedestrian crossings of minor roads (fig 8.32).

To divide a cycle track
In some circumstances, cyclists travelling in the opposite direction on a two-way cycle track should be separated, for example where the flows are high, where the track is narrow or where there are tight bends or steep gradients with poor sight-lines. In these situations, a 50mm wide broken line should be provided down the centre of the track.

To give or reinforce instructions
Carriageway markings are used to tell cyclists to give way where a cycle track crosses another cycle track. Where cycle tracks meet busy roads and 'stop' signs have been provided, these can be supplemented by stop markings on the carriageway.

Carriageway markings can also be used to tell cyclists which direction the route goes and where it goes to. However, since carriageway markings are not particularly visible from a distance, they will be inadequate on their own, and should be supplemented with signs.

8.33 Poor maintenance leads to decaying facilities and a public exhibition of the low priority accorded to cyclists. The remains of an advisory cycle crossing at Aix-en-Provence, France

8.8 MAINTENANCE OF CARRIAGEWAY MARKINGS

Many cycle facilities created only with carriageway markings have disappeared over a period of time due solely to lack of maintenance. Lack of clarity leads to misunderstandings and dangerous situations, for example where a motorist believes that a lane is so eradicated that he need not keep out of it. Maintenance checks should therefore be carried out at least once a year on facilities not in the highway and at least every six months on facilities in the highway, where wear and tear are much greater.

Action checklist

1. Obtain a copy of any government, state and local regulations pertaining to signs and carriageway markings.
2. Walk over a proposed route and decide which type of sign is required to mark each section, each junction, and all other facilities. At the same time decide what carriageway markings are required.
3. Approach each junction on the route from the motor vehicle's direction and decide which signs are required to warn them to expect cyclists.
4. Draw all the signs and carriageway markings onto a map and produce a complete list of all the signs which are required.
5. Decide what size each sign should be (small if cyclists and pedestrians are required to read it – large if motor vehicle drivers must read it).
6. Decide what height each sign needs to be above the ground.
7. Discuss the proposals with the police, cyclists and where necessary, state or national government.
8. Order all the signs and posts required.
9. Instruct the works department to erect the signs and paint the carriageway markings onto the road to the specifications given.
10. Check that the work has been properly carried out and that the lighting works.
11. Make arrangements for the signs and carriageway markings to be included in existing maintenance schedules and periodically check that maintenance work has been carried out.

9 Bicycle parking

There are two reasons why bicycle parking facilities are critically important to any plan for the development of cycling. From the cyclists' point of view the availability of secure bicycle parking is a pre-requisite to any bicycle trip. From a local authorities' viewpoint, the provision of parking facilities discourages cyclists from leaving their bicycles in positions which could cause an obstruction or be a danger to pedestrians, particularly the blind.

The extent to which lack of secure parking is a deterrent to cycling is shown from a survey carried out in the City of Baltimore, USA, which shows that 25% of cyclists had been victims of a bicycle theft, and of these 20% had given up cycling.

9.1 This thief has done well

9.1 PARKING POLICIES

There are persuasive arguments for providing parking facilities even if nothing else is done to assist cyclists. In London alone, over fifty bicycles are reported stolen every day. At an average value of £55 each this represents a loss of £1,000,000 a year to London residents. Furthermore, a survey from the District of Columbia, USA, suggests that unreported thefts may be three times as many as reported thefts. More important, however, from a public policy viewpoint is the fact that the cost of providing parking is far cheaper than the cost of investigating and prosecuting the thieves.

Action will be required by a wide variety of people and organisations to provide a comprehensive network of parking facilities. Local authority parking policy statements must therefore be framed in a way which encourages, and if necessary requires, action by others.

9.1.1 Local regulations

In many countries regulations controlling the construction of new buildings state how many car parking places should be provided, depending on the use of the building. The implementation of this concept to bicycles will vary from country to country depending on the regulations available. In the UK, the Development Policy Control Notes (drawn up by central government) could be amended. Alternatively, conditions could be attached to the granting of planning permission for developments, requiring that a specific number of bicycle parking facilities be provided. In the USA, a number of states have formulated bicycle parking ordinances for incorporation into local zoning regulations. In Palo Alto, California, for example, city developers are required (in most cases) by zoning ordinance to dedicate 10% of the total required parking space to secure bicycle storage facilities. This ordnance also defines the type of storage facilities which should be provided. In Montgomery County, Maryland, the zoning ordinance stipulates that all owners of parking lots containing more than 40 parking spaces must provide one bicycle parking stand or locker for each 20 car parking spaces. Not more than 20 bicycle parking stands or lockers are required in any one lot. It also states that 'bicycle parking facilities shall be so located as to be safe from theft. Interior storage and lockers are encouraged. They shall be properly repaired and maintained. Facilities that are used for overnight parking must be protected from the weather when they are part of an enclosed parking facility.' If enforcement is felt to be too strong a measure, then encouragement could be given in the form of reduced rates (property tax rebates in the USA).

Clearly, authorities pursuing such policies must take the lead by providing parking at their own buildings, and, where the authority is responsible for parking on the highway, for provisions there as well.

9.2 ESTIMATING DEMAND

There are so few statistics available to help an engineer to estimate the demand for bicycle parking facilities in public places that any method used will only give a rough answer. The following method is a basis from which to make estimates:

SUGGESTED BICYCLE PARKING SPACE PROVISION BY LAND USE

Land uses	Amount of bicycle parking space required
Residential uses	
One-family or two-family dwelling or flat	None
Apartment house, tenement house, or multiple dwelling	One for each two dwelling units
Bed and breakfast/rooming house	One for each five guest bedrooms
Motel and hotel	One for each twenty employees
Dormitory, sorority, or fraternity house not a part of a campus development	One for each two beds
Schools	
Nursery and primary school	One for every twenty students plus one for each twenty teachers and other employees
Secondary school	One for every twenty students plus one for each twenty teachers and other employees
College or other institution of higher learning; business, trade, or other school and accessory uses located on campus	For each building, one for every twenty seats plus one for every twenty teachers or other employees
Institution uses	
Hospitals	One for each twenty employees
Places of public assembly (except hotels)	
Churches	One for every ten seats
Arena, armory, assembly hall, auditorium, concert hall, convention hall, dance hall, public hall, stadium, community centres, skating rinks, theatres	One for each ten seats of first 10,000 seats; plus one for each twenty seats above the first 10,000

Source: *District of Columbia Bikeway Planning Study*, 1975.

Produce map of existing facilities
If no map already exists, then someone will have to go out and walk the streets to discover what facilities have been provided. Taking a map of the area to a local cyclists' meeting and asking them to identify all the facilities they know would provide a useful starting point, and involves them in the planning process.

Discover extent of current problems
First look at the results of origin/destination surveys and discover where bicycle journeys begin and end. Then go out and mark on a map every place where bicycles are regularly parked. Visits to places where bicycles have been seen should be undertaken at different times of the day and on different days of the week. In this way a map can be produced identifying current requirements for short-term and long-term parking.

Determine current growth in bicycle usage
The collection of bicycle usage data and the application of growth factors are described in Chapter 4. A growth rate of 5–10% in the demand for bicycle parking might be appropriate in an area which is not providing other facilities.

Estimate trip generation
Where the development of cycling is planned, make an estimate of the number of trips which will be generated by the plans. From this and the figure for current growth in bicycle usage make an estimate of future requirements. This could add 15% to current requirements in an area where new routes are being provided and bicycle use is growing.

Total requirements
By adding anticipated future needs to current requirements a total for each site can be produced and put on a map identifying which sites require short-term and which long-term facilities. Another basis for calculating demand is to set standards according to different types of land use. This could also be used as a guide for other organisations wanting to know how many spaces to provide. The box shows suggestions from the District of Columbia, USA.

9.3 LOCATION OF FACILITIES

Unlike the parking of all other vehicles, bicycle parking cannot easily be controlled. If parking facilities are not conveniently located then cyclists can ignore them and use nearby railings, lamp posts or parking meters. Cyclists, in common with other road users, want to minimize the distance they have to walk from the parking area to their destination. The location of facilities is therefore determined by the distance a cyclist is willing to walk. This distance will depend on the time the cyclist is intending to stay at the destination and the suitability of nearer alternatives. A rough estimate might be to assume a maximum distance of 100–150m for all-day parking and 25m or less for short-term parking. The planner should therefore as a general rule think in terms of providing plenty of small clusters of facilities rather than one large parking area.

Bicycles are less likely to be stolen if they are at sites passed by many people who all act as a deterrent to the thief with a hacksaw or bolt-cutters. Busy streets are therefore more suitable than quiet back streets. Where long-term parking facilities are being provided they can often be sited near a factory gate-house or railway ticket office so that someone can be made responsible for keeping an eye on the bicycles.

9.2 It is essential that the bicycle frame and both wheels can be locked to a permanent fixture. The Universal parking stand (Sheffield, UK)

9.4 DESIGN CRITERIA

There are two sets of criteria, those of the cyclists' whose needs must be met if the facilities are to be used, and those of the local authority who must consider, among other factors, costs and the needs of other people.

9.4.1 Cyclists' requirements

Security

This is undoubtedly cyclists' major requirement. Ideally, the cyclist should be able to secure the bicycle and all its accessories (lamps, pump, etc). This requirement can only be met by bicycle lockers. Where this is not feasible, it is essential that the bicycle frame and both wheels can be locked to a permanent fixture. In general, there are two types of thief who need to be foiled. The petty thief, who needs £50–£100 at short notice and has no experience or tools, can be foiled by a good lock and cable. The expert, with bolt-cutters and other equipment, will only be deterred by mechanisms which are more difficult to break than the bicycle frame itself. In the UK, the most common bicycle locking device is a cable (or chain) connected to a padlock. These are available in varying lengths and strengths – a long steel cable being the best compromise between a light insecure cable and a heavy case-hardened chain. Cables which can lock both wheels and the frame of the bike to a stand need to be at least 1.8m long. In the USA, many designs of bicycle parking facilities only require a padlock because the stand itself holds the bicycle frame and wheels secure.

Weather protection

This is important at all sites where bicycles are parked for more than one hour – for example at railway stations, factories and offices. It is not essential at short-term parking stands, for example at shopping centres, but it is nevertheless an advantage – if only to provide cyclists with a little shelter while they prepare to set off.

The only protection that is required is a roof to keep the rain off; 'all-in' enclosures are a positive disadvantage because they provide good cover for the potential thief. Some bicycle parking facilities on the market have metal roofs as an integral part of their design. However, these are often unstable and rather unsightly. A more economical and attractive solution would be to use preformed plastic and wood. Alternatively where bicycle parking facilities are being provided as part of a new construction, the weather protection can be designed as an integral part of the building.

Suitability

Parking stands must accept all types of bicycles and all wheel sizes. Some facilities on the market do not satisfy this condition and checks should therefore be made before a particular design of facility is bought. Furthermore some types of facility damage bicycles, in particular wheels can be buckled when bicycles are gripped by the wheel and the bike is knocked sideways by someone entering the next bay.

Convenience

Facilities which require the bicycle to be lifted off the ground will not be well-used by women and old people. For example, a hook in the ceiling provides the most dense method of storing bikes, but cyclists would have to lift their bikes onto the hooks. Even wheel-rim holders inclined at a steep angle will present problems for weaker people. At a large site, different types of facilities could be provided to take advantage of the minimal space required by vertical stalls without excluding the weaker members of the community.

9.4.2 Local authorities' requirements

Having fulfilled cyclists' requirements, local authorities must consider the problems created by parking facilities for other members of the community.

Obstruction

There are two considerations here – legal and practical. In the UK, the 1978 Transport Act gives local authorities specific powers to provide bicycle parking racks in the highway. Anyone may provide parking facilities off the highway without danger of creating an obstruction. Employers, public transport operators, local authorities and other organisations can therefore construct racks on their own property – though statutory authorities, and, indeed, companies or associations, must possess the general power to do so.

9.3 Space requirements can be reduced by raising alternate handlebars. Note that these facilities have been provided in the carriageway (Antibes, France)

9.4 A Class II facility securing the frame and both wheels

9.5 A Class III facility securing only one wheel

There are difficulties for cyclists when parking facilities are not provided. In this situation, cyclists will tend to lock their bicycles to the nearest lamp post or railing. In doing this a cyclist would strictly be creating an obstruction of the highway, but a court would not look upon a prosecution kindly, applying the 'de minimis' rule – 'the law is not concerned with trifles'. But if, for example, a blind person tripped and was injured by the bicycle, the cyclist might well run into financial trouble and the insurance might not cover damages arising from what would be an unlawful obstruction.

The second consideration relating to obstruction is practical. In some circumstances, a parking facility itself could obstruct the pavement and provide a hazard for blind people.

Cost and availability

The cost of buying (or constructing) and installing facilities will be an important consideration where a large number are being provided. In some countries, it is likely that no information will be readily available on manufacturers of facilities, their technical specifications, delivery times and costs. The engineer will therefore be faced with gathering this information himself. Government transport departments, local authorities known for bicycle provisions, bicycle manufacturers, touring clubs, and pressure groups might all provide starting points.

Maintenance

Broadly speaking, parking facilities should require minimal maintenance and be vandal-proof, since facilities which gain a reputation for being broken will be ignored by regular cyclists. Facilities which have many moving parts should be avoided.

Whatever type of facility is finally chosen, an administrative mechanism should be devised to ensure that they are checked at least four times per year so that the local authority always knows their condition. This could be done, for example, by asking a local cycling club to act as vigilantes and submit regular reports to the engineers' office.

Ease of construction

Designs which are simple to install are less likely to be incorrectly or badly fitted and will be cheaper to provide.

Space requirements

There are two considerations here: firstly the facilities themselves require different sizes and shapes of spaces, secondly some designs require a larger manoeuvring space.

The British Standard (BS 1716) stipulates that facilities should be no less than 61cm apart unless the handlebars of alternate bicycles are raised by more than 20cm, *or* the bicycles are parked in a skew pattern. In either of these cases the absolute minimum is 30cm. This is very small indeed; wherever possible facilities should be 70cm apart.

The minimum gangway for convenient withdrawal of bicycles is 2.0m for square pattern stands and 1.4m for a skew pattern. Wider gangways are advisable where stands are installed in schools and public places and particularly where a gangway is common to two rows of stands.

9.5 THE CHOICE OF APPROPRIATE FACILITIES

9.5.1 Classes of facilities

Research has led to the development of three classes of facilities:

Class I Lockers or controlled access areas where bicycles may be stored, protected from theft, weather and vandalism.
Class II Devices which lock the bicycle frame and wheels.
Class III Bicycle stand or other fixed objects to which a bicycle may be secured.

The provision of Class I facilities is a significant step forward in protecting bicycles. Storage areas can be controlled either by leasing keys to bicycle owners or by a paid attendant.

In urban areas, spaces in existing car parks can be adapted to provide bicycle parking facilities, though experience from the USA suggests that car park owners are reluctant to do this unless regulations are made.

Class II bicycle parking devices are designed to secure the bicycle frame and wheels, but accessories are not protected. Weather protection may be provided. In the USA, coin-operated and key-operated facilities are available. In most other countries cyclists have to provide their own chain and padlock; and in the USA, padlocks are the most popular because coin and key operated systems are expensive to buy and require more maintenance.

Class III are the most predominant type of facility in most countries. Cyclists have to provide their own locking device, and since any additional weight is a burden to a cyclist, they tend to carry light-weight locks, none of which, according to an American consumer report, will last longer than two minutes. This class of facility is only really suitable for short-stay parking.

9.5.2 Charging for use

The basic argument for asking people to pay for the use of facilities is sound; it costs money to provide and maintain the facility, so cyclists should pay for their use. However, practical experience has shown that this is too simplistic. If a cyclist can obtain the same degree of security without using the facility (for example, by chaining up to a nearby railing), then they are unlikely to use it. In general, cyclists are only willing to pay for bike lockers or enclosed storage spaces (Class I facilities) if they provide additional security and weather protection.

Other rationales therefore have to be found for providing facilities. This is not difficult – many organisations already provide free car parking facilities, employers for their staff, shops for their customers, colleges for their students and hospitals for their visitors, to name but a few. However, where an organisation's business is selling parking space, there is no rationale for providing facilities free – so to be successful they should concentrate on Class I facilities.

Two methods of charging have proved successful for bicycle lockers and enclosed storage spaces: day payments and leasing. The advantage of daily payments is that the facility is available to everyone on a first-come first-served basis, but the economics only work if collection of the money is only part of someone's job, preferably someone who is already collecting money for something else. The advantage of leasing is that it is cheaper to administer and cyclists are guaranteed their spaces. In return for a fee, cyclists obtain a key to a locker or enclosed storage space. Levels of charging will be determined by local conditions. The following examples of locker charges are a rough guideline: in 1978 Bay Area Rapid Transit (BART) in San Francisco charged 25 cents a day or $5 per month for a lease; in 1980, Poland Street Garage in central London charged 50 pence per day. BART also provides Class II facilities free of charge.

TWO EXAMPLES OF CLASS I FACILITIES FROM WASHINGTON D.C.

1. Union Station

A good example of a controlled storage area is that in Union Station, the Amtrack and commuter rail terminal in Washington, D.C. A caged area for bicycle storage is provided inside the station, administered and maintained by the National Park Service. For a small fee, cyclists obtain a key to the storage area. Most of the bicycle-rail commuters use the storage for overnight parking, using their bicycles for the work-trip end of their journey.

2. Silver Spring Station

The first ten lockers installed at METRO's Silver Spring Station were offered for lease at $70 per year. All lockers were leased for a full year prior to the station's opening day (without the benefit of advertising). Based on an installed cost of $320 per double locker unit, the METRO locker rentals will cover the capital investment in three years. Since all the lockers were leased for a full year on the first day offered, almost half of the capital cost was covered immediately after installation. With demonstrated high demand, 16 more lockers have been ordered for the Silver Spring Station and the District of Columbia has 250 on order to be installed at stations throughout the city.

9.5.3 Common types of facilities

A wide variety of bicycle parking facilities are now on the market. The traditional designs widely used in Europe and the USA have recently been supplemented by a number of new and improved types manufactured in the USA. While space does not permit the inclusion of a complete list of every type used, p 92 shows examples of designs covering as wide a range of parking principles as possible. The majority of the designs shown come from the UK and the USA.

9.5.4 Layout of facilities

The basic measurements for spacing facilities were described in section 9.4, 'Design criteria'. When a design has been chosen, consideration should be given to the most economical use of space possible with that design. Fig 9.15 shows layouts for various types of design.

Storage facilities can stand out like a sore thumb if careful consideration is not given to the design of the roofing and their position relative to other buildings. They should not just be considered as another piece of street furniture and placed at any convenient point. The use of trees, bushes and low level walls can greatly enhance an area and also provide a simple screen for the parked bicycles. However, care should be taken to ensure that these do not provide the potential thief with good protection.

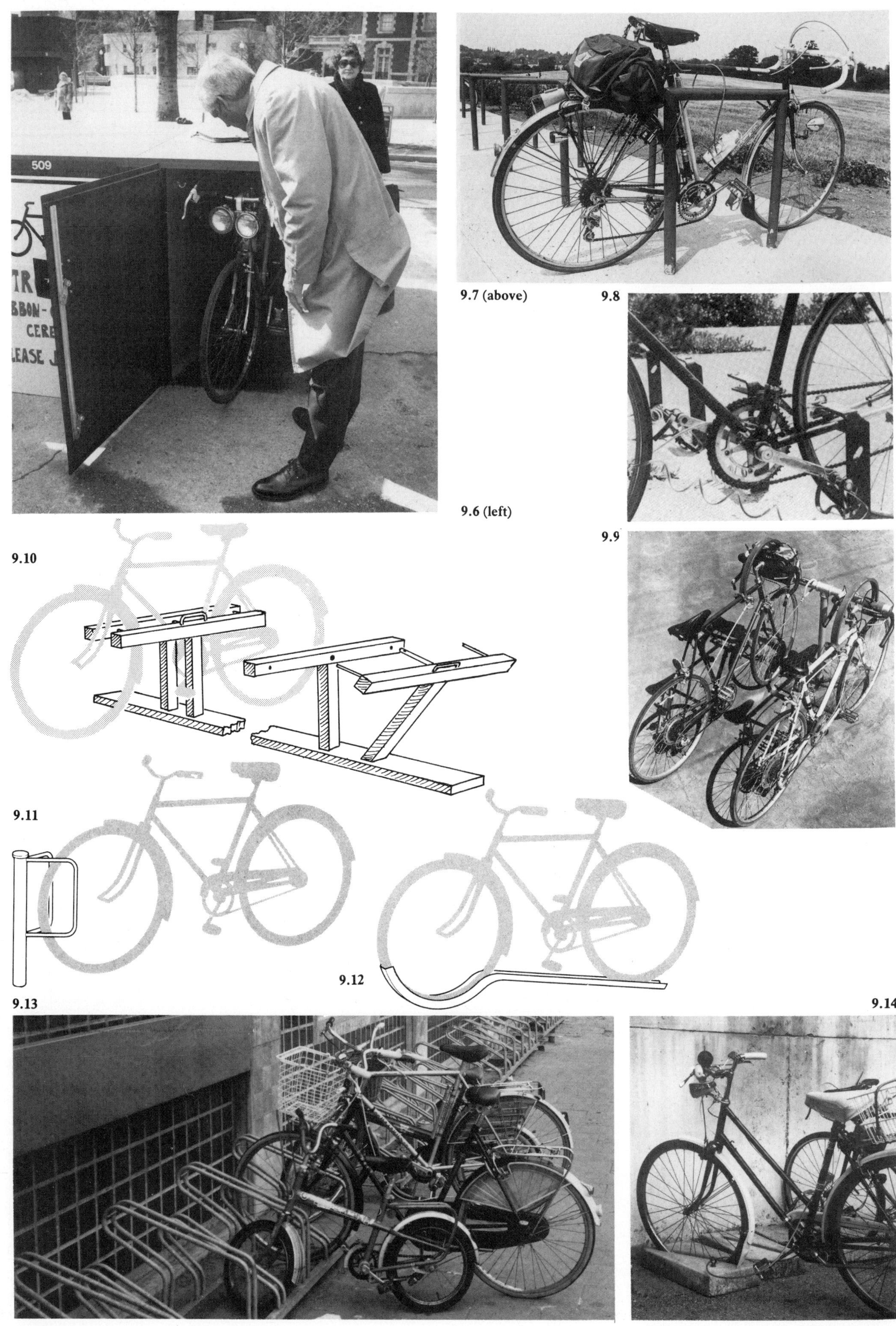

9.7 (above)

9.8

9.6 (left)

9.9

9.10

9.11

9.12

9.13

9.14

Type	Comments	Advantages	Disadvantages
Bike locker (Class I) **9.6**	An ideal solution for long-term parking	Secures bicycle and accessories Good weather protection	Very expensive compared to other facilities Requires some maintenance
The universal stand (Class II) **9.7**	Not produced by a manufacturer but easily constructed in a work-shop	Enables cyclists to lock the frame and both wheels to the stand Relatively cheap	The stand requires more space than other designs when no bicycles are parked in it Paint can be chipped off bicycle frame if the bicycle is knocked while parked
Rally rack (RR300) (Class II) **9.8**	Other models without a cable to secure the front wheel (RR200) and without any front wheel security (RR100) are available A good Class II rack made in the USA	Secures rear wheel and frame with a single lock Steel plate prevents removal of front wheel (see fig 9.4) Virtually maintenance free Good aesthetic appeal	Expensive
Rack III (Class II) **9.9**	Used at many locations throughout the USA	Secures both wheels and frame with one lock	Moving parts may require maintenance Not suitable for small wheel bicycles
Park-a-bike (Class II) **9.10**	A solid but unattractive design available in the USA	Secures both wheels and frame with a single lock Relatively easy to use	Cable vulnerable to bolt- or wire-cutters No aesthetic appeal
V Wheel Grip (Class III) **9.11**	Widely used at public buildings in the UK Only suitable for short-term parking	Compact and simple design Virtually maintenance free Accepts all sizes and shapes of wheel Highly versatile and therefore suitable for many different shapes (see section 9.5.4 'Layout of facilities')	Requires a particularly long cable to link both wheels and the frame to the rack An awkward obstruction could be created if the rack was placed on a busy pavement Can buckle bicycle wheels
Rim holder (Class III) **9.12**	Used at factories and railway stations in the UK A somewhat dated design	Both wheels and frame can be secured to the rack with a medium length cable Accepts all sizes and shapes of wheel	Space consuming Unsightly Large manœuvring space required
Standard rack, arch rack and loop rack (Class III) **9.13**	Old designs without many advantages	Relatively cheap	All require a particularly long cable to link both wheels and the frame to the rack Wheels can be buckled if bicycle is knocked sideways in any of these
Concrete blocks (unclassified) **9.14**	Very unpopular among cyclists in the UK Not an acceptable solution to the parking problem	Blocks set into the ground are practically invisible Cheap	Wheels very easily buckled if bike is knocked sideways Fallen leaves and other debris must be regularly cleaned from the groove Impossible to lock bicycle to holder unless a metal loop is set into the concrete

Action checklist

1. Identify the criteria which a bicycle parking facility must satisfy to meet the needs of cyclists and discuss these criteria with local cycling organisations.
2. Identify the criteria which local planners and engineers should consider before taking a decision to buy a particular design.
3. Estimate the current and future demand for long and short-stay parking facilities at different sites.
4. Gather information about different types of storage facilities available from manufacturers and about non-proprietary designs.
5. Discuss this information with local cycling organisations to gain a cyclist's perspective on the information gathered; but remember that members of clubs are not necessarily representative of a broad range of cyclists.
6. Evaluate each storage facility against cyclists' and engineers' criteria to produce preferred alternatives. If no suitable facility is available, consider constructing a facility to suit local requirements.
7. Produce an overall design for each site where facilities are to be provided.
8. Prepare a maintenance schedule which will ensure that facilities are regularly checked.
9. Install the racks and carry out a simple evaluation programme to check that sufficient have been provided, that cyclists find them convenient and that they are being regularly maintained.

9.6 SHOWERS AND LOCKERS

There are two further considerations which apply particularly to the provision of facilities at work places. Many people have to wear clothes for work which are unsuitable for cycling. In particular a regular cyclist will ruin many types of modern shoe and wear through even the best material for suit trousers in a matter of months. Commuter cyclists therefore require changing facilities and personal lockers in which to store cycling clothes and office suits.

Secondly, cyclists with longer journeys are likely to arrive hot and sweaty and not in a condition which is likely to be appreciated by fellow workers. Showering facilities have therefore been provided in a number of American offices and are becoming increasingly popular.

a. Universal stand

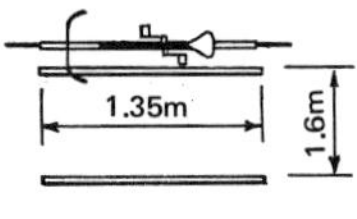

b. A short-term parking stand

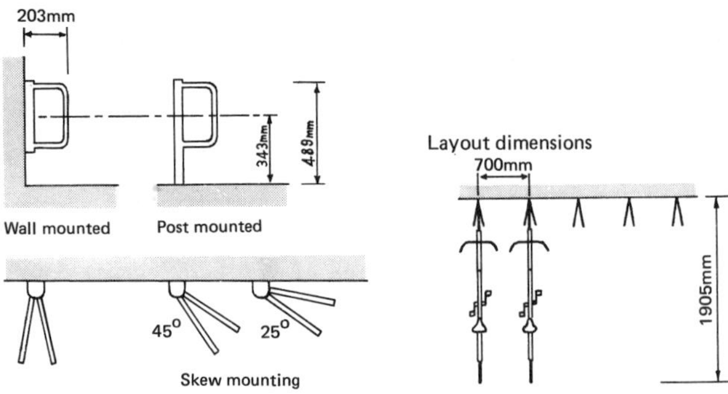

Density of bicycles can be increased by staggering heights

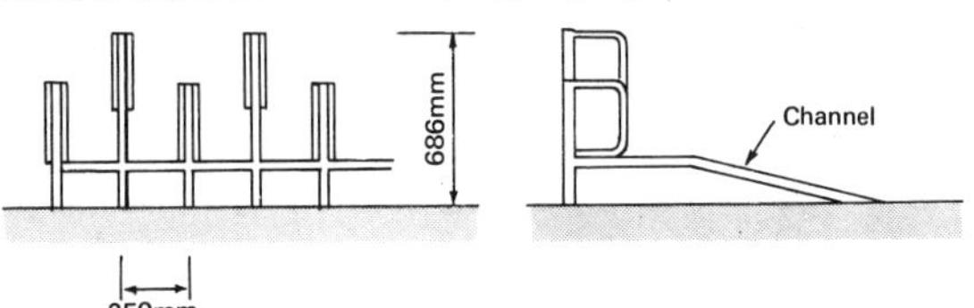

c. Wedge-shaped lockers

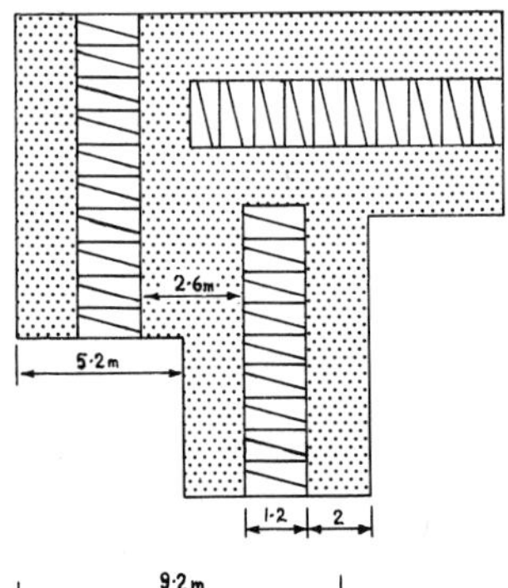

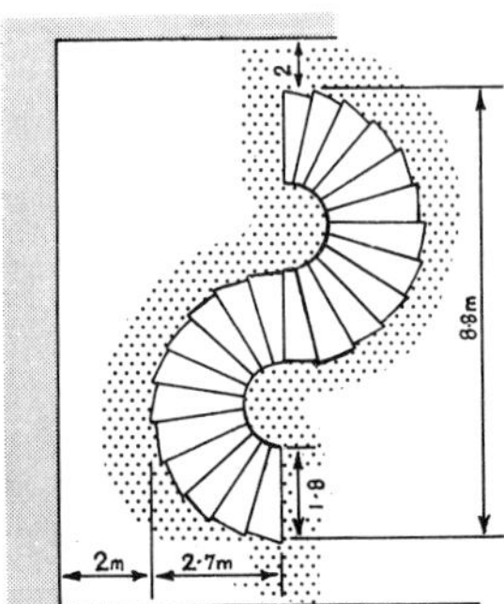

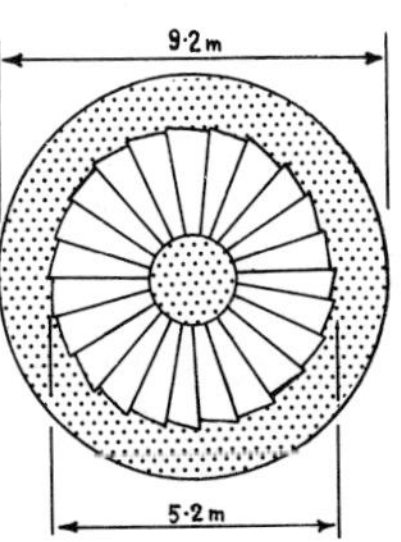

9.15 Layout of bicycle parking facilities

10 Education and encouragement

Before taking a car on the road without supervision, the average UK adult receives twenty-five hours of training and has to pass an oral and practical test. Requirements in other countries are similar, the more stringent including a written examination. This massive educational effort aims to teach people how to control their vehicle and behave according to a common set of rules.

It is therefore extraordinary that the same countries allow cyclists to use the same road system and expect them to know and behave according to the same set of rules with no formal training whatsoever. Moreover children, with a weaker perception of speed and direction, with less physical ability to control their bicycles and with less commonsense, share the roads. As a result, thousands of children are killed or injured each year in accidents caused by their own ignorance or bad behaviour.

The major difficulty in tackling this problem is that both motorists and cyclists believe that the other needs to be controlled and educated. From the cyclist's viewpoint, the roads were relatively safe before the use of private motor cars and heavy goods vehicles became widespread; therefore, since motor vehicles cause the problem, the solution lies in controlling their use. However, from the motorist's point of view, the accident problem is caused by cyclists not understanding or obeying the rules of the road. Research suggests that in the case of fatal child accidents, the children were at fault in 90% of accidents in Australia and 61% in the UK. Motorists justifiably argue that proper education of cyclists is required to reduce this appalling toll of bicycle/motor vehicle accidents.

This chapter first sets out how an education programme can be developed and improved and then describes the individual components of such a programme.

A final section discusses the importance of publicity and promotion in educating public opinion and so encouraging favourable attitudes towards bicycle planning.

10.1 THE DEVELOPMENT OF AN EDUCATION PROGRAMME

There are three essential prerequisites for a successful education programme. Firstly, it must tackle the behaviour of both cyclists and motorists. Secondly, it must support enforcement. Without the threat of enforcement, people tend to consider their own interests (eg, getting somewhere quickly) and not the risks they are taking.

The third essential ingredient of an education programme is its permanence. A number of behavioural studies have shown that unless people's habits, and particularly those of children, are regularly reinforced, they tend to return to their former ways. An education programme will therefore have to both train new cyclists and drivers, and improve the behaviour of existing cyclists and drivers.

Since there are limitations on the potential success of education programmes, trade-offs with other areas of an overall bicycle plan may have to be considered. If there is competition for funding between education programmes and engineering work, and safety is the major criterion for allocating funds, then in some circumstances the physical measures to improve cyclists' safety could be a more cost-effective solution in the long-term.

The resolution of these priorities will vary from one area to another and will depend on a number of factors including the number and type of accidents, the cost effectiveness of different measures, the availability of funding and the political acceptability of the proposed actions. Most countries already have some form of children's bicycle education. In many, the number of local authorities allocating resources to this problem has increased in recent years. It is therefore likely that a considerable body of experience and practical knowledge already exists. However, the accident statistics from almost every country indicate that current efforts are inadequate.

The first priority in any area will therefore be to determine the exact nature of the safety problem (as described in Chapter 5). These local statistics can be used to focus attention on the problem, and to argue for the allocation of sufficient funds to tackle the problem on a realistic basis. They will also assist with the determination of priorities within the overall programme.

In the majority of cases school children will undoubtedly be the group requiring the most attention. In the UK, over 40% of pedal cyclist casualties are under 15 years old. Within this group, statistics from a number of countries show that the largest proportion of accidents involve boys aged between 9 and 15.

Improvement of motor vehicle drivers' awareness of cyclists will also be a priority in most areas. Since this is a large group of people to communicate with, it may require the allocation of considerable resources.

10.1 Bicycle education at schools is a critical component of an education programme

Given that financial and staff resources will have limitations, the effective use of available resources will be of the utmost importance. However, the range of people and organisations interested in bicycle safety is wide. The development of an organisational structure which incorporates all these people is a useful way of maximizing resources: the creation of a bicycle education group, consisting of road safety officers, the police, local cycling clubs, interested teachers, parent-teacher associations and keen individuals would bring together a wide range of people with access to a variety of different resources. This group could well be a sub-section of the overall steering group (see section 3.4 'Preliminary consultation').

Once the overall priorities have been determined, each area of work will require detailed planning. In areas where there is already some form of bicycle education, a review of current practices will be a prerequisite for integration with other aspects of bicycle planning.

From a study of education programmes in different countries it is clear that the keys to a successful programme are enthusiasm and commitment. All too often education work becomes a bureaucratic process without innovation and forward drive. The lessons which have to be taught may remain similar over periods of time, but when they compete with the developing range of other material being taught, new ideas, new communication methods and new teaching material are required to ensure that the subject is not seen as being out of date.

There is a combination of many sources of funds and a large reservoir of untapped enthusiasm amongst cyclists; what is required is a plan which harnesses and develops these two essential ingredients.

10.1.1 Integrating education with other plans

The importance of integrating educational activity with other aspects of a bicycle programme cannot be underestimated. Data required by education officers may affect the amount and type of information on safety and usage which is collected, and the need to monitor the effectiveness of different aspects of the programme will require coordination with other departments.

The materials used to publicize safety problems and to teach cyclists and motorists to behave according to a common code should highlight actions which are being taken to improve the safety of cycle routes and junctions, the type of signs that have been used to mark cycle facilities and the places where bicycle parking facilities have been provided.

Since reinforcement is an important part of the education process, coordination with the police is essential. Police officers can play a vitally important role, stopping motorists and cyclists who make mistakes and, in the case of young people, reminding them of the correct behaviour (see Chapter 11, 'Enforcement').

The timing of highlights in an education programme can also be coordinated with other developments in a bicycle programme to maximize the publicity gained.

Finally, coordination will be particularly important when trade-offs have to be made between different aspects of the plan or between different budgets. Good working relationships and an understanding of other people's work are essential if sound decisions are to be made.

10.1.2 The effectiveness of education

Remarkably little work has been done on the effectiveness of education programmes. A study of thirty children in the UK, half of whom received training, concluded that 'A national Cycle Proficiency training course had succeeded in bringing about improvements in certain important aspects of children's cycling behaviour and some of this improvement had been maintained after a lapse of two months'. It also found that the improvement was greater under the protected conditions of an experimental road system than in the normal conditions found on public roads, where children made decisions on their own, unaware that they were being observed. The study concluded that 'the children had not transferred the whole of their training to practical use' (*Evaluation of a Cycle Proficiency Training Course*, 1979).

One attempt has been made to link accident involvement

with training and although the sample was small, the study found that children who did not have training were involved in three times as many accidents as those who did, despite the fact that trained children cycled more.

10.1.3 Funding education programmes

The major limitation on education programmes is the availabiltiy of funds. Within a local authority there will generally be intense competition between different departments, and even if road safety is allocated a reasonable budget, those concerned with bicycle safety will have to fight for a share of it. In the local authority context, the sources of funds include the following:

- Road safety budgets: this is likely to be the single largest source of funds.
- Employment development: this new source of funds has become available following the rapid growth in unemployment in many countries. In the UK, this money can be used for projects which will benefit the community or the environment.
- Physical education budgets: since cycling is a form of physical exercise money allocated to physical education can be used to teach cycling, and therefore bicycle safety.
- Community development budgets: some authorities have budgets for the development of voluntary activities. These coule be used when volunteers are involved in bicycle education.
- Other existing budgets: some activities described in this chapter can be undertaken at minimal extra cost, for example sending publicity to drivers with road-tax documents.

The availability of funds widens considerably if part of the safety education programme is not directly connected to the local authority. Many of the sources of funding given below would be unwilling to allocate money to pay for work which 'the local authority should be doing'. However, if some parts of bicycle education are structured in a way which distances them from the local authority, then these other sources become available. For example, a Bicycle Education Group could be created as a separate organisation, which is serviced and partially funded by the local authority. This independence would often satisfy other funding sources that their money was being spent on work which otherwise would not be undertaken. But it need not result in the local authority losing control over how the money is spent. The authority would expect to receive accounts and would control the staff allocated to the group. Within this wider context the following sources of funds become available:

Bicycle manufacturers and traders

It is in their interest to improve the safety record of cycling. Although funds may be limited, manufacturers in a number of countries have funded educational activities.

Trust funding

This is a significant source of funds for charitable organisations. Trusts are established especially to further educational work, and although competition is strong, a good case can undoubtedly be put for bicycle education.

Fund-raising

Within the context of an active organisation, fund-raising efforts could be launched. Sponsored bicycle-rides are renowned as good fund-raisers.

Parent-teacher associations

In many cases, these exist to help schools with activities which do not take place or cannot be funded within the existing regime. Bicycle education is such an area. In addition, skills and other resources besides money can be brought in through this channel.

Paying for courses

Although favouring those who can afford it, money can be raised by charging a small fee for bicycle safety courses.

10.2 EDUCATING CHILDREN

A considerable body of material has been published about bicycle education for children, most notably by the Royal Society for the Prevention of Accidents in the UK and the Geelong Bike Plan in Australia. This section draws together many of the techniques which have been tried, to enable those authorities that already undertake education work to inject new ideas into their programmes, and to present an overall picture for those that do not.

10.2.1 School education

The goal of bicycle education in schools is to teach all children how to ride bicycles safely in all traffic conditions. The goal can be broken down into a number of requirements which will be essential to any course of bicycle education. These include:

an ability to ride safely in traffic
an understanding of the rules of the road
habits of care and alertness
an ability to make decisions in traffic and respond to the hazards of the roads
knowledge of how to maintain bicycles.

This is clearly a massive task which will require considerable resources.

An important method of encouraging children to participate in bicycle safety education is to make the award of a Cycle Proficiency Certificate a condition of cycling to school or keeping a bicycle in school grounds. The aim should be to create a climate in which this award is highly desirable, thus encouraging excellence in this subject.

Organisation

School bicycle education should be organised to maximize the use of resources (equipment, teaching materials and specialist knowledge) and the involvement of teachers. In practice this usually requires a combination of the resources of a road safety department and their staff, and the interest of individual teachers in each school. However the road safety department may also have to take responsibility for motivating teachers and developing their interest. Teacher involvement is particularly important for follow-up work including the establishment of bicycle clubs and the organisation of other activities.

Children's accident types

Analysis of the types of accidents in which children are involved identifies areas of training which should be given special attention. Although little research has been done comparing the different types of accidents in which children and adults are involved, there is evidence to suggest that they

10.2 Bicycle education should be fun

are similar. The four main types of accidents which are identified in section 5.2.1 'Common locations and types' should therefore be used as a basis for teaching manoeuvres which require special attention.

Three other factors are important in children's bicycle accidents. UK research shows that:

80% take place in daylight hours
60% take place at or near road junctions
less than 5% are caused by mechanical defects.

UK RECOMMENDED SYLLABUS OF TRAINING

Session 1
Maintenance and adjustment of the bicycle, correct riding position, use of handlebars, pedalling skilfully to maintain adequate speed, application of brakes.

Session 2
Position of foot on pedals, 'ankling', braking in different conditions, starting and stopping, parking.

Session 3
Highway code, riding safely in all circumstances, road sense, turning left at different types of junction.

Session 4
Turning right at different types of junction, overtaking parked and moving vehicles.

Session 5
Practical revision, turning right, awareness in looking behind before making any manoeuvres.

Course content

Research in the UK has indentified the need to educate children to conceptualize the road and road crossings in a way which will make them consistently aware of the dangers of the roads. In particular, children fail to understand that 'safe' ways of making manoeuvres are not inherently safe, but depend on individual behaviour. Secondly, in order to avoid making material too theoretical and therefore not part of a child's daily life, local examples and photographs are essential.

The importance of practical training cannot be underestimated. While schools may be reticent about taking responsiblity for children on the roads, the lack of on-road training may lead to a greater risk of accident involvement in the future.

Course duration and timing

The duration of a course will depend primarily on the extent to which bicycle education is a continuous part of a child's education. In the UK, the course leading to a National Cycling Proficiency Certificate (fig 10.4) consists of seven lessons each lasting $1\frac{1}{4}$ hours. In Australia, the Bike Ed Course takes two terms, with at least one hour per week devoted to it. In America, the district of Columbia was recommended to allocate a minimum of six hours classroom instruction per year, plus additional time for practical work.

The most opportune time to instil good habits is when children start to cycle to school. Although this varies, it is likely to be the beginning of a new school year or term. Visits by external trainers or work by school teachers should therefore be concentrated at these times.

Age of training

The fact that bicycle accidents increase steeply from the age of 5 or 6 in most countries suggests that bicycle education should start at a very early age. However, the incidence of child bicycle accidents peaks with the 12–15 age group, so to achieve the maximum effect for given resources, education should be concentrated on this group. Furthermore, research in the UK has shown that older children tend to learn more from a given course than younger children. These points, together with the fact that many lessons are forgotten after only six to eight months, give considerable strength to the argument for continuous training throughout school life. However, in most schools curriculum time is at a premium, so choices will have to be made. A reasonable compromise might be to have intensive training for three groups: the 5–6 age group, the 8–10 age group and the 12–14 age group. Thus each child would be taught once and reminded twice.

Training teachers

Most developed countries make considerable efforts to train people how to teach their subject. It is therefore surprising to discover that very little is done to train people how to teach bicycle safety. The fact that this subject necessarily includes a wide range of skills and that many people come in to schools to teach it without any teacher training, make special training sessions an essential part of any education programme.

The major qualification for all teachers of bicycle safety is that they are regular cyclists themselves. Only by experiencing the problems and difficulties faced by cyclists on the road can teachers be in a position to explain them accurately and

10.3 Off-road training should be as realistic as possible. It should be supported with on-road training

10.4 UK cycle proficiency certificate

THE ROYAL SOCIETY FOR THE PREVENTION OF ACCIDENTS

NATIONAL CYCLING PROFICIENCY
CERTIFICATE

AWARDED TO

WHO HAS COMPLETED A COURSE OF INSTRUCTION IN THE NATIONAL CYCLING PROFICIENCY SCHEME AND PASSED THE TEST FOR SKILFUL CYCLING

CERTIFICATE NO. ------------------

PRESIDENT

DATE ------------------------------

10.5 The Australian Bike-Ed kit

convincingly to children. As a leading American bicycle education expert has said, asking a non-cyclist to teach cycling 'is like hiring a one-legged man to teach dance'. The other essential qualification is enthusiasm for the subject.

One of the most suitable ways of training teachers is by one or two day in-service training courses organised for a whole area. This provides an opportunity to go into the subject in depth and for teachers from many schools to mix with road safety officers, police officers and others who are involved with bicycle safety.

Teaching materials

One of the major problems of teaching any safety subject is to make the dangers seem real and not just the concern of 'the teachers'. The use of films and video cassettes not only gives the subject a real dimension but is also likely to have a much greater educational impact. Video can also be used to great effect by filming children before a course begins and showing the film which demonstrates their own mistakes. This is likely to be particularly popular since children enjoy watching themselves and their friends on the screen. Video can also be used to film correct and incorrect ways of handling difficult local situations.

Another way of introducing the local element into bicycle safety education is to provide teachers with a pack of information including:

data on the number of local accidents
the types of accidents and the ages/sex of those involved
a map showing where accidents occur
a map showing safer routes for cyclists
details of local laws prohibiting cycling in certain places.

In most countries other materials are available nationally, including photographs, film-strips and wall charts. These will add colour and interest to the course.

Assessment

The importance of good assessment procedures cannot be overstressed. To a large extent the quality of a scheme which culminates in a award of a certificate is controlled by the examiners. Requirements must therefore be laid down to guide examiners. Some errors by candidates merit automatic failure. The Australia Bike Ed course requires 85% proficiency; in addition, failure to stop completely at a stop sign, to give way or to signal and look behind before merging, all result in instant failure.

Adding some fun to safety education

Since the enthusiasm of the children is an essential component of successful bicycle safety education, steps should be taken to make it fun. In Australia and the USA, bike rodeos, which consist of a series of games and competitions, are often arranged to fulfil this function. If a rodeo is organised it provides an excellent opportunity to get local press coverage and thereby raise safety consciousness among a wider group of people.

10.2.2 Education by parents

It is startling to see a society in which the priority structure typically gives more individualized training to the family pet than to a child learning about bicycles

(*Eugene Bikeways Master Plan*, 1974)

Parental guidance is a major factor influencing children's behaviour. Sadly, many parents do not seem to recognise bicycle safety as an area of lasting priority. One reason for this may be that the child's first bike is often a toy and the major hurdle perceived by the parent is to teach the child to balance the bike. Once this is achieved a few words are spoken about 'watching out for cars' and 'riding slowly' and the child's safety is left in the hands of fate.

The major aim, therefore, is to instil in parents the importance of systematically teaching children about the hazards of the roads and how to overcome them. The problem can be split into two parts: firstly, alerting parents to the existence of the problem, and secondly, giving them the information to either teach the children themselves or send their children to local classes.

Arming people with some basic information about bicycle safety requires communication media which allow a considerable amount of information to be presented. One way of doing this is to include a leaflet with every new bicycle sold. Further copies of the leaflet could be left at bicycle shops, toy shops, libraries and other public places. To catch parents of existing cyclists articles could be written for the local authority's news-sheet, adverts could be placed in local newspapers and articles could be distributed to organisations which have newsletters.

In situations where regular school bicycle education is not available, or where this can be supported by other activities, courses should be provided outside school hours. Although only children who least need the education are likely to attend, there are many advantages to systematic professional training over good instruction given by a responsible parent. Furthermore, the lessons learned by one child are often passed on to others.

Classes could be held at local community centres, bicycle club rooms or other public centres, and they should be staffed by people who have attended training courses. All a successful course requires is a little publicity, enthusiastic organisation and some interesting activities.

10.3 EDUCATING ADULT CYCLISTS

The greatest difficulty in attempting to teach bicycle safety to adults is finding ways of communicating with those cyclists who most need the training. Attention should therefore be directed at attempts to communicate through carefully chosen media.

Accident statistics suggest that the most important group, after school children, is the 17–25 age group. The popular interests of this group of people should therefore be identified and communication about their interests should include local safety facts and figures, details of accident black-spots and tips about surviving in traffic.

Another effective means of communication is undoubtedly television. Since this is expensive, a campaign should be aimed at cyclists and other road users. However, this medium suffers particularly from the problem that some people return to their old habits when the campaign is over.

The organisation of other activities can also have a 'spin-off' effect on adult bicycle safety. The establishment of a strong network of clubs with an active programme of interesting activities will put people into contact with more conscientious cyclists. Club runs, treasure hunts and map-reading contests all provide valuable opportunities for safety points to be made.

10.4 EDUCATING MOTOR VEHICLE DRIVERS

Considerable effort is already put into road safety campaigns, to persuade people not to drink and drive, to wear seat belts and so on. The task of those responsible for bicycle safety is to ensure that this aspect of road safety is built into campaign plans.

Large numbers of cyclists are the innocent victims of the incorrect behaviour of motor vehicle drivers. Furthermore, practically every cyclist can reel off a list of near misses, incurred or seen in recent weeks. The purpose of educating motor vehicle drivers is two-fold: firstly, to improve their behaviour, and secondly, to show cyclists that both aspects of the bicycle safety problem are being tackled.

The time to start is when people learn to drive. Information about accident types and the characteristics of bicycles should be given during driving lessons to sow the seeds of maturity and courtesy which are essential elements of safety on the roads. This information should be included in the *Highway Code* and other documents used by learner drivers. It should also be included in drivers' tests.

When people learn to drive other types of vehicles, such as heavy goods vehicles, buses and coaches, further instruction should be given on the responsibilities of vehicle drivers. In particular, drivers of large vehicles should be taught and questioned about the space which should be given to cyclists when overtaking.

However their actions will only affect a small proportion of the current driving population. Further action will be required to improve the behaviour of existing drivers. Like adult cyclists, most drivers believe that they behave well. The first task will therefore be to tell people precisely what the problem is. Advertising will often be the most effective method of communication, though the difficulties of permanently modifying people's behaviour should not be underestimated. Other ways of reinforcing the message could include the distribution of posters and leaflets at petrol filling stations, car parks and auto shops and the inclusion of leaflets with all official post connected with motor vehicles, such as road tax, driving licences and insurance returns. Fleet truck drivers, bus and coach drivers and drivers of public utility vehicles are an easier audience to reach. Information could be distributed at meeting places or included with company circulars.

The magnitude of this task should not be underestimated and the fact that the communication channels are so few means that they will have to be used heavily to achieve results.

10.5 ENCOURAGEMENT

The importance of publicity and promotion has been badly underestimated by many authorities in the UK and other

10.6 The UK Secretary of State for Transport and the Mayor of Middlesbrough create publicity for the opening of the town's first cycle route

countries. In general, the effort put into publicising a bicycle plan should at least equal that put into, say, the engineering.

There are two main types of publicity work, each with its own goals. Regular reporting should keep the public informed about the development of plans in the area, while special campaigns should aim to focus public attention on a particular event or issue (eg, the opening of a new cycle route, or children's road safety).

10.5.1 Developing a strategy

A strategy should identify how the goals are going to be achieved. The details will depend on the methods of communication available, the budget for publicity and the availability of personnel. It is important, however, that the many groups of people who will be involved in implementing the strategy should also be involved in its development (see section 3.4 'Preliminary consultation'). In particular, local bicycle groups usually provide a core of enthusiastic volunteers who should be carefully listened to and consulted.

10.5.2 Tactics

The key to a successful strategy is the use of as wide a variety of tactics as possible, thus creating sufficient interest to generate widespread discussion within the community. Minimal resources can be stretched to their utmost by working with cyclists, bicycle traders and manufacturers and anyone else involved in the bicycle plan who can offer useful resources, such as teachers and police officers. As many of the following methods as possible should be used to help make the subject an important issue: the media (local television, radio and newspapers), leaflets and posters, competitions, exhibitions, public speaking and newsheets. Most authorities have publicity departments whose expertise can be drawn upon; furthermore, the use of all these tactics is well documented elsewhere.

10.5.3 Evaluation

It is important to decide on a means of measuring the effectiveness of the campaign and to set up a system to gather the necessary information to monitor the effects of publicity (see Chapter 12, 'Monitoring, evaluation and feedback'). After the completion of the campaign a review should take place so that successes and failures can be noted and lessons learned which will be useful for the next campaign.

10.5.4 Encouragement in Geelong – an example

Geelong, a town some 50 miles due west of Melbourne, Australia, has a five-year bike plan. Equal weighting is given to the four elements of the plan – education, engineering, enforcement and encouragement.

The scale of the encouragement programme can be seen from their 1979 progress report:

'The encouragement programme seeks to promote an awareness of improved facilities, safety education and enforcement programmes and of the benefits of cycling. In 1978/79 the encouragement programme was largely an information exercise aimed at making the community more aware of the Geelong Bike Plan. A wide variety of methods were used for promoting safe cycling in Geelong. These included:

Radio: A saturation programme on the local station 3GL consisting of jingles, bicycle weather forecasts, endorsements by prominent personalities and competitions.

Newspapers: Regular press releases, daily bicycle cartoons and the distribution of bicycle leaflets to every house in the Geelong area.

Schools: The sale of 3,500 bicycle safety flags at a subsidised price. A bicycle book subsidy was also made available to all schools in the Geelong area.

Films: Members of the public were offered free entrance to a special screening of a popular film for all those arriving by bike. Also five bicycle films were purchased for use by schools and community organisations. These included a Walt Disney film and a film produced for planning professionals.

Exhibitions: Displays were mounted at a Municipal Office and at an open day at a Spastic Centre.

Clubs: A Geelong bicycle touring club was formed.

Public lectures: These were given at schools and universities, on the subject of the Geelong Bike Plan. Articles were prepared for journals and newspapers.

Promotional material: Support to free name engraving on bicycles project and the distribution of safety pamphlets by the Police Bike Team.

Research: A research grant was provided to the Australian Road Research Board to investigate latest overseas trends in bicycle planning, education and enforcement.'

Geelong Bike Plan On The Move, 1979

Action checklist

1. Use local data to pinpoint exactly what education is required, who requires it and what priority it should be given.
2. If no coordinating body for bicycle education exists, bring together representatives of all interested organisations, including the police, the education department, parent-teacher associations and bicycle clubs.
3. With the help of this group draw up a full inventory of all current activities, both those which are directly relevant to bicycle education and encouragement and those which may have a spin-off effect.
4. Together, agree the goals for bicycle education and encouragement in the area.
5. Draw up a plan which aims to achieve these goals. This may include the creation of a complete bicycle education and encouragement programme, or the improvement of existing programmes.
6. Identify the various sources of funds to pay for the programmes, including as wide a variety as possible. Determine how the controllers of existing budgets could be persuaded to increase them.
7. Identify areas of education and encouragement work which should be coordinated with other aspects of an overall plan for cycling in the area.
8. Vigorously pursue the activities undertaken, and regularly review all the individual activities and the overall programmes to determine whether the desired goals are being achieved. If they are not, modify activities accordingly.

11 Enforcement

For many years measures to force cyclists to obey the rules of the road have been lax, and as a result some cyclists have taken the liberty of doing as they please. This problem has been compounded by inappropriate traffic management measures which make little sense to cyclists and are therefore not adhered to by a significant proportion of the cycling population.

The other side of the enforcement coin is the inconsiderate behaviour of many motor vehicle drivers, who treat cyclists as second-class road users – partly because cyclists do not obey the rules of the road. The effect of these often strongly held attitudes is that cyclists feel that bad motorist behaviour should be punished more harshly and more often, and motorists believe that good behaviour by cyclists should be more rigorously enforced. The net result is that if either party is pulled up for bad behaviour they feel victimized.

A pre-requisite for any enforcement programme is therefore an understanding by both groups that most roads have to be shared and that an acceptable common code of behaviour is in everyone's best interest.

Most of the work on enforcement measures has been carried out in the USA, where it became a significant issue following the rapid rise in bicycle use in the 1970s. However, the down-turn of the economy and, in particular, the reduction of public sector expenditure has led to the curtailment of a number of enforcement schemes before conclusive evaluation of the measures could be carried out. It is therefore only possible to make tentative conclusions about the potential of different measures.

A number of clear-cut discoveries have, however, been made. Firstly, education and enforcement are inextricably linked; on the one hand, it is practically impossible to enforce measures without the support of a good education programme, and on the other, education has been found to need the support of enforcement measures to change people's behaviour.

Secondly, in many communities there is little concern about the accident problem and therefore no desire to see that

11.1 Enforcement is often a low priority

behaviour is improved. The community therefore has to be made aware of the seriousness of the bicycle safety problem and the reasons why measures are being taken to combat it, before the programme is launched. A number of enforcement programmes have found that success depended on extensive media coverage. This led to support from the community for the programme, which in turn made police officers feel justified in their action.

Thirdly, the enforcement authority must give reasonable priority to the enforcement programme to ensure its success. In particular, experience in the USA has shown that the provision of a regular budget is a singularly effective way of assuring the success of a programme.

Fourthly, the single town approach, rather than the regional approach, seems to be more effective, probably because the programmes depend heavily on individuals convincing members of the enforcement authority that this an important issue.

Responsibility for enforcement measures will fall primarily on the local police force, so their involvement and enthusiasm for the whole bicycle programme is essential. One of the most successful methods of achieving this has been to allocate specific responsibility for bicycle work to one person who is enthusiastic about the programme. However, it may well be that the planning or engineers' department has to take responsibility for motivating interest within the police department in the first place.

Fifthly, in-service training is essential. Highly trained police officers find it difficult to regard 'ticking off' bicycle offenders as an important function. A one-day seminar or equivalent activity is therefore required to make officers aware of the problem and the issues.

Finally, the continuing success of the programme depends on support from senior officers and regular reminders by them of the value of the programme.

The range of measures available to tackle the enforcement problem will vary from country to country depending on the legal framework and their political acceptability. The costs will not be large, since the main resource required for such a programme is the time of police officers. This chapter describes that advantages and disadvantages of different measures and shows how they can be linked together to form a realistic programme.

11.1 ENFORCEMENT MEASURES

This section describes the measures which are appropriate for improving the behaviour of different groups of road users.

11.1.1 Measures for young cyclists

Since accidents are more prevalent in the younger age groups, enforcement will often concentrate on this group. The measures available include:

Verbal warnings

These are suitable for minor offences. Children should be told that they have done wrong and why it is important to do it correctly. Other safety points can also be included in the warning. With older children (say 9–15 years) the warning can be given more significance by taking the child's name and address.

11.2 With older children warnings can be given more significance by taking names and addresses (Geelong, Australia)

Warning to parents

When children commit more serious offences, the verbal warning can be supported by a letter sent to their parents informing them of the error and requesting their assistance in teaching the child to ride safely. A leaflet containing the basic rules of the road should also be sent with the letter. In some states in the USA the police take the child home and deal with the matter immediately, verbally encouraging parental action.

Laying charges

Children who are of a certain age (10 or over in the UK) can have charges laid against them for serious offences. However, widespread use of this measure is likely to be unpopular with both the community and the courts.

When repeated warnings are issued to children or parents, the police in Victoria, Australia, require the child and the parents to attend the nearest police station for a formal caution by the officer in charge.

In some American states, a system of 'peer courts' has been developed where children are admonished by people of their own age – responsible, mature children picked from Scout and Guide groups and other similar organisations. Although convictions are not recorded, punishments can include compulsory attendance at a safety course, essays, copying out the rules of the road and other similar measures. These have been found to work successfully in a number of states and are reported to be gaining support.

11.1.2 Measures for adult cyclists

Whilst verbal warnings and laying charges are also available for dealing with adult offences, it has been found that the former is too weak and the latter too strong for the average offence. In some states of the USA and in Victoria, Australia, a system of 'ticketing' appropriate for cyclists has therefore been devised. Cyclists are issued with a 'ticket' (a traffic infringement notice, fig 11.3b) which describes the offence and this is followed by a caution notice (fig 11.3c) which is sent to the offender. If the offence is repeated, the police have discretion to issue another warning or to prosecute the cyclist. In some American states, a 'bicycle citation notice' can be issued, requiring the cyclist to attend safety classes. Tick-

Form No 547

VICTORIA POLICE

19

To: ....
....
....

Dear Sir/Madam,

On ..../..../19.... .... was reported as having committed the following traffic violation:

It has been decided that this matter would be most suitably dealt with by a Caution, rather than by a Children's Court. This Caution is not a Court and does not determine innocence or guilt, but aims to assist the child and avoid a formal Children's Court hearing at an early age.

The Caution will be conducted at ...... a.m. at .... on ..../..../19.... It is desirable that both parents or guardians attend with .... on that date.

Please contact my office on the above telephone number if you are unclear about the procedures or feel that an alternative date is necessary.

Yours faithfully,

....
Rank: ....

PLEASE REMEMBER: The life of your child may depend on his knowledge and observation of road laws.

VICTORIA POLICE

BICYCLE OFFENCE REPORT ORIGINAL

To .... D.O.B. ....

of ....
(full address)

On................day............../.........../19........at................. A.M. / P.M. You were intercepted

riding a bicycle in .... (Street)

....(Location) and that an Offence was committed as indicated hereunder by a cross **X**

KIND AND PARTICULARS OF OFFENCE

☐ Disobey Road Sign	☐ Careless riding
☐ Disobey Traffic Signal	☐ Failure to yield right of way
☐ Wrong side of street	☐ Lighting offences
☐ Failure to signal	☐ Riding more than two abreast
☐ No hands on handlebars	☐ Dangerous overtaking
☐ Improper (Turn)	☐ Travelling at dangerous speed
☐ Illegal passenger	☐ Endangering pedestrian safety
☐ On footpath	☐ Unroadworthy bicycle
☐ Hitching onto another vehicle	☐ Other (Specify)

COMPLETE FOR JUVENILE

PARENT or GUARDIAN ....

ADDRESS...

.... SIGNATURE .... DISTRICT
( )

RANK .... NO. ....

.... STATION

Form No 546

TEL

OUR REF

VICTORIA POLICE

TO 19

BICYCLE OFFENCE
CAUTION NOTICE

Dear Sir/Madam,

On ..../.........../19.........., ... was reported as
(NAME)
having committed the following traffic violation

Although in this case it is not proposed to institute proceedings, you are warned that a repetition could lead to a prosecution, and may also be the cause of serious injury to the cyclist, and to others.

Yours faithfully,

( )

PLEASE REMEMBER ! The traffic laws are everybody's business and we ask your co-operation in making the roads safe for all.

Geelong Bike Plan

11.3 (a) **(top left)** Warning letter sent to parents of children committing traffic violations, (b) **(bottom left)** the ticket issued to adults who commit bicycle offences and (c) **(above)** the caution notice which follows the ticket

eting can also be used for children's offences, warning letters being sent to their parents.

Four American states and many municipalities have provisions for impounding bicycles to punish violators of local traffic ordinances. Periods of impounding vary – in Davis, California, the maximum is 30 days. In many cases impoundment is at the discretion of the police and there is no right of appeal or for a court hearing.

11.1.3 Measures for motor vehicle drivers

In most countries there are already many procedures for the prosecution of motorists who commit traffic offences. In some American states, ticketing is used to enforce good behaviour. The problem of ensuring that motorists do not infringe the rights of cyclists is that most police officers do not use the available measures because they are unaware of the problem. In some cases, they hold the motorists' view that cyclists just 'get in the way' of their cars. The best way for an officer to learn the problem is to use a bicycle for a period of time.

Assuming it has been accepted that motorists and cyclists both need enforcement to improve their behaviour, one way of ensuring fair treatment is to monitor the number of warnings and citations issued and inform police officers whether they are being too harsh or lenient to either party. These figures could also be published to show cyclists and motorists that treatment was fair (fig 11.5).

11.2 THE ORGANISATION OF ENFORCEMENT MEASURES

There are a number of ways of organising law enforcement including the use of:

traffic police
all uniformed police officers
traffic wardens
specially appointed officers.

The advantages and disadvantages of these methods are shown in fig 11.6. In Victoria, Australia, the second option has been used because it was felt that the enforcement would be widespread and cost effective. It was coupled with the publication of a booklet on police department procedures and the appointment of two officers in each district to organise bike safety seminars.

11.3 THE USE OF LICENSING

Two other enforcement measures have been tried. Both have considerable potential in theory, but neither has been reported to be outstandingly successful.

11.3.1 Licensing cyclists

The major benefit of requiring cyclists to hold a licence is that they can be tested on the rules of the road and proficiency in using a bicycle before taking to the road. However, the cost of organising such a system, the need for it to be state or nationwide and the problem of 'foreign' cyclists would seem to outweigh the benefits. There are no reports of successful cyclist licensing schemes.

An alternative which would maximize the benefits while minimising costs would be to require children under the age of, say 15, to pass a proficiency test before cycling on the roads. Another alternative, which has been applied in a number of countries, is to introduce a minimum age for cycling on public roads (see section 13.1.4 'General controls on the cyclist'). This reduces accidents below the age set and also alerts parents to the fact that cycling on roads is an activity which requires a certain level of skill.

11.3.2 Bicycle registration

The primary aim of a registration scheme is to discourage theft and assist in the recovery of stolen bicycles. It can also be used to improve the mechanical standards of machines on the road, and as a means of identifying riders who give false names and addresses when issued with warnings.

A simple system requires that bicycle frames are stamped with a number which is recorded locally against the owners' name and address (manufacturers already stamp bikes with frame numbers in some countries). If a renewable licensing system is used, then a sticker is required in addition to the frame number to indicate that the licence has been renewed.

Fees varying from $1to $5 for a two-year licence have been charged and riding a bicycle without a licence has been made an offence. The administration is usually carried out by the body responsible for vehicle registration.

In the USA, two states (Utah and Hawaii) and a number of municipalities currently have compulsory registration. It has been tried in other areas, but it was found that without state-wide or even nation-wide registration, it was not an effective deterrent against theft.

11.4 Enforcement of motorists' behaviour is an essential component of an enforcement programme

Summary of Geelong police bike patrol action	Motorists	Cyclists
Verbal warnings	132	520
Traffic infringement notices	77	–
Open court summonses	46	–

11.5 Publishing details of actions taken shows cyclists and motorists that the behaviour of both groups is being tackled

11.4 TWO EXAMPLES

The best way to show the feasibility and effectiveness of the measures described in this chapter is to look at two towns where they have been used.

11.6 The advantages and disadvantages of different methods of organising enforcement

	Traffic police	All uniformed officers	Traffic wardens	Specially appointed officers
Advantages	Officers have good knowledge of traffic law	More widespread law enforcement	Uses existing staff	Officers become experts in their fields
	Legal changes not required	No additional expenditure required		Momentum would be easier to maintain
Disadvantages	Officers in motor cars do not appreciate cyclists problems	Harder to convince all officers to give this priority	Wardens have less authority	High cost
			Wardens are not empowered to deal with criminal offences	Coverage would not be widespread

11.4.1 An example from Australia

In Geelong, Australia, a trial was carried out to establish the feasibility of involving a large number of police officers in bicycle enforcement, to test administrative procedures for handling offenders and to discover how officers, cyclists and motorists and the non-cycling public reacted to the scheme.

The administrative system was based on tickets ('bicycle offence reports' for cyclists and standard tickets for motorists). Publicity included posters entitled 'We care about cyclists' to emphasise the safety rather than the punishment aspect of the programme, and a widely distributed 'Bicycle Law Enforcement' booklet setting out the background to the problem for officers and the general public.

Before the trial was launched, a conference held for police in charge of police stations was addressed by the Assistant Commissioner to stress support from senior police. Regular press releases were issued and all school principals were informed about the trial.

In addition to verbal warnings, the following actions were taken against offending cyclists:

Bicycle Offence Reports issued to adults	77
Bicycle Offence Reports issued to children	244
Second adult offences	0
Second child offences	5
Third child offences	1
Court actions	0

The following conclusions were drawn from the trial:

- the overwhelming majority of police readily accepted the recommended procedures
- this type of enforcement readily fits into present duties
- it does not produce administrative problems and requires little follow-up work
- the methods used were politically acceptable, the only comments received being favourable ones from the parents of children cautioned.

As a result of the success of this trial the procedures are now being implemented throughout the state, and the appointment of a Bicycle Co-ordinator within the police department is being considered.

The trial is seen in Australia as a major reinforcement of the rights of cyclists as legitimate users of the road, with the same responsibilities as other drivers.

Action checklist

1. Identify people within the enforcement community who are concerned with road safety and whose interest in bicycle safety can be aroused.
2. Build these people into the overall process of developing cycling in the area, to increase their perspective on the problem and knowledge of the issues.
3. Identify which areas of cyclist-motorist behaviour are causing most problems locally and which enforcement issues are politically important.
4. Identify enforcement measures which are appropriate, legally possible and politically acceptable and draw up a programme of activities designed to tackle the most pressing problems.
5. Obtain support for the programme from local cyclists and from the highest levels within the police authority.
6. Ensure that educational work is undertaken on those aspects of the behavioral problem which are to be the focus of the enforcement programme before the launch of the enforcement measures.
7. Organise a thorough briefing for all the police officers who will be involved in the programme.
8. Launch the programme with the maximum amount of publicity possible.
9. Monitor the activities of the different aspects of the programme by collecting data from police officers on the number of warnings issued, the types of offences which are most prevalent and on other actions taken against motorists and cyclists.
10. Use this information to refine the programme and ensure that the activities become a permanent feature of police officers' duties.

11.4.2 An example from the USA

In Cranford, New Jersey, a five-member Cranford Bicycle Board was established to plan a programme of education, media coverage and police enforcement.

The enforcement programme is operated by regular police force members who stop juvenile offenders, check their bicycles for proper registration and equipment and if necessary, after a first and second violation, send warning letters to parents with a request that they help teach bicycle safety at home. Following a third violation, the juvenile is required to bring his or her parents to meet with a traffic safety officer. A fourth violation requires a Juvenile Court appearance (although this has never occurred).

Adult cyclists are summoned to appear in Traffic Courts and pay an average fine of $15.

Every year, about 700 cyclists are stopped, 60 bicycles impounded and ten adults receive citations. All patrol cars carry bicycle racks for impounding bicycles that are stolen, unregistered, or have serious mechanical defects.

Each year, all officers attend a 45-minute briefing on bicycle enforcement. The enforcement effort is backed by an intense education and publicity campaign which may involve up to fifty officials and citizens at a time. For two months, each spring, the Bike Board conducts a Bicycle Safety Alert – a saturation media campaign involving the distribution of banners, bumper stickers, signs and buttons.

Schools have co-operated by integrating bicycle safety into their work. People learning to drive cars are taught how to share the road with cyclists. Fourth and fifth graders are only permitted to ride to school after they have shown their proposed routes to the principal and discussed their rights and responsibilities.

The programme is said to have worked well, combining police activities with a well-planned media and safety programme involving many sectors of the community.

12 Monitoring, evaluation and feedback

The purpose of monitoring is to provide data which enables people to determine how successful something is, and to identify ways of improving it. The success or failure will be measured against a set of predetermined goals and objectives, the formulation of which was described in Chapter 3.

Most plans will contain a number of objectives, and the activities designed to achieve one will often affect the achievement of others. A monitoring scheme will therefore have to attempt to disaggregate the effects of various activities on the achievement of each objective (fig 12.1).

Monitoring will often start at a very early stage in the development of a bicycle plan, because data will be required on the situation before any activities are undertaken, to enable 'before and after' comparisons to be made.

Monitoring will involve a combination of the use of data which is already collected and the gathering of new data. A major task will therefore be co-ordination with other people with responsibilities for data collection. Since data on most aspects of cycling is often not collected, existing data collection activities may require amendment.

The aim of this chapter is to show how monitoring schemes should be established. A significant component of monitoring work will be concerned with the use and safety of bicycles. This chapter should therefore be read in conjunction with sections 4.5, 5.4 and 5.5.

12.1 MONITORING THE EFFECTS OF INFRASTRUCTURE CHANGES

This section describes the establishment of monitoring systems which are designed to enable planners to evaluate the effects of infrastructure changes.

12.1.1 Regular monitoring

The first stage in the creation of a regular monitoring system is to establish precisely what data is already collected. This will almost certainly include reports of injury accidents and in some area, estimates of the use of bicycles.

In addition to this information some base line data will also be available. This may include:

- results of questionnaires indicating the proportion of the population that cycles regularly, what measures would persuade people to cycle, and what people think the local authority should do
- existing cycle flows and origins/destinations of cyclists' journeys
- age and sex of the cycling population
- ownership of bicycles
- journey characteristics for bicycles and other modes.

12.1 The effect of different activities on various objectives of a plan to develop cycling

Examples of activities	Objectives affected: Making cycling safer	Improving cyclists' environment	Reducing traffic congestion	Reducing dependence on oil	Increasing fitness of population
Attack danger spots	●				
Improve routes used by cyclists	●	●	●	●	●
Organise education programmes	●				
Build enforcement activities into police officers' regular duties	●				
Publicize the benefits of cycling				●	●
Create residential precincts	●	●			

SAMPLE QUESTIONS TO INCLUDE IN SURVEYS OF CYCLISTS' ATTITUDES

During the last three months, how often have you travelled by bicycle?
Did you ride a bicycle before the cycle route was created?
Did the introduction of the cycle route lead you to:
start cycling for the first time
take up cycling again
use your bicycle more often?
Do you think the cycle route should be continued or discontinued?
Why do you want the cycle route continued?
Would you describe the ...... section of the route as very satisfactory, satisfactory, unsatisfactory or very unsatisfactory?
Why is it unsatisfactory?

Information will also be known about the current and expected structure of the area, of employment and of the local population.

Evaluation of this data will help to determine exactly what additional data should be collected regularly. As a minimum, the monitoring system should provide answers to the following questions:

Has the number of trips made by bicycle changed?
What are the characteristics of bicycle trips (journey purpose, multi-mode, new trips, etc)?
What are the possible causes of changes in bicycle use?
Has the number of accidents involving cyclists increased?
Have the characteristics of accidents changed?

This data should be collected at least four times a year, though authorities that do traffic counts monthly will be able to obtain more details. It should be evaluated against previous data and attempts should be made to identify the reasons for changes. It should also be compared with national data and if possible, with data from similar towns which are not taking steps to encourage cycling.

The resulting reports should be distributed as widely as possible among people involved with the bicycle plan, decision makers and the press. The reports will form an important part of a strategy designed to increase people's awareness and understanding of cycling.

To discover the success of individual components of a bicycle plan, further monitoring exercises will be required.

12.1.2 Monitoring routes developed for cyclists

The development of a route for cyclists will usually involve the combination of a number of different measures including the enhancement of existing streets, the use of routes where cycling was previously not allowed and the provision of special cycling facilities. The purpose of monitoring the whole route is to determine the overall effect of the measures on cyclists, motor vehicles and pedestrians and to gain an insight into people's attitudes towards the measures. Four data gathering exercises will be required:

Usage

Counts of cyclists and other road users should be made at a number of different points on the route and at 'control points' off the route before any infrastructure changes are introduced, immediately after their introduction and at quarterly intervals after that. This will determine how the measures have affected the routes cyclists take and whether any new trips or transferred trips have been generated. The change of usage may be in the region of 10–25%. However, the effect of other factors such as weather, school games days or early closing may be of the same magnitude. Care is required in identifying which, if any, of such factors, are influencing usage.

Journey times

Most infrastructure changes will affect the journey times of one or more modes. Despite the fact that changes will often be small, measurements of journey times before and after the infrastructure changes will be essential to counter the often exaggerated claims of proponents and opponents of the changes. A sample of between six and ten journeys by each mode for a representative journey undertaken simultaneously would provide a reasonable data base. The journey time measurements should be made a short period before, immediately after and, say, six months after the changes, when minor operating problems will have been ironed out.

Attitudes

Cyclists, motor vehicle drivers, pedestrians, residents and traders should all be asked for their opinions on the measures introduced. A structured questionnaire will simplify the analysis of results but if a measure is completely innovatory, an open-ended question should be asked to identify aspects of the measure which have been missed by the question deviser.

The first attitude surveys should be conducted immediately after the implementation of the changes to gauge initial reactions and identify possible modifications. The second should be conducted twelve months later to determine more permanent attitudes and to discover whether there are any other problems which could be ironed out.

The information should be gathered from a combination of household interviews and roadside interviews. The sample sizes will depend, among other things, on the length of route, the number of different types of area it passes through and the money which is available for the work. At least one or two questions in the household survey should be the same as

Household interviews	**Phase 1 (rounded figures)**
Residents living on the routes	300
People living in the study area	1,000
Car drivers living in the study area	450
Cyclists living in the study area	450
Roadside interviews	
Cyclists on the route	500
Cyclists off the route	150
Pedestrians	60
Traders interviewed	16

12.2 Sample sizes used for attitude surveys on 6km cycle route in Peterborough

questions in the roadside survey to enable checks to be made on the accuracy of the study. Furthermore, by asking questions about the frequency of bicycle trips, the results of the attitude survey and the usage counts can be interconnected.

In order to evaluate the data, information will have to be collected on new developments in the area such as housing, employment changes and major roadworks, all of which may influence the use of bicycles and attitudes towards the cycle route.

Accidents

Although it is unlikely to be statistically significant, accident data should be collected and analysed because accidents can become a political problem as a result of increased reporting or exaggerated reports of near-misses, by opponents of the scheme. Historical details over as long a period as possible will be valuable in gauging whether accident rates have changed.

The data from these four exercises should be gathered to enable officials, elected representatives, people involved with the bicycle plan and the general public to judge the success of the scheme.

12.1.3 Monitoring special facilities

When new features have been introduced (such as a road closure or a cycle-pedestrian path in a park) they will need to be observed to determine whether users are behaving as intended. Surveys should consist primarily of personal observation, with the surveyor making detailed notes to minimize the extent to which preconceptions affect the conclusions drawn. Surveys should be carried out immediately after the introduction of a facility to determine how it performs when users are familiarizing themselves with it, and then three and six months later to determine behavioural patterns when the learning process has been completed. Surveys should be undertaken in the peak hour and in an off-peak hour and should, if possible, be supplemented with periodic informal observations.

If this qualitative analysis does not identify problems which have been reported but not observed, or if quantitative analysis is required, film or video recordings can be made, enabling detailed analysis of behavioural patterns to be undertaken. A carefully positioned camera can provide a valuable insight into exactly what happens on the ground. It can also be used to check that bicycle counts have been taken accurately and to check oral accounts of problems. However, time-lapse photography is an expensive and time consuming process. If the feature is unique, it will often be appropriate for a national agency to carry out such work.

MONITORING IN PETERBOROUGH

An experimental cycle route running from an outer residential area to Peterborough city centre was opened in July 1977. Studies were carried out:

- to determine the effect of the route on bicycle usage
- to record the opinions of cyclists, motorists, residents and business people
- to investigate the response of users to different features of the route.

The studies included peak hour and 16 hour traffic counts, taken once a month or once a fortnight, on the same day of the week, over a period of 20 months, at ten sites on the route and 6 elsewhere; 150 hours of time-lapse photography were obtained from 9 sites on the route. Attitude surveys were carried out in four places, spread over a year, to determine the views of residents, people living on the route, car drivers, cyclists, pedestrians, traders and employers. Journey time experiments were also undertaken.

These studies gave data which enabled the researchers to conclude, among other things, that:

- the introduction of the facility did lead to an increase of flows on the route relative to a decline in the rest of the town
- a quarter of cyclists interviewed had taken up cycling or been encouraged to cycle more by the introduction of the route
- a new housing development added approximately 10% to bicycle flows along one part of the route
- 92% of residents, drivers, pedestrians and traders felt the route should be continued
- motorists liked the routes more as they became used to them
- no difficulties were encountered on a narrow (1.8m wide) section of cycle-pedestrian track
- motor vehicles regularly encroached a cycle lane to pass vehicles waiting to turn right
- the contra-flow lane was not very popular with either motorists or cyclists
- traffic light phasing at one junction did not give cyclists sufficient time to cross
- there were too few accidents to draw statistically significant conclusions about the effect of the route on safety.

12.2 MONITORING EDUCATION WORK

The main purpose of most educational programmes will be to improve safety. Monitoring the effect of a programme as a whole will therefore be primarily concerned with accident data. In a medium size town it is likely that the number of accidents resulting in death or serious injury will be too small to be statistically significent. Therefore, unless the programme is carried out over a larger area, figures for accidents resulting in slight injury will have to be used, despite their unreliability. The incidence of these is likely to be in the region of 1 per 1,000 population, so in a town of 100,000 people there will be about 100 such accidents per year. The first measure of the success of an education programme is whether this figure can be reduced and held down.

Given that political support is an important component of any programme, views should be sought on the education programme. Often this can simply be a matter of adding two or three questions onto the end of another suvey to determine whether people have heard about specific parts of the programme, whether they have done anything about it (for example sending their children to a proficiency course) and if not, why not. In addition, further information can be gathered from people who attend educational activities, and where appropriate from their parents.

Monitoring people's behaviour before and after training and monitoring different methods of teaching the same material will help to find how effective training is and which methods are most effective. Usually this detailed work will be most appropriately carried out at the regional or national level, given the time and expense involved and the wider applicability of the results.

Using observers and time-lapse photography, the behaviour of different groups of people can be monitored in a variety of situations. This is most easily done with school children since some can be picked for training and some remain untrained for a period to be used as a control group.

Violation	Number of arrests and verbal warnings issued	Number of injury accidents at which the cyclist was deemed to be at fault
Failure to stop at stop signal or stop sign	5900	560 (1 fatal)
Not carrying a light	3500	73 (1 fatal)
Driving on wrong side of road	1300	420
Pedestrian violation	760	43
Incorrect turning procedure	350	530 (8 fatal)
Failure to give car right of way	230	1200 (18 fatal)
Reckless driving	10	230 (1 fatal)
Other driving violation	9100	1100 (12 fatal)

12.3 Comparison of arrests, verbal warnings and accidents involving bicycles (Source: California Highway Patrol computerised record, 1979)

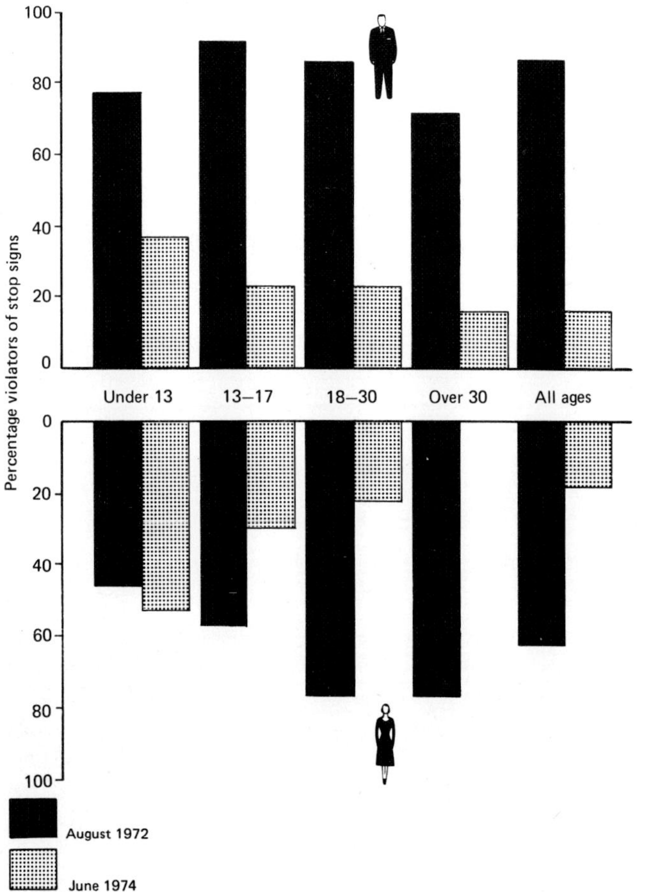

12.4 Reduction of bicycle violations in Santa Barbara from August 1972 to June 1974

12.3 MONITORING ENFORCEMENT WORK

Since the purpose of enforcement work is to improve safety, the fundamental measure will again be accident data. Other data can also be collected, such as the number of verbal warnings, citations or court summonses issued. However, it will be difficult to determine whether the number issued has changed because of increased police activity or worse behaviour. Experiments in the USA suggest that this measure is more appropriate for monitoring police activity. This can be valuable, since people's behaviour will only improve if there is persistent work by the police.

Data on the number of warnings issued can usefully be compared with data on the occurrence of accidents in which the cyclist was deemed to be at fault. This will identify whether enforcement work is concentrating on the manoeuvres which cause the most accidents. However, a number of qualifications must be attached to this type of comparison; firstly the allocation of fault at accidents is determined by individual officers, who may categorize errors in different ways. Secondly, the enforcement of correct behaviour is easier for some categories (eg, not carrying lights) than others (eg, reckless driving).

However, data from the California Highway Patrol (fig 12.3) does shed some light on the problem. It suggests that law enforcement agencies should concentrate more on 'incorrect turning procedures' and 'failure to give cars right of way'.

One method which has been used in Santa Barbara, USA, to determine the effect of enforcement on behaviour, is to follow cyclists until they have an opportunity to violate or comply with a traffic regulation. The survey showed an overall reduction of observed violations from 55% to 21% over a two-year period, even though the number of bicycles increased by an estimated 70% (fig 12.4).

12.4 MONITORING PUBLICITY CAMPAIGNS

The purpose of a considerable proportion of publicity work will be to assist in the achievement of other goals, for example publicizing the existence of new routes for cyclists. However, some publicity work will be designed directly to achieve an objective, for example giving parents the information they require to teach their children about safety. Monitoring can be undertaken to determine the effectiveness of this work by asking relevant questions in attitude surveys. Since these are likely to be undertaken to determine people's attitudes to a variety of issues, little extra expenditure will be incurred. The following questions for parents could be used to determine the effects of a parent education programme:

Do you give your children any training before allowing them to ride on the roads?
What rules of the road did you teach your children?
How often do you cycle on the roads with your children?
Do you ever carry out a visual check to see whether your child's behaviour has deteriorated?

Attitude surveys should also be used to determine the effectiveness of different publicity methods by asking people what they can recall from a particular campaign.

Other methods of monitoring the effectiveness of publicity may be available for little extra effort. For example, the success of a campaign to persuade people to attend safety classes can be measured by the number who actually appear.

12.5 THE COST OF MONITORING

To undertake all the work described in this chapter would clearly be beyond the resources of many authorities. However, the value of the data cannot be underestimated. Without facts and figures, the effect of often expensive and time-consuming projects will not be known.

A number of techniques can be used to minimize the costs incurred. Firstly, other authorities may be introducing similar ideas, enabling monitoring to be co-ordinated and costs shared. Secondly, if it can be argued that the results will have nationwide value, central government can be approached for financial assistance. Thirdly, work on different aspects of monitoring should be co-ordinated to ensure that opportunities for gathering data are not missed. In particular attitude surveys, which are expensive to conduct, should be co-ordinated to gain an insight into different parts of a plan to develop cycling. Finally, some monitoring can be done at minimal cost, for example monitoring press coverage and letters to the press.

12.6 FEEDBACK

The primary purpose of much of the monitoring work undertaken will be to learn lessons which can be then applied to future developments. It is essential therefore that administrative mechanisms are created to ensure that these lessons are applied. This could include annual or bi-annual reviews of progress and a formal process of reporting on the implementation of lessons learned, both of which should be built into the original planning process (see Chapter 3). Since the implementation of any programme is likely to take a number of years and since much of the work will be on-going, written records which can be passed on from one person to another will be important.

Action checklist

1. Check that regular monitoring activities collect data on bicycles.
2. Formulate precise objectives at an early stage in the development of a plan.
3. Decide which activities are to be monitored, to measure the achievement of these objectives.
4. Establish which methods of monitoring should be used to measure these activities.
5. If necessary, raise further funds from other agencies to help pay for the work.
6. Ensure that monitoring systems are established so that 'before and after' comparisons can be made.
7. Establish administrative procedures to ensure that lessons learned are applied to future projects.

13 Legal considerations

A planner or engineer is not expected to be a legal expert, but a broad understanding of the law involved in any proposals will reveal possible legal constraints and difficulties. Moreover, where a scheme involves novel or complex ideas, a good working relationship with the legal department may be vital to its success. Since every jurisdiction has its own legal framework, it has not been possible to present this chapter in terms which are applicable to most countries. We have therefore picked two, the UK and the USA, and described the laws and regulations in each in considerable detail. In addition, interesting examples from other countries have been included.

Since changes and amendments are continually being made to the law, it is essential that planners and engineers check with the legal department before embarking on a scheme.

13.1 THE UNITED KINGDOM

13.1.1 The legal framework

In England and Wales, local authorities are treated in law as corporations created by Statute. As such, their power to do anything must derive from a Statute or regulations made under it (see section 13.2 below); if an authority does something not authorized by law, or fails to comply with procedure laid down in the law, it runs the risk of having its action treated as *ultra vires* and held invalid by the courts. This would result in the proposal being withdrawn with obvious political embarrassment. In certain cases, the District Auditor (a central government appointee responsible for inspecting the annual accounts of a local authority) may apply for a court order if an item of account is contrary to the law; the court then has the power to order the person responsible for incurring or authorizing the illegal payment to repay the amount personally (Local Government Act 1972, s. 161).

Legal provisions may also dictate the manner in which the cyclist may ride his machine, and this area of the law can be important in the preparation of proposals. There is little point, for example, in building into a plan a manoeuvre which it would be illegal for the cyclist to perform. The guidance on the law in the following sections is not a complete analysis of all the legal considerations or problems likely to be encountered in planning for bicycles, and should not be taken as a substitute for proper consultation with the relevant department. But it will give a good understanding of the structure of the law and the type of legal issues involved.

Some of the statutes quoted apply to Scotland with modifications as specified in a particular section, eg, the Road Traffic Regulation Act 1967. If a Statute is applicable only to England and Wales, other legislation along broadly similar lines may be in force (eg, Town and Country Planning (Scotland) Act 1972).

13.1.2 Sources of law

Statutes

The basis of legislation in England and Wales is the Statute or Act of Parliament, which must pass through both Houses of Parliament and receive Royal Assent before becoming law. These days, Statutes, or particular sections in a Statute, are often only brought into force when a Secretary of State makes the appropriate regulations, known as 'Commencement Orders'; a section in the Statute itself (usually the penultimate section entitled 'Commencement etc. . .') will indicate whether or not this mechanism has been adopted.

Some Statutes, known as Private Acts, give special powers to a particular body, often a local authority or a statutory undertaker such as a Water Authority. The powers are generally restricted to a specified local area. Private Acts are promoted by the authority itself, and the procedure for passing through Parliament is very different from that for Public Acts. But once all the stages are passed, they have force in law equal to any other Statute.

THE MAIN STATUTES REFERRED TO IN THE UK SECTION OF THIS CHAPTER

Countryside Act 1968
Highway Act 1835
Highways Act 1980 ('HA 1980')
Local Government Act 1972
New Towns Act 1965
Road Traffic Act 1972 ('RTA 1972')
Road Traffic Regulation Act 1967 ('RTRA 1967')
Transport Act 1978
Town and Country Planning Act 1971 ('TCPA 1971')

Regulations

Statutes will often give the Secretary of State the power to make regulations, orders (including Commencement orders) and rules by way of 'statutory instruments', sometimes known as delegated legislation. The Statute will create the essential framework and structure of the law, while details of its implementation and applicability are left to Government departments. Statutory instruments, which are generally subject to Parliamentary approval, and have the same force of law as the Statute itself, are cited by their title and number, eg, S.I. 1980/123.

Circulars

Government departments regularly publish circulars which generally consist of advice to local authorities and similar bodies explaining the provisions of new Statutes and regulations, and suggesting methods of implementation. They do not have the force of law, but provide a useful indicator of Government policy and thinking. Circulars are cited by their issuing department and number, eg, DoE 19/1980.

By-laws

Statutes will often give public authorities power to make local by-laws or regulation orders, which once made will have the force of law. Penalties for non-compliance, the scope and purpose of the by-laws or orders, and the procedure for making them are laid down in the enabling Statute. By-laws generally require confirmation by Central Government. Failure to have regard to the defined scope and purpose, or to follow the required procedure for making them, can result in the by-law or order being declared *ultra vires* and of no effect.

Court decisions

The Courts play a vital role in interpreting legislation, especially where the applicability is not precisely clear. In addition, the courts have themselves developed certain principles of law (the rules of natural justice, for example). Parliament has the constitutional power to override decisions of the courts, and may therefore, by express wording in a Statute, exclude these principles from its operation. Otherwise, all legislation will be interpreted in the light of these 'common law' principles. Decisions of the higher courts (the Court of Appeal and House of Lords) carry more weight than those of lower courts, and cases of importance will be published in one or more of the series of law reports; they are cited by the names of parties and the abbreviation of the law report series (eg, Thornton *v* Kirklees Metropolitan Borough Council [1979] 2 All ER 349.

13.1.3 Definitions

Definition of bicycle

The term 'cycle' and 'bicycle' are not generally defined in legislation in England and Wales, other than in broad categorizing terms such as:

> *'cycle' means a pedal cycle or pedal bicycle not being in either case propelled by mechanical power*
>
> (Road Vehicle Lighting Regulations, S.I. 1971/694)

The courts have, on occasion, attempted more precise definitions, such as:

> *a mechanical contrivance to facilitate the progress of footpassengers, the motive power being supplied by the legs of the passenger* (Smith *v* Kynnersey [1903] I KB 790)

USEFUL LEGAL DEFINITIONS

Bridleway. A highway over which the public have the right of way on foot or horseback, or leading a horse or driving animals but no other right of way (s. 329, Highways Act 1980). The Countryside Act 1968, granted members of the public the right to ride bicycles along a bridleway under certain conditions.

A bridleway is a 'road' for the purposes of the offences of reckless, careless, or drunken cycling, and carrying more than one passenger (s. 18–21, Road Traffic Act 1972).

Carriageway. A way constituting or comprised in a highway, being a way (other than a cycle track) over which the public have a right of way for the passage of vehicles (s. 329, Highways Act 1980). The American equivalent is the 'roadway'.

Cycle track. A way constituting or comprised in a highway, being a way over which the public have the following, but no other right of way, that is to say, right of way on pedal cycles with or without right of way on foot (s. 329, Highways Act 1980).

Footpath. A highway over which the public have the right of way on foot only, not being a footway (s. 329, Highways Act 1980).

Footway. A way comprised in a highway which also comprises a carriageway being a way over which the public have the right of way on foot only (s. 329, Highways Act 1980). The American equivalent is a 'sidewalk'.

Highway. A way over which the public have a right of way. A somewhat narrower term than 'road' (q.v.) since there should be some evidence of permanent dedication as a public right of way.

Road. Any highway *and* other road to which the public has access (s. 196, Road Traffic Act 1972; s. 104(1) Road Traffic Regulation Act 1967). A wider term than 'highway' (q.v.) but the term 'public' in the second limb of the definition has been interpreted by the courts to mean the general public and not simply a particular class of members of the public (eg, hotel guests using the driveway to a hotel).

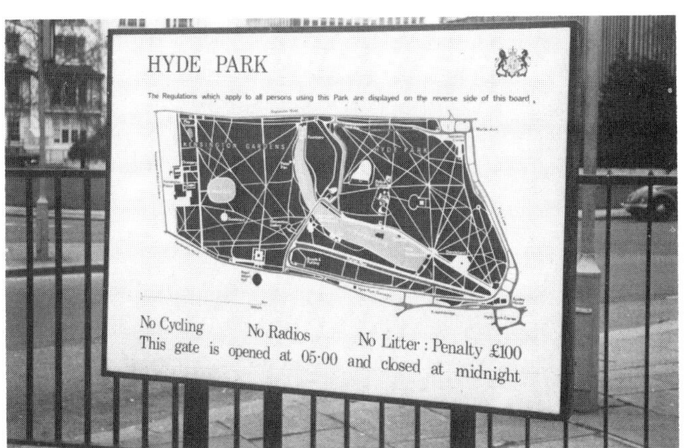

13.1 By-laws are often used to prohibit cycling

MOPEDS

A moped used to be defined as a motor bicycle with an engine of under 50cc cylinder capacity and equipped with pedals by means of which it was capable of being propelled. Since 1st August 1977 the statutory definition has been tightened up as a result of the introduction of faster machines which nevertheless adhered to this definition. The term now means a motor cycle with a maximum design speed not exceeding 30 mph, a kerbside weight of less than 250kg, and an engine of under 50cc cylinder capacity, whether or not pedals are attached.

The courts have held that a moped that is being pedalled without the engine running is still a mechanically propelled vehicle, at least for the purpose of excise and MOT regulations. Where a statute or regulation defines a pedal cycle as a vehicle 'not being propelled by mechanical power' (see section 13.3), a moped being pedalled will be excluded. However, where a statute makes no such definition (see for example, the definition of a cycle track in Highways Act 1959), a moped being pedalled probably comes within the term 'pedal cycle'. Care should therefore be taken in the framing of Traffic Regulation and other Orders, if this is likely to give rise to a problem.

The definition and treatment of mopeds and motor-assisted cycles varies considerably within European countries. Generally, the definition incorporates a speed limit (30kph in Denmark, 45kph in France) and requires that pedals available for propulsion are attached to the machine.

Mopeds are required to use cycle tracks where they are available in many European countries including Belgium, Italy, France and Denmark, though in the latter case this does not apply in urban areas unless specifically signed. In the UK, all traffic signs which use the bicycle symbol are now specifically defined in terms of 'pedal-cycles'. Where a local authority wishes to permit mopeds to use a bicycle facility, supplementary 'and moped' plates should be added to the bicycle sign.

ELECTRICALLY ASSISTED BICYCLES

Section 24 of the 1981 Transport Act gives the Secretary of State the power to make regulations defining certain types of electrically assisted pedal cycles not to be treated as motor vehicles for the purposes of the Road Traffic Act 1972 and the Road Traffic Regulation Act 1967. Such cycles therefore would not require licence plates or insurance, cyclists would be permitted to ride without crash helmets, and they could be ridden on cycle lanes and tracks, in the absence of specific Traffic Regulation Orders.

The section goes on to make it an offence for anyone under the age of 14 to drive such a bicycle on the road, punishable with a fine not exceeding £50.

Definition of 'vehicle'
Where the term 'vehicle' is used in legislation in England and Wales, it will, unless otherwise specified, include bicycles. The term 'carriage' which is not often used in modern legislation, has also been intepreted by the courts to include bicycles.

Wheeling a bicycle
A feature of urban cycling is the convenience of quickly dismounting and wheeling or pushing a bicycle. But the law in England and Wales essentially makes no distinction between the cyclist riding and the cyclist pushing a bicycle. There is no general statutory provision for a person pushing a bicycle to be treated as a pedestrian.

There is little case law on the subject, and what does exist is not consistent. In one case concerning a cyclist pushing his bicycle up a hill, a court declared:

> *if it had been necessary to decide whether he was a cyclist or a pedestrian, I would have held the deceased to have still been a cyclist, and not a pedestrian at the time of the accident*
> (per Roche J, Harper *v* Associated Newspapers (1927) 43 TLR 331)

But a recent decision of the Divisional Court held that someone pushing a bicycle was still a 'footpassenger' for the purpose of zebra crossing regulations (Crank *v* Brooks, Divisional Court, 16th May 1980, unreported). A cyclist is possibly still bound by traffic regulation orders or traffic signs when dismounted unless the order is expressly applicable only to bicycles being ridden. Individual cases are unlikely to be pursued or treated seriously by the courts, but this type of manoeuvre should not be incorporated into a proposal without giving some thought to the legal difficulties.

13.1.4 General controls on the cyclist

Before a driver can take a motor vehicle on the public roads, he must comply with a considerable number of legal requirements (age, insurance, MOT, etc) and have reached a level of proficiency in driving. In contrast, there are few restrictions on cyclists.

Driving licence
No country requires cyclists to pass any sort of proficiency test before taking to the public road, nor is any driving licence required.

Age
In common with most countries, there is no age restriction for bicycle users in England and Wales. In Denmark, however, there is a minimum age of 6 years, unless accompanied by a rider over 15; Austria prohibits riders under 12 on the public roads unless accompanied by an adult.

In some jurisdictions, local regulations or laws may provide age restrictions in certain cases. For instance, Traffic Ordinances in San Francisco provide that 'No person of fifteen (15) or more years shall ride a bicycle upon any sidewalk in any district'. Traffic Regulation Orders with similar age restrictions would be invalid in England and Wales since they must relate to a class of vehicle rather than a class of vehicle user (see section 13.5 'Rules of the road').

Registration
Registration of bicycles is not required in England and Wales. Registration systems are in force in some other jurisd-

ictions, essentially as a method of making the theft of bicycles more difficult. The United States Model Traffic Ordinance (on which local regulation may be based) provides that the penalty for violation of traffic laws by cyclists may include the removal or detention of licence plates, if they are required by a registration system.

Children and the law

While children of any age may ride a bicycle in England and Wales, those under 10 years old cannot be guilty of a criminal offence. No conviction of a child between 10 and 14 years can be made unless it is proved that the child knew he was doing wrong, for example by evidence of concealment.

Similar provisions exist in many other countries. The definition of 'bicycle' in the American Uniform Vehicle Code is drafted to exclude children's bicycles in order to ensure that children are not covered by any of the criminal provisions in the Code.

Equipment

Legislation in most countries makes certain requirements for the equipment a bicycle must carry. This area of the law primarily concerns the bicycle user rather than the planner or engineer. But in proposing routes that are likely to be used extensively at night-time, it may be relevant to be aware of lighting requirements for bicycles. Most countries, including England and Wales, require the use of white front lights and rear red reflectors. The use of rear red lights at night-time is also required in law in England and Wales, but not in all countries.

13.1.5 Rules of the road

There are a number of criminal offences in England and Wales which relate specifically to the use of bicycles.

Reckless cycling

Section 17 of the Road Traffic Act 1972 makes 'reckless cycling' a criminal offence. This is the most serious offence related to the riding of bicycles, and the 'reckless' element has been interpreted in England and Wales to imply that the rider has taken a conscious risk, or has ignored the possible consequences of his action, when riding in such a manner as to create an obvious and serious risk of causing physical injury or substantial damage to property (see R *v* Lawrence (Stephen) [1981] RTR 217).

Careless cycling

Section 18 of the Road Traffic Act 1972 ('RTA 1972') creates the less serious offence of 'careless cycling'. The offence is committed when the rider falls below the standards that can be expected of a reasonably competent and prudent cyclist, whether or not he was aware of this at the time of the offence. There is no detailed statutory code in England and Wales specifying the standards to be expected, and in the final analysis it is a matter for the courts to determine in each and every case. The Highway Code, however, provides some useful guidance.

Drunken cycling

It is an offence under s. 19, RTA 1972 to ride a bicycle on a road, including a bridleway, or other public place whilst unfit to do so through drink or drugs. Under s. 12, Licencing Act 1872 it is an offence to be in charge of any carriage (a term that would include a bicycle) on the highway or other public place when drunk, and this would be an appropriate offence for someone drunkenly wheeling or pushing a bicycle.

Carrying passengers

It is an offence under s. 21, RTA 1972 to carry a passenger on a bicycle not constructed or adapted to carry more than one person. In other countries, such as Holland, carrying passengers is allowed.

The Highway Code

The Highway Code (issued and periodically revised by the Department of Transport) provides the best guide to the rules of the road applicable to cyclists. Failure to comply with the Code is not an offence in itself, nor will it *necessarily* lead to a conviction of reckless or careless cycling. But its observance or non-observance can be relied upon as evidence in criminal or civil proceedings (s. 37(5), RTA 1972). The following sections therefore indicate some of the most pertinent provisions in the Code concerning the riding of a bicycle. Quotations are from the current (1978) Highway Code.

Riding on the road

Keep to the left, except when road signs or markings indicate otherwise or when you intend to turn right or when you have to pass stationary vehicles or pedestrians in the road (para. 39).

Never drive so fast that you cannot stop well within the distance you can see to be clear (para. 46).

Leave enough space between you and the vehicle in front so that you can pull up safely if it slows down or stops suddenly (para. 47).

Do not ride more than two side by side (para. 130).

You should always give clear arm signals to let drivers behind you know what you intend to do especially at roundabouts and junctions (para. 135).

Turning left

Before turning . . . left . . . always glance behind and make sure it is safe. Give a clear arm signal to show what you intend to do (para. 130).

Before and after the turn keep as close to the left as safety and the length of your vehicle will allow (para. 100).

Give way to pedestrians crossing the road into which you are turning (para. 100).

Turning right

When it is safe, give right turn signal and as soon as you can do so safely, take up position just left of the middle of the road or in a space marked for right turning traffic (para. 97).

Alternative right turn

On busy roads and at night if you want to turn right, it is often safer to stop first on the left handside of the road, and wait for a safe gap in the traffic before you start to turn (para. 132).

Local traffic regulation orders could be made prescribing such a course for cyclists turning right at junctions. But there are likely to be problems of enforcement, and the proposed introduction of such orders might well meet with resistance

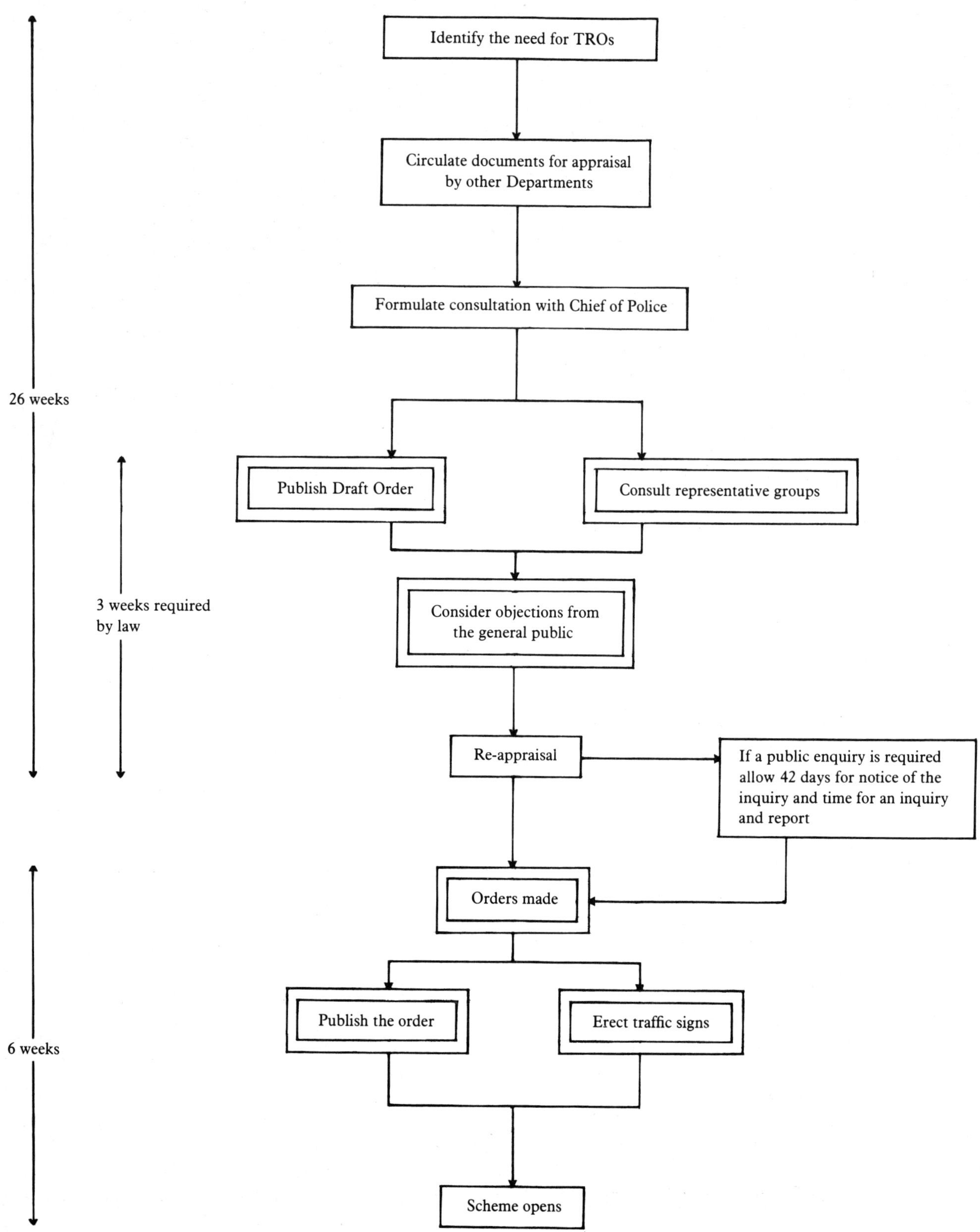

Notes: Legally required steps are marked in double lined boxes.
No provision is made for procedures relating to financial approval.
Where another authority is involved (eg, the GLC and a London Borough Council), add more time for legally required consultations.

13.2 The procedure involved in making a Traffic Regulation Order

13.3 The advantage of experimental TROs is that they can be brought into effect more quickly than full orders. This untidy road closure was part of the ill-fated Balham, London, traffic management scheme

from cyclists who felt they were being treated as second-class road users.

Roundabouts

Again, the course advised for cyclists is that to be taken by drivers of motor vehicles. Unless road markings indicate otherwise, precedence must be given to vehicles on the right.

When turning left, *approach in the left hand lane: keep to that lane in the roundabout* (para. 103).

When going forward, *approach in the left hand lane: keep to that lane in the roundabout.* But 'if conditions dictate', the approach may be in the right hand lane, and then that lane should be kept to (para. 103).

When turning right, *approach in the right hand lane: keep to that lane in the roundabout* (para. 103).

If there are more than two lanes on the approach, *use the clearest convenient lane on approach and through the roundabout suitable for the exit you intend to take* (para. 104).

Alternative route at roundabouts

The Highway Code suggests an alternative route for cyclists who feel unable to follow the above procedures because of 'inexperience or any other reason': '*You should either stay in the left hand lane of the roundabout . . . or get off your cycle and walk*' (para. 134).

13.1.6 Traffic regulation orders

In England and Wales the making of Traffic Regulation Orders ('TROs') by Highway Authorities is likely to play a major part in the implementation of bicycle plans. The statutory basis, contained in the Road Traffic Regulation Act 1967 ('RTRA 1967'), provides great flexibility in the type and scope of Orders than can be made. The procedural requirements, which are essential for an Order to take effect, are, however, fairly complex and will inevitably result in the process taking some time (see fig 13.2).

Section 1 of the RTRA 1967 (dealing with TROs outside Greater London) provides a number of purposes for which TROs may be made. These range from 'facilitating the passage on the road of any class of traffic' to 'preserving or improving amenties'; these categories should be sufficiently wide to include any proposals requiring TROs.

The scope of TROs as defined in s. 1(3) RTRA 1967 is equally wide: prohibiting, restricting or regulating the use of the road or any part thereof by vehicular traffic or by such

EXPERIMENTAL TRAFFIC ORDERS

Section 9 of the RTRA 1967 allows Highway Authorities to make TROs relating to an 'experimental' scheme of traffic management. The scope and purpose of such TROs are the same as those for full Orders, but they will be limited to a duration of 18 months.

The advantage of experimental TROs is that they can be brought into effect more quickly than full Orders, since the procedural requirements for making them are less complex. The police must still be consultated, but draft Orders need not be published for public comment, nor need representative organizations be consulted. Experimental TROs can be converted to full Orders at a later stage.

Their obvious value is that their use allows the public time to adjust to, and appreciate the benefits – and the pitfalls – of a new scheme before it is made permanent.

The term 'experimental' is not defined in the Act. The TRO does not have to be novel in its type or scope, but it should probably be new to the area of implementation, and the Authority should genuinely regard it as an experimental measure.

traffic of any class, or by footpassengers. A number of specific examples are given, without prejudice to the above general statement, and these include regulating or prohibiting traffic to go in any specified direction, or specifying parts of the carriageway to be used. But a number of restrictions should be noted.

- TROs do not apply to animals: only vehicles (a term including bicycles) or footpassengers may be specified
- TROs cannot deny access to premises by footpassengers
- TROs preventing access to premises for more than 8 hours out of 24 can be made only for a limited number of reasons, and will require the consent of the Secretary of State if opposed by owners or occupiers of such premises
- TROs cannot regulate the speed of vehicles: provision for the making of speed limits is in s. 77 RTRA 1967.

The power of the Greater London Council to make TROs is governed by s. 6 RTRA, which specifies slightly different criteria from those in s. 1. In particular, the need to obtain consent from the Secretary of State for Orders restricting access for more than 8 hours our of 24 does not apply. Consultation with Borough Councils within whose area the affected road lies is required.

In addition the Commissioner of Police (either City or Metropolitan) possesses limited powers to make regulations for experimental traffic schemes with the consent of the GLC.

Consultation with the Chief Officer of Police is always necessary prior to the making of a TRO (s. 84C RTRA 1967). The police are likely to be particularly concerned with problems of enforcement and demands on manpower. Self-enforcing TROs (eg, no entry to a street, with a physical barrier in place) are therefore likely to be favoured. Orders with which drivers or cyclists are unlikely to comply unless supervised will be less favoured (eg, Orders specifying unusual manoeuvres for cyclists). For similar reasons TROs drafted in imprecise language or involving any doubt in their applicability should be avoided.

In addition to consultation with the police, other detailed requirements for the procedure are contained in regulations: see Local Authorities Traffic Orders (Procedure) (England and Wales) Regulations 1969, S.I. 1969/463. The procedure will involve consultation with representative bodies of those likely to be affected, publication of draft Orders, time for public objections, and a possible local public inquiry (see fig 13.2).

On the making of a TRO, the authority must, by provisions in the above regulations, 'forthwith take such steps as are necessary to secure . . . the erection on or near the road of such traffic signs in such positions as the authority may consider requisite for securing that adequate information as to the effect of the Order is given to persons using the road'.

Neither the governing Statute nor the regulations expressly state that a TRO will be invalid unless an appropriate sign is erected – in contrast to equivalent provisions in some State law in the United States. But case law suggests that if an Authority failed to take the steps described above, the TRO would have no effect.

Contravening a TRO is a summary offence with a maximum fine of £100. The failure to comply with certain traffic signs is also an offence (see section 13.13 below).

13.4 The parking of motor vehicles on cycle tracks may amount to an obstruction of the highway

13.1.7 Cycle tracks

Cycle tracks beside carriageways

Cycle tracks running alongside an existing carriageway may be constructed by Highway Authorities under s. 65, Highways Act 1980. Although the Act uses only the word 'construct', Authorities have been advised by the Department of Transport that: *'The amount of "construction" work involved may be minimal or even non-existent, depending on the circumstances of the particular case'* (Local Transport Note 1/78, para 4.11). This interpretation will be relevant where an existing pavement or part of the carriageway is being converted for use by bicycles using this power.

Cycle tracks independent of existing carriageways

Cycle tracks that do not run alongside existing carriageways may be constructed under s. 24, Highways Act 1980: this gives Highway Authorities the power to construct 'highways', a term that includes cycle tracks (s. 329, Highways Act 1980). Traffic Regulation Orders must be made to exclude motor vehicles from the new highway.

Prohibition of non-cyclists

There is no legal right to drive a motor vehicle along a cycle track, but a driver commits no criminal offence in doing so; owners of the sub-soil or the Highway Authority could probably sue the driver in civil courts for nuisance or trespass (see Pratt & Mackenzie, Law of Highways). A stronger deterrent would be to make a TRO excluding motor vehicles from using the cycle track since breach of the Order is a criminal offence.

Where it is desired to restrict the riding of horses or other animals, this must be achieved by means of local by-laws rather than TROs. These will require confirmation by Central Government.

Parking on cycle tracks

The parking of motor vehicles on cycle tracks may amount to an obstruction of the highway, a criminal offence under s. 137, Highways Act 1980. The courts, however, will con-

CONTROLLING BICYCLES ON PAVEMENTS

A local order in Bellevue, Washington, USA provides that:

Every person operating a bicycle upon any sidewalk shall operate the bicycle in a careful and prudent manner and at a rate of speed no greater than is reasonable and proper under the conditions existing at the point of operation, taking into account the amount and character of pedestrian traffic, grade and width of sidewalk, and condition of surface; and when because of the width of such sidewalk or the amount of pedestrain traffic thereon, riding a bicycle on such a sidewalk would endanger or unreasonably inconvenience pedestrians, such person shall stop and dismount from such bicycle.

Such an elaborate, and essentially exhortatory, order would almost certainly be unacceptable in England and Wales, if not void for uncertainty.

sider the reasonableness of each particular case to determine whether or not there has been an obstruction. TROs may also be made prohibiting or restricting the parking of motor vehicles on cycle tracks.

Mandatory use of cycle tracks

There is no general statutory provision in England and Wales that cyclists must use a cycle track. The American Uniform Vehicle Code, in contrast, provides that, *where a usable path for bicycles has been provided adjacent to the roadway, bicycle riders shall use such path and shall not use the roadway*

(UVC @ 11–1205)

In England and Wales, TROs can be made to that effect.

13.1.8 Cycle-pedestrian tracks

The footway

In England and Wales 'driving a vehicle' on the pavement beside a carriageway (known in law as 'the footway') is a criminal offence under s. 72, Highway Act 1835, and riding a bicycle along this part of the highway is therefore illegal. Cyclists may use this part of the highway in England and Wales only if the footway, or part of it, is 'removed' in law under s. 66, HA 1980, and converted into a cycle track with appropriate TROs made to exclude motor vehicles.

The footpath

There is no criminal offence of riding a bicycle along a footpath, defined in HA 1980 as a highway over which pedestrians have the sole right of way but which does not run alongside an existing carriageway. Appropriate TROs can be made prohibiting cycling alongside specified footpaths where it is felt this is a problem.

Where a proposal involves the use of a footpath for cycling, it may be necessary to obtain covenants from the owners of the sub-soil not to sue such cyclists in civil actions for nuisance or trespass. Alternatively, the Highway Authority must stop up the footpath, and provide a new way allowing a wider class of taffic; motor vehicles would be excluded by appropriate TROs. This procedure is, however, likely to be complex. For further guidance on this, see Local Transport Note 1/78, para 4.9.

Pedestrianization schemes

Where the Secretary of State has made an order converting a street into a footpath as part of a pedestrianization scheme under s. 212, Town and Country Planning Act 1971, exemptions may be made for specified classes of vehicle to drive or ride in the area, even though it is in law a footpath. Such exemptions may include bicycles (see section 13.1.9 'Closing up streets').

Controls on cycle-pedestrian tracks

Where shared tracks for bicycles and pedestrians are planned, extra controls over the behaviour of cyclists should be considered. The criminal offences of reckless and careless cycling will still apply (see section 13.1.5 'Rules of the road'), but there is no general obligation in law for cyclists to give way to pedestrians except when they are riding along bridleways (see section 13.1.11 'Bridleways, parks and new towns').

Local TROs could be made to this effect, but unless they are clear in their application, there may be problems of enforcement. Advisory notices may have an effect and the placing of street furniture such as seats and shrubs in pedestrianized areas under s. 212, Town and Country Planning Act 1971 may be the most effective method of ensuring that cyclists and pedestrians do not become a danger or nuisance to each other.

Residential precincts in England and Wales

No specific provision exists in law for the creation of residential precincts (the equivalent of the Dutch *Woonerven*). They are quite distinct from shopping precincts in that there is no legal discouragement to the use of private motor vehicles within the area, though the design ensures that through traffic is unlikely to make use of it. The use of orders under s. 212, Town and Country Planning Act 1971 (see section 13.9, 'Closing up streets'), even though it permits exemptions for classes of traffic, is inappropriate for the creation of equivalent areas in England and Wales.

The use of a carefully worded set of TROs coupled with appropriate design features could, however, create the components of a *Woonerf*. The purpose of a residential precinct is probably not inconsistent with the general legal duty of Highway Authorities when framing TROs 'to ensure the expeditious, convenient and safe movement of vehicular and other traffic, including pedestrians' (s. 84(1), RTRA 1967).

Bollards and other obstructions can be placed at either end of, and within the restricted area, and these design features can be effective in reducing traffic flows and speed. Speed limits of less than 30mph require the approval of the Secretary of State, but on present policy this will not normally be given (Local Transport Note 2/78, para 3.22). The placing of street furniture of any permanence, however, is not permitted (see 13.1.9 below).

Avoiding the impression of a division between a carriageway and footway – an essential feature of a residential precinct – can probably be achieved by the removal of the footway under s. 66, HA 1980. The whole highway then becomes a carriageway, in contrast to pedestrianization schemes where the carriageway is converted into a footpath. There is no general legal restriction on the use of carriageways by pedestrians, but design features would have to ensure the continuing safety of pedestrians in the street.

Otherwise, the Highway Authority might be considered to be in breach of its general duty under s. 66(1), HA 1980 to provide footways for pedestrians where consideration of safety and traffic conditions demand their need.

13.1.9 Closing up streets

Alteration of carriageway widths

Highway Authorities possess the general power to widen highways under s. 72, HA 1980, either by coming to an agreement with adjoining land-owners or by using compulsory purchase powers (s. 239, HA 1980; s. 122, TCPA 1971).

Authorities also have the power to vary the relative widths of the footway and carriageway (s. 75, HA 1980). In addition, they may provide, alter, or remove footways under s. 66, HA 1980. Using these powers, an Authority could remove the whole or part of an underused footway in order to construct a cycle track or extra lane for bicycles. But Highway Authorities are also under a general duty to provide a proper and sufficient footway where they consider this to be necessary and desirable for the safety or accomodation of pedestrians.

Traffic restricted streets

TROs may be made to restrict traffic in a street in a number of ways, ranging from prohibiting all vehicles for certain times of the day to allowing the entry of only certain types of vehicles (for example, buses or delivery vehicles) for 24 hours a day.

TROs can be made for only certain reasons (see section 13.1.6), and there are special constraints when it is intended to restrict access for more than 8 hours out of 24. Under s. 69, RTRA 1967, a Highway Authority may place bollards and other obstructions at either end of the restricted street, as well as placing street furniture such as seats or tubs within the street. But works which would make the re-opening of the road to vehicles unreasonably difficult or which would alter the nature of the surface of the road are not permitted under s. 69.

Pedestrianized streets

While appropriate TROs can prohibit all but the minimum of traffic in a street, other powers exist to create a fully pedestrianized area. Under s. 212, TCPA 1971 a local planning authority can apply to the Secretary of State for an Order converting an existing street into a 'footpath or a bridleway'. Once the Order is made it will be illegal for any vehicle to drive in the area, unless the use of specified classes of vehicles is permitted in the Order. The Order may include bicycles in the list of exemptions. On the making of a s. 212 Order, the local authority may carry out extensive works 'to give effect to the Order, to enhance amenities, and generally for purposes beneficial to the public' (s. 213, TCPA). The works may include repaving the former carriageway and the provision of flowerbeds, and represent considerably wider powers than those available following the making of a TRO.

General advice on the provision of pedestrian facilities is given in Local Transport Note 2/78.

Bollards and other obstructions

The form of bollard or obstruction which may be placed on a highway where traffic is prohibited by TROs may be as the Authority considers 'appropriate for preventing' the passage of vehicles included in the Order. They may be designed to obstruct vehicles of any description, and be fixed or moveable. Gaps may therefore be left for cyclists. No detailed design criterion is prescribed by law, nor is authorization from Central Government required. But s. 69, RTRA 1967 does prohibit the placing of any bollard or obstruction which would

- prevent the passage of foot-passengers
- or alter the nature of the surface of the highway
- or be such that re-opening the road to vehicles would be 'unreasonably difficult'.

Road humps

The restrictions in s. 69, RTRA 1967 mean that Highway Authorities may not create road humps or depressions as a method of restricting or preventing traffic flow. At present, only the Secretary of State for Transport (with the consent of the relevant Highway Authority) has the power to create road humps or depressions, and then only for an experimental period of 12 months (s. 17 RTRA 1967).

13.1.10 Legal standards for highway surface and maintenance

Maintenance of the highway

Since the costs and difficulties of maintaining routes used by cyclists may be an important element in considering a proposal, the legal duties of Highway Authorities in relation to highway maintenance will be relevant.

The law concerning maintenance in England and Wales makes no direct reference to the bicycle. Highway Authorities simply have a general duty under s. 41, HA 1980 to maintain highways, a term that will include cycle tracks and footpaths. The precise standard of maintenance required by law is finally a matter for the courts; in one case a court noted, 'It is the duty of the road authorities to keep their public highways in a state fit to accommodate the ordinary traffic which passes or may be expected to pass thereon.'

Pot-holes and minor defects in the surface of the road represent a greater danger to cyclists than to drivers of motor cars. The standard of maintenance required by law for cycle tracks and parts of the highway known to be used by cyclists is therefore higher than that for highways used solely by motor vehicles. A special procedure exists in HA 1959 for members of the public to enforce the duty to maintain the highway (see box).

Claim for damages

A claim for damages by an injured cyclist may be made against the Highway Authority for breach of the statutory duty. But the cyclist must prove damage, either to himself or his machine, and must have been a lawful user of the highway: a cyclist illegally riding along a footpath or pavement is unlikely to succeed.

Where the grounds for breach of duty are that the Highway Authority *failed* to take steps to maintain a highway (rather than that it positively took action that was negligent), the Authority will have to show that in all the circumstances it took such steps as were reasonably required to ensure that the highway was not dangerous to traffic (s. 58, Highways Act 1980); this means that factors such as the Authority's

FORCING LOCAL AUTHORITIES TO MAINTAIN THE HIGHWAY

Section 56, HA 1959 provides a special procedure for members of the public to enforce the duty of Highway Authorities to maintain the highway. An individual must serve a notice requiring the Authority to state whether the stretch of road is a public highway and whether the Authority is liable to maintain it.

Within six months the individual may apply to the local magistrates' court for an Order that the highway is out of repair and that it must be put into repair. If successful the individual will be entitled to any costs incurred.

13.5 A typical example of a cycle track which does not have regular maintenance

scheme for inspection of highways, and financial constraints will all be relevant.

Finally, it must be remembered that the law does not require perfect standards of maintenance: 'A highway is not to be criticised by the standards of a bowling green'

(Littler *v* Liverpool Corporation [1968] 2 All ER 343).

13.1.11 Bridleways, parks and new towns

Bridleways

Bridleways are defined in HA 1980 as highways with the right of way for persons on horseback and pedestrians only. But by s. 30(1), Countryside Act 1968, members of the public have the right to ride bicycles along a bridleway, 'but in exercising that right cyclists shall give way to pedestrians and persons on horseback'. This right for cyclists may be excluded by appropriate TROs.

13.6 The legal basis for the provision of cycle routes in new towns is simpler than in other areas (Milton Keynes, UK)

Parks

The control of behaviour within parks will generally be affected by means of by-laws or local regulations. The introduction of a cycle route may require changing existing by-laws or introducing new ones, and this could involve discussion with another local authority or particular committees or officers concerned with parks.

However, no one set of laws governs the administration of parks and open spaces, and the extent of legal difficulties in introducing cycle routes within a particular park or open space will depend on the type of park, relevant local Private Acts of Parliament and even the original conveyance deeds. For instance, a local authority generally may not use a 'public recreation or pleasure ground' governed by the Public Health Act 1875 for any purpose inconsistent with public recreation: the provision of a commuter cycle route through such a public recreation ground might therefore be *ultra vires*. But cycle routes have been successfully introduced into parks and provided early consultation is made with the legal department to establish the legal position, it should be possible to resolve most problems.

Royal parks

Royal parks are kept under supervision by a Central Government Department (the Department of the Environment in most cases) using powers conferred by Parks Regulation Act 1872 and Parks Regulation Amendment Act 1926. The Secretary of State may make regulations that are considered necessary to properly manage the park, to preserve order and to prevent abuses. Regulations are laid before Parliament in the form of a Statutory Instrument; see, for example, the Wakehurst Place Regulations S.I. 1980/361, one of which forbids anyone to enter the park with a bicycle.

New towns

Some of the most comprehensive provisions for cyclists in England and Wales have been made in the New Towns. No doubt the luxury of starting with a clean slate is the primary reason for this, but the legal basis for the development of cycle routes is simpler in New Towns than in other areas. The New Towns Act 1965 governs the exercise of powers within areas designated by the Secretary of State as a site for a New Town. All development of land (which includes land for the construction of cycle tracks and other facilities) primarily rests with the New Town Corporation for the area. Proposals for development are made by the Corporation and require approval from the Secretary of State.

13.1.12 Parking

Highway Authorities or other public authorities are under no legal obligation to provide parking facilities for bicycles. Local authorities have the discretion to do so under s. 28, RTRA 1967, as do Parish Councils with the consent of the County Council (s. 46, RTRA 1967).

Using these powers, facilities such as bicycle parking stands may be erected and they may be placed on parts of the highway including the pavement (s. 12, Transport Act 1978). But they must not be placed in a position that might be dangerous to pedestrians or other highway users; the law allowing the provision of facilities does not relieve an Authority from liability to someone injured by a negligently positioned parking stand.

Areas of the pavement adjoining shop fronts may not be part of the highway but still belong to the owner of the fronting premises. Detailed maps of the highway should reveal its extent, and where appropriate, permission from frontage owners may have to be obtained before parking stands can be erected.

Where a pedestrian scheme has been implemented under s. 212, TCPA 1971, authorities possess wide powers to place objects or structures within the area as appear to them to be desirable 'for the purpose beneficial to the public'. The public can, of course, include cyclists and parking stands may be included in the street furniture placed within the pedestrian zone.

Parked bicycles

If parking stands or other parking facilities are not provided, cyclists will be forced to leave their bicycles elsewhere, and this can put them in legal difficulties. Leaving a vehicle on any part of the road (which includes the pavement) in a position likely to cause danger to other road users is an offence under s. 24, RTA 1972. Even when no danger is caused, a cyclist who, say, rests a bicycle on the pavement against a wall or fronting premises, may be guilty of causing 'an obstruction to the highway', an offence under s. 137, HA 1980. Nobody need be actually obstructed for the offence to be committed, but there must be proof of some unreasonable use of the highway (see Nagy *v* Weston [1965] 1 All ER 78). Individual cases may well be dismissed on the principle of *de minimis non curat lex* – the law is not concerned with trivia.

But an argument that can be raised against ambitious proposals is that they may result in a large number of bicycles being left on pavements or in other areas. The proper provision of adequate parking facilities may well be the answer. But, in any event, TROs could be made to contain the problem. A local ordinance in the United States, for example, provides that 'No person shall park a bicycle in a street enough to include a similar provision, but there may be difficulties in enforcement (see section 13.6 'Traffic Regulation Orders').

13.1.13 Traffic signs

Erection of signs

Highway Authorities in England and Wales possess the general power to erect traffic signs, but the form of traffic sign is controlled by Central Government. By s 54(2), RTRA 1967, signs shall be of a size, colour and type prescribed in regulations issued by the Secretary of State, except where he or she authorizes the erection of a type not so prescribed.

Traffic signs include 'any object or device for conveying to traffic on roads of any class warnings, information, requirements, and restrictions'; the term 'roads' will include all highways, and therefore cycle tracks and footpaths. Present regulations prescribing traffic signs are contained in S.I. 1981/859, and contain only some seven signs directly relating to bicycles. They may be used without authorization from the Secretary of State.

Where signs of a different type are proposed (including any of the bicycle signs prescribed in the regulations but different in size from those prescribed), Government authorization is required from the Regional Office of the Department of Transport. In Local Transport Note 1/78 Annex, the Government suggested a range of possible signs relating to bicycles. Some, but not all, of these have now been prescribed in the 1981 regulations, and their use does not require authorization. Use of any of the remaining signs in the Annex will still formally need authorization, but this will normally be a simple procedure.

Where the sign proposed is of a novel type not included in the regulations or Local Transport Note 1/78, negotiations for authorization can be expected to be complex and lengthy – a matter of months rather than weeks.

Failure to comply

The failure to comply with certain mandatory traffic signs is an offence under s. 22, RTA 1972. These signs include, among others, thoese indicating 'Stop' at major roads, red traffic lights, and 'No Entry' signs. A person riding a bicycle must certainly obey such signs, and it appears that someone wheeling a bicycle must still comply with the signs. For details of mandatory traffic signs, see Traffic Sign Regulations and General Directions 1981, S.I. 1981/859.

Action checklist for UK Law

Many authorities have developed their own procedures for checking the features of a scheme and their legal implications. The following checklist has been drawn up to assist with the identification of legal problems at the earliest stage.

1. Identify the particular elements of a proposal (eg, street closure, route through park, cycle lane, parking facilities).
2. Identify which elements involve either a change of existing facilities (eg, cycle lanes, street closure), or construction work (eg, cycle track, parking facilities, barriers).
3. Determine whether there is clear statutory authority for each element. If so, are any particular limitations or special procedural requirements imposed by the Statute (eg, the type of barrier that may be erected, or the need for consent from the Secretary of State)? If there is doubt about the statutory authority for a particular element, the position should be checked with the legal department.
4. Identify parts of the proposal which involve land not vested in the authority preparing the proposal (eg, parking facilities at a shop frontage, routes through a park). Early consultation with, and agreement from the particular landowners will be necessary. Compulsory purchase orders will be available in many cases, but their use will involve added time and expense.
5. Determine whether there are any elements likely to involve particular legal problems (eg, routes through parks, shared cycle-pedestrian facilities). Early consultation with the legal department should iron out any difficulties.
6. Identify whether there are precedents elsewhere for particular elements in the proposal. The existence of a precedent will be of particular use where an element in the scheme has not been created before by the authority and would appear to pose legal problems; information concerning the precedent and the legal procedure adopted should be ascertained at an early stage.

13.7 Bicycle parking stands may be placed in the highway under s. 12 of the Transport Act 1978 (Sheffield, UK)

13.2 THE UNITED STATES OF AMERICA

13.2.1 The legal framework

In the USA plans for the development of cycling are inextricably bound up with complicated legal provisions. Planners or engineers must determine from the law both their powers and duties and must also consider traffic rules that will affect the cyclist. Legislation must be considered at a number of levels. Federal laws and regulation will be of particular relevance where they govern highway grant programmes, and increasingly, general planning policies. State laws and regulations are likely to be of more immediate concern. Streets and Highways Codes will define types of routes that may be provided and details of funding arrangements for State highway and transport programmes, while the State Vehicle Codes will lay down rules of the road which must be followed by the cyclists using those routes. Finally specific local powers and traffic rules may be contained in municipal ordinances.

The guidance below concentrates on some of the most important legal provisions that a planner or engineer may have to consider. With fifty different sets of State laws, and innumerable local ordinances, the examples of provisions are extremely restricted. Provisions quoted therefore are largely drawn from the Uniform Vehicle Code and Model Traffic Ordinance (1979 version unless otherwise stated), together with a number of examples mainly from California State and local laws. These of course are no substitute for study of the actual provisions in force in any particular locality, but should give an understanding of the nature of legal controls, and of problems that may be encountered.

13.2.2 Definitions

Definition of 'vehicle'

In many jurisdictions, the definition of a vehicle in the State Vehicle Code will exclude a bicycle. For example,

> *a vehicle is a device by which any person or property may be propelled, moved or drawn upon a highway, excepting a device moved exclusively by human power or used exclusively upon stationary rails or tracks.*
>
> (California Vehicle Code @ 670)

Where this is the case, the rider of the bicycle is likely to be treated as the driver of a vehicle for certain provisions of the Code which provides that:

THE UNIFORM VEHICLE CODE AND MODEL TRAFFIC ORDINANCE

The Uniform Vehicle Code and Model Traffic Ordinance referred to extensively in the text, are a specimen set of traffic laws and ordinances. They have no legal force in themselves, but are used as a guide by State legislatures and municipalities in drafting their own traffic rules.

The UVC and MTO are produced by the National Committee of Uniform Traffic Laws and Ordinances, an independent non-profit organisation, with the aim of encouraging sound and uniform traffic laws and ordinances. Revisions are made every four years.

MOPEDS

Mopeds are defined in UVC @ 133.1 as a motor-driven cycle with pedals to permit propulsion by human power with a motor of not less than 2 brake horsepower and a design speed of less than 30mph. Where a State Vehicle Code excludes devices moved 'exclusively' by human power from the definition of vehicle, a moped will remain a vehicle (see People v Jordan (1977) 142 Cal. Reporter 401). Similarly, where the definition of 'bicycle' uses the words 'solely' or 'exclusively' a moped will not be included in that definition.

Every person riding a bicycle upon a roadway or any paved shoulder has all the rights and is subject to all the duties applicable to the driver of a vehicle (by this Division and Division 10) except those provisions which by their nature cannot apply.

(California Vehicle Code @ 21200)

The structure above has the advantage of making it clear that someone pushing a bicycle is not to be treated as the driver of a vehicle (see section 13.1.3 for the unclear position in UK law). But the approach and especially the phrase 'which by their nature cannot apply' has been criticized for being complicated and uncertain in its application. The revised version of the Uniform Vehicle Code therefore includes devices moved by human power within the definition of a vehicle (UVC. @ 1.184). When this revision is adopted by States, some traffic laws will have to specifically exclude bicycles (for example, licensing and registration requirements).

Definition of 'bicycle'

The present definition of a bicycle in the Uniform Vehicle Code is:

Every vehicle propelled solely by human power upon which any person may ride, having two tandem wheels, except such vehicles with a seat height of no more than 25 inches from the ground when the seat is adjusted to its highest position, and except scooters and similar devices.

Other definitions may be found:

A bicycle is a device upon which any person may ride propelled exclusively by human power through a belt, chain or gears and having either two or three wheels.

(Calif. Vehicle Code @ 231)

Definition of 'highway' and 'roadway'

The definition of the 'highway' contained in the Uniform Vehicle Code is:

The entire width between the boundary lines of every way publicly maintained when any part thereof is open to the use of the public for the purpose of vehicular travel.

(UVC @ 1.122)

The 'roadway' (equivalent to the UK term 'carriageway') is defined as:

That portion of the highway improved, designed and ordinarily used for vehicular travel, exclusive of the sidewalk, berm or shoulder is used by persons riding bicycles or other human powered vehicles.

(UVC @ 1.158)

Both these definitions are drafted with reference to 'vehicular traffic'. Consequently, where the term 'bicycle' is excluded from the definition of a 'vehicle', any bikeway designed exclusively for bicycles and distinct from existing highway routes will not be a 'highway' at least for the purposes of the Vehicle Code. This will have implications for rights of way at intersections (see below) and other rules relating to highways. Whether a distinct bikeway of this type is treated as a highway may also affect funding arrangements related to highways, though specific provisions may clarify the point:

The Legislature finds and declares that the construction and maintenance of such non-motorized transportation facilities constitutes a highway under Art. XXVI of the California Constitution, and justifies the expenditure of highway funds and the exercise of the power of eminent domain therefore.

(California Streets and Highways Code, @ 156.10 (c))

13.2.3 Federal policy

The framework set by the federal government, such as it is, was described in section 2.3.2. Two components of that framework which are not discussed elsewhere are highlighted here because they contain measures which may affect planning and design aspects of proposals to enhance cycling.

Air pollution

The Clean Air Act requires States to prepare State Implementation Plans (SIPs) providing for 'implementation, maintenance and enforcement' of national air quality standards (42. USC @ 7401). Included in the Plans, which are subject to the approval of the Federal Environmental Protection Agency, must be emission limitations, schedules and timetables and other such measures as may be necessary, including land use and transportation controls (s. 110 (a) (2)(b)). While the parts of the SIP dealing with transportation, often known as 'Transportation Control Plans' are not obligatory, there is great flexibility in the type of transportation control that may be included. A number of SIPs have already included a variety of measures designed to encourage bicycle use. Apart from the construction of particular bikeways, these have included such diverse measures as:

- the preparation of a city map, rating each street for difficulty of riding (Portland, Oregon)
- the development of storage facilities for bicycles (Chicago, Ill.)
- the replacement of impediments such as drainage gratings and the improvement of road surfaces (Boston, Mass.).

Urban transportation planning

Urban areas with a population of over 50,000 are required to have a 'continuing, cooperative and comprehensive' transportation planning process (known as the '3C process') as a condition for receiving Federal capital operating assistance (Urban Mass Transportation Act 1964, as amended, USC 134). Metropolitan Planning Organisations are designated by State Governors for the purpose, and Federal regulations implementing the process are contained in 23 CFR Part 450. Part of the 3C process should include consideration of the needs of cyclists, since the regulations state that consideration should be given to 'energy conservation' and that the process should include 'an evaluation of alternative transportation systems management improvements to make more efficient use of existing transportation resources'. (23CFR

@450.120 (a)(6) and (8)(ii)). Appendix A to the regulations contains advice on actions which should be included in the process, and 'it is expected that some actions in each category will be appropriate for any urbanized area' (Appendix A.4). Category (a)(3) provides examples of provisions for pedestrians and bicycles which include:

- bicycle paths and exclusive lanes
- pedestrian malls and other means of separating pedestrian and vehicular traffic
- secure and convenient storage areas for bicycles
- other bicycle facilitiation measures.

13.2.4 Rules of the road

Familiarity with relevant provisions of vehicles codes and local traffic ordinances are clearly an important consideration when preparing plans to improve cycling conditions. Legal provisions relating to rules of the road are considerably more detailed and extensive than those in the UK, where a single and flexible traffic offence of 'careless driving' (or, in the case of cyclists, 'careless cycling') regulates standards of behaviour in most traffic conditions.

Most of the provisions of the Code governing rules of the road will refer exclusively to the operation of vehicles upon 'the highway' (UVC @11.101). Some provisions, however, may be expressly stated to apply elsewhere; for example, UVC @11.1201 states that a number of provisions will apply to bicycles operated 'On any highway or upon any path set aside for the exclusive use of bicycles' (UVC @11.1201, 1968 version).

If a bicycle is a 'vehicle', bikeways will become highways in their own right, and cyclists on such bikeways will be governed by the general provisions.

'Reckless cycling'

The Uniform Vehicle Code provides that any person who drives 'any vehicle' in wilful and wanton disregard for the safety of persons or property is guilty of reckless driving (@11.901(a)). In many jurisdictions, this offence will apply only to cyclists on the roadway, but where the bicycle is directly included in the definition of a vehicle, the offence will apply to cyclists on all parts of the highway.

Position on the roadway

Any person operating a bicycle or a moped upon a roadway at less than normal speed at the time and place and under the conditions then existing shall ride as close as practicable to the right-hand curb of the roadway.

(UVC @11.1205(a))

Three exceptions to the general rule are provided: when overtaking, when preparing for a left turn, and when reasonably necessary to avoid obstructions such as parked vehicles and surface hazards.

In many State Vehicle Codes the equivalent provision is stricter, and requires all cyclists, whatever their speed, to ride 'as near as practicable' to the right-hand side of the roadway, exercising due care when overtaking another vehicle.

Left turns

The general rule for left turns is that vehicles must approach the turn in the lawfully available extreme left-hand lane and make the turn whenever practicable (UVC @11.601(b)). Bicycles following this manoeuvre, especially at night-time

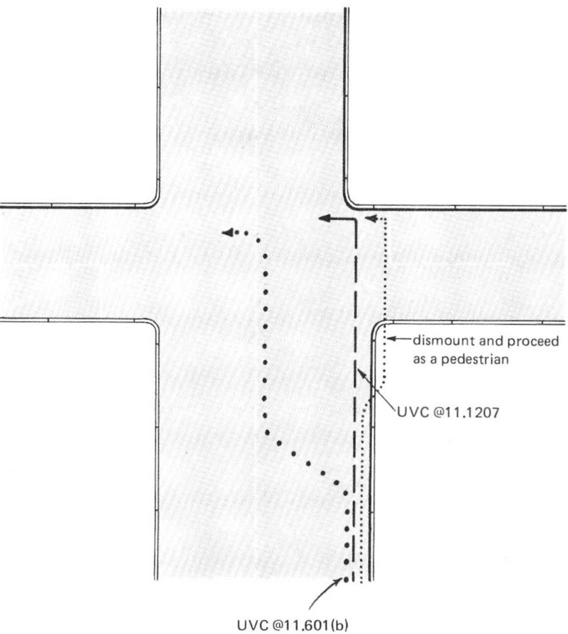

13.8 Possible left turn manoeuvres for cyclists at intersections

or at busy intersections, may be put in a vulnerable position. Cyclists can dismount and follow the route used by pedestrians, but the Uniform Vehicle Code provides an alternative route for cyclists and moped riders (UVC @11.1207): the rider approaches the turn as close as practicable to the *right* curb or edge of a roadway, crosses the intersection, and makes the turn from as close as possible to the edge of the roadway on the far side. Although this manoeuvre may be safer for the cyclist, it is not without legal difficulties: cyclists must comply with traffic control devices regulating traffic on the road in which they wish to proceed. Therefore they may have to wait on the other side of the intersection for a green light and in that position may well be blocking traffic wishing to turn right on red if this is permitted (see UVC @11.202(c)).

The Vehicle Code does however give powers to the State Highway Commission and local authorities to use official traffic control devices to direct cyclists on a specific course (UVC @11.1207(c)).

Rights of way

The general rule at uncontrolled intersections is contained in UVC @11.1401:

The driver of the vehicle on the left shall yield the right of way to the vehicle on the right.

Where a bikeway intersects with a highway, this rule will apply where the bikeway is itself a 'highway'. Since it may be unrealistic to expect drivers of motor vehicles to yield right of way at such an intersection, official traffic control devices should be considered; alternatively, preferential rights of way may be indicated by stop or yield signs, as authorized under @15.109.

State Vehicle Codes or local ordinances may themselves provide other rules. In Chicago, for example, an ordinance requires every person operating a bicycle on a roadway to yield the right of way to other moving vehicles at all times.

Pedestrians

Where cyclists are not prohibited from riding on sidewalks, they must yield right of way to pedestrians (UVC @ 11.1209(a)). On a separate bikeway, rules applicable to pedestrians on highways will apply, assuming the bikeway is considered a highway under the Code. Pedestrians therefore would have to yield to all bicycles on the bikeway except when crossing on a crosswalk (UVC @ 11.506). Suitable yield signs may authorize preferential rights of way and the State Vehicle Code itself may provide particular rules governing the bikeway:

No person shall proceed along a bicycle path or lane where there is an adjacent pedestrian facility.

(Calif. Vehicle Code @ 21966)

13.2.5 Bike paths

Construction

Provisions in the State Streets and Highways Code will generally indicate the types of bicycle paths that may be constructed, whether independent of existing routes or not. Careful consideration must be given to the terminology used, and especially to the definition sections, since there appears to be little consistency at present in the way that terms such as 'bikeway', 'bike path' and 'biketrail' are used in legislation.

An example of an authorizing section is:

The Department may construct and maintain non-motorized transportation facilities approximately parallelling any State highway where the separation of non-motorized traffic from motor vehicle traffic will increase traffic capacity or safety of the highway.

(Calif. Streets and Highways Code @ 156.10(a))

Mandatory use of bike paths

One of the most controversial sections of UVC provides that:

Wherever a usable path for bicycles has been provided adjacent to the roadway, bicycle riders shall use such path and shall not use the roadway.

(UVC. @ 11.1205(b))

This provision or an equivalent is found in many jurisdictions. Strenuous efforts have been made to take this clause out of UVC because it may require cyclists to use a badly designed or even a dangerous bike path and because the term 'usable' is imprecise. In the final analysis, the definition of 'usable' will be a matter for court judgement in each particular case. In some jurisdictions, the word 'usable' is omitted, and only those paths designated by official traffic control devices must be used. In other jurisdictions, the requirement has been repealed altogether (see, for example, Repeal of Mandatory Bikepath Use Act, 1979, Texas); traffic planners then have to rely on the safety and convenience of the bike path itself to attract the cyclist.

13.2.6 Bike lanes

The UVC allows authorities to erect official traffic control devices directing specified traffic to use a designated lane on the roadway (UVC, 11.309(c)). 'Bicycle only' lanes may therefore be created in existing roadways, but careful consideration must be given to whether or not motor vehicles should be expressly excluded from travel in the bicycle lane, and, in particular, to the problems of vehicles wishing to turn right across the path of the lane (see section 6.2.5 'Cycle lanes'). Rules governing the motorist's duty to signal and approach the right turn from as close as practical to the right-hand kerb or edge of the roadway will govern the situation (see UVC @ 11.601(c)), but may not provide the safest guidance. Local traffic ordinances will often give the power to designate bicycle lanes. Section 5.32 of the Davis (Calif.) City Code, for example, provides:

The City Engineer, upon approval of the Safety Advisory Committee, is authorized to erect or place signs upon any street, or adjacent to any street in the city indicating the existence of a bicycle lane and otherwise regulating the operation and use of vehicles and bicycles with respect thereto.

The provision itself is authorized by the California Vehicle Code (@ 20207) permitting the establishment of such lanes on city streets.

Mandatory use of cycle lanes

The State Vehicle Code or local ordinance may provide rules that will apply to all bicycle lanes; for example:

Any person operating a bicycle upon the roadway at less than the normal speed of traffic moving in the same direction shall ride within the bicycle lane. (Calif. Vehicle Code @ 21208)

Three exceptions to the general rule are then provided – when overtaking, when turning left, and when reasonably necessary to avoid obstacles and debris.

Traffic control devices may also require use of the lane, and failure to comply with such a device is an offence (see UVC @ 11.201).

13.2.7 Exclusion of bicycles

Exclusion from controlled-access roadways

The use of any class or kind of traffic found to be incompatible with the normal use and safe movement of traffic may be regulated or prohibited (UVC @ 11.313). Bicycles may be included within a class of traffic, and in some jurisdictions are expressly mentioned in equivalent provisions.

If an existing controlled-access roadway appears likely to form a suitable link in a bicycle route, careful study of the relevant legal provisions must be made. In some States a blanket ban exists on bicycles, and no discretion to permit their use is allowed. Other examples of general bans exist: the Iowa State Vehicle Code prohibits all traffic incapable of attaining and maintaining a speed of 40mph in its interstate system.

The precise terminology used will determine whether this can be allowed. If the term 'roadway' is used, bicycles may still be able to use a shoulder or path running beside the roadway, while the term 'highway' will probably include the entire width of the public way. Some jurisdictions use terms such as 'expressway' and 'freeway', and in the absence of specific provisions, these too will include the whole width of the highway.

Exclusion of specified traffic

Under the Model Traffic Ordinance, the city traffic engineer is authorized to prohibit classes or kinds of traffic from 'heavily travelled' streets or part of such streets which would be incompatible with normal and safe movement of traffic (MTO @17.4). The term 'street' would include the whole highway, and not simply the roadway (UVC @1.172). Where it is intended to prohibit bicycles from the roadway of such streets, but to allow them to use a shoulder or path running beside the roadway, provisions must be framed to include only the roadway.

13.2.8 Bicycles and pedestrians

Riding on sidewalks

In England and Wales there is a general prohibition against riding bicycles on sidewalks. In most jurisdictions in the United States, cycling on sidewalks is permitted, subject to exceptions; both the State Vehicle Code and Local Traffic Ordinance must be consulted for details. The revised Uniform Vehicle Code provides that bicyclists may not ride on sidewalks where such use is prohibited by official traffic control devices (UVC. 11.1209). Some local traffic ordinances restrain cycling on sidewalks by age, and others prohibit all cycling on sidewalks in certain general localities; for example:

> *No person shall ride a bicycle upon a sidewalk within the central traffic district.*
>
> (Davis, Calif. City Code, Sec. 5.26)

Rules on sidewalks

Where cycling is permitted on sidewalks, particular rules will govern the cyclist's behaviour. For example:

> *A person propelling a bicycle upon or along the sidewalk, or across the roadway upon and along a crosswalk, shall yield right of way to any pedestrian and shall give audible signal before overtaking and passing such pedestrian.*
>
> (UVC @11.1209)

13.2.9 Play streets

Sections 4.6 and 4.7 of the Model Traffic Ordinance provide for the establishment of 'play streets' by the City Engineer. Once established, no one should drive a vehicle in a play street unless they have business or a residence in that area, and then any such driver 'shall exercise the greatest care in driving upon any such street'. This provision should be compared with the Dutch *Woonerf* regulations since the concepts are similar.

13.2.10 Parking

Parking of bicycles

Increased bicycle use will lead to increased bicycle parking requirements, and this may lead to congestion and obstruction of the sidewalk. Controls over the manner and position of parking may be formulated, and the Uniform Vehicle Code provides that:

> *A bicycle parked on the sidewalk shall not impede the normal use and reasonable movement of pedestrian and other traffic.*
>
> (UVC, @11.1210(b))

The Model Traffic Ordinance (1962 version), which provides the model for many municipal ordinances, provides more detailed controls:

> *No person shall park a bicycle upon a street other than upon the roadway against the curb or upon a sidewalk in a rack to support the bicycle or against a building or at the curb, in such manner as to afford the least obstruction to pedestrian traffic.*
>
> (Sec. 12.18)

In addition, official traffic control devices may prohibit or restrict the parking of bicycles on the sidewalk (UVC @11.1210).

Fixing bicycles to posts

Cyclists will often wish to lock their bicycle securely to some fixed object. At one extreme, local ordinances may prohibit attaching bicycles to certain objects, for example parking meters, whether or not an obstruction is caused.

A more positive approach may be found in ordinances which expressly permit the securing of bicycles to public poles. Section 12.14 of the Model Traffic Ordinance, as revised in 1975, provides an example of such a provision.

> *Any person may park near, and secure a bicycle to, any publicly owned pole or post for a period of not more than twelve consecutive hours, unless an official traffic-control device or any applicable law or ordinance prohibits parking or securing bicycles at that location. No bicycle shall be secured to any tree, fire hydrant, or police or fire call box. No bicycle shall be secured in any manner as to impede the normal and reasonable movement of pedestrian or other traffic.*

Provision of parking facilities

Adequate and well-designed parking facilities and parking places for bicycles can help minimize obstruction problems on the sidewalk. Local ordinances may permit the Chief of Police to designate parking places for bicycles and to authorize the erection of parking facilities. In Burlingarne, Calif., this ordinance is expressed in strong terms:

> *The Police Department shall provide and set up suitable racks adjacent to the curb or gutter at such places in business districts of the city as may be deemed advisable for the parking of bicycles by persons who have occasion to stop temporarily in such districts.*
>
> (Code Sec. 13.52.150)

The provision of off-street parking facilities can be required in new developments where appropriate zoning powers exist. The schedule of off-street parking requirements in the Zoning Regulations of Palo Alto, Calif., now includes requirements for bicycle facilities both in terms of numbers and of quality (see section 9.1.1 'Local regulations').

In addition, police powers may be available to require owners of existing residential and office buildings to provide parking spaces for bicycles.

Literature guide

This section is designed to introduce readers to the major publications on bicycle planning and the related subjects. It concentrates particularly on documents which are easily available, rather than listing every report or article ever published on the subject.

Bicycle Forum *Published by:* Dan Burden, 317 Beverly, Missoula, MT 59801, USA.
This is the only magazine devoted primarily to bicycle planning and has developed a reputation for top quality reporting. It has covered education, enforcement, facilities and recreational cycling. The back issues are an excellent source of information.

The Bicycle Planning Book *Author:* Mike Hudson and Associates. *Published by:* Open Books/Friends of the Earth. *Available from:* Friends of the Earth, 9 Poland Street, London W1. 1978
This book sets out the arguments for a more systematic approach to bicycle planning. It describes UK government and local authority activities and has a section of bicycle planning abroad.

Bicycle Transportation for Energy Conservation *Author:* US Department of Transportation. *Published by:* US Department of Transportation, Office of the Secretary, Washington D.C., 20590. 1980
This report was required by the National Energy Conservation Act 1978. It sets out estimates of the potential savings resulting from increased utilitarian cycling, identifies the obstacles and constraints on increased bicycle use and presents an ambitious programme of measures designed to increase the current levels of use by a factor of between three and five.

The Bike-ed Course *Author:* J. R. Newlands. *Published by:* Road Safety and Traffic Authority, Melbourne, Victoria, Australia. 1979
This kit consists of 7 teaching manuals, 15 posters, 100 colour slides and 7 photocopy masters. The subjects covered include sharing the road with others, bike mechanics, riding skills and a road test. It is the most spectacular kit available.

Bikeway Planning and Design Manual *Author:* Barton Aschman Associates Inc. *Published by:* US Department of the Interior, National Park Service, National Capital Region, 1100 Ohio Drive, S. W., Washington D.C., 20242. 1979
This is one of the most recent American Design Manuals, which was prepared for a division on the National Park Service. It sets out the goals and objectives of bicycle planning and discusses the principles of bicycle facility design. It also gives design standards and describes monitoring procedures.

Bikeways – State of the Art 1974 *Author:* De Leuw, Cather and Co. *Published by:* US Department of Transportation FHWA. *Available from:* National Technical Information Service, Springfields, Virginia, 22151.
This is an early report on developments in bikeway planning in the USA. It concentrates on the provision of special facilities for cyclists.

Combined Pedestrian and Cycle Subways – Layout and Dimensions. *Author:* UK Department of Transport. *Published by:* Department of Transport, 2 Marsham St, London SW1. 1979
This note gives design, layout and dimensional requirements for new cycle-pedestrian subways. The advice given would also be useful to authorities considering converting existing subways into shared facilities.

Comparison of On-road and Off-road Cycle Training for Children *Authors:* P. Wells, C. S. Downing, M. Bennett. *Published by:* Transport and Road Research Laboratory, Crowthorne, Berks, UK. 1979
This is the report of an experiment which compared the effectiveness of bicycle training on and off public roads. It concluded that the road-trained group performed significantly better than the playground trained group on all the manoevres tested.

Cycle Routes in Peterborough – Interim Report *Authors:* S. Quenault, J. Morgan. *Published by:* Transport and Road Research Laboratory, Crowthorne, Berks, UK. 1979
This describes the results of traffic studies and attitude surveys carried out before and after the opening of the cycle route in Peterborough.

Cycle Routes in Portsmouth *Authors:* S. Quenault, J. Nicholson, T. V. Head. *Published by:* Transport and Road Research Laboratory, Crowthorne, Berks, UK.
This report was published in three volumes: (1) Planning and Implementation, 1977 (2) Traffic Studies, 1979 (3) Attitude Surveys, 1979.
It describes the complete programme of research carried out by the TRRL into the Portsmouth cycle route experiment.

Cycling as a Mode of Transport *Published by:* Transport and Road Research Laboratory, Crowthorne, Berks, UK. 1980
This is the report of the proceedings of the 1978 symposium on cycling held at the TRRL. It includes eight papers on bicycle use, safety, law, design criteria, bicycle routes in The Hague and Tilburg, the US Bikeway Demonstration Program and cycle routes in Peterborough. It is a valuable compendium of information and experience.

Cycling Transportation Engineering *Author:* John Forester. *Published by:* Custom Cycle Fitments, 782 Allen Court, Palo Alto, California, 94303. 1977
A polemical report which sets out the author's views on the myths and mistakes of bicycle planning. The subjects covered include: the problems confronting cyclists, methods of undertaking deficiency surveys and road width criteria.

Demonstration Cycle Routes in Tilburg *Author:* Ministry of Transport and Public Works. *Published by:* Ministry of Transport and Public Works, Plesmanweg 1–6, The Hague, Netherlands. 1977
A detailed description of the cycle route in Tilburg, illustrated with many before and after photographs.

Design and Construction Criteria for Bikeway Construction Projects *Author:* US Department of Transportation. *Published by:* US Department of Transportation, FHWA, 400 Seventh St, S.W., Washington D.C., 20590. 1980
This is a draft document issued to solicit comments on the proposed FHWA document 'Guide for Bicycle Facilities'. It stresses the importance of the existing road system and suggests a methodology for making improvements. It also gives a number of design standards for the construction of bikeways.

District of Columbia Bikeway Planning Study *Author:* Barton Aschman Associates Inc. *Published by:* Barton Aschman Associates Inc., 1739K St, Northwest, Washington D.C., 20006. 1974/5
This set of twelve memoranda were prepared to provide documentation on technical aspects of the District of Columbia Bicycle Transportation Plan and Program. They provide useful background information on a wide range of bicycle planning issues.

Effective Cycling *Author:* John Forester. *Published by:* Custom Cycle Fitments, 782 Allen Court, Palo Alto, California, 94303. 1978
This is the book for a course designed to teach adults how to ride defensively in traffic. The course includes reading assignments from the book and practical work.

Evaluation of a Cycling Proficiency Training Course using two Behavioural Recording Methods *Authors:* M. Bennett, B. Sanders, C. S. Downing. *Published by:* Transport and Road Research Laboratory, Crowthorne, Berks, UK. 1979
This report compares the behaviour of children who have received training with those who have not by studying 15 children before and after training and comparing them with a control group. The project also evaluated the effectiveness of different behavioural recording methods.

Geelong Bike Plan *Author:* Geelong Bike Plan Committee. *Available from:* Geelong Bike Plan, State Public Offices, Cnr Fenwick and Little Malop Streets, Geelong 3220, Australia. 1977
This is the most comprehensive bike plan in Australia and has been awarded two Australian planning prizes. It uses the four Es methodology (Education, Enforcement, Engineering and Encouragement) and has formed the basis for Geelong's ambitious plans. The original is out of print, but summary and microfiche editions are available.

Guide for Bicycle Routes *Author:* American Association of State Highway and Transportation Officials. *Published by:* ASSHTO, 444 North Capitol, Washington D.C., 2001. 1974
Many US regulations refer to this document. The Federal Highways Administration (FWHA) has proposed that, since this document is now somewhat out of date, these references should be to a new document, the draft of which appeared in the Federal Register on August 4th 1980 under the title 'Design and Construction Criteria for Bikeway Construction Projects' (see above).

Residential Roads and Footpaths – Layout considerations *Author:* UK Department of Transport. *Published by:* Her Majesty's Stationery Office, 49 High Holborn, London WC1. 1977
This is the UK government advice to local authorities on the layout of residential roads and footpaths.

Planning and Design Criteria for Bikeways in California *Author:* California Department of Transportation. *Published by:* Caltrans, Office of Bicycle Programs, PO Box 1499, Sacremento, California, 95807. 1978
This report establishes criteria for the development of bikeways in California, and is one of the most respected design guidelines available. It sets the role of bikeways in context and describes design, construction and layout details for different types of bikeways.

Regional Workshops on Bicycle Safety *Published by:* US Department of Transportation, National Highway Traffic and Safety Administration (NHTSA). *Available from:* National Technical Information Service, Springfield, Virginia, 22161.
This is the report of ten regional workshops designed to improve information exchange between people involved with bicycle safety. As well as looking at accidents, the workshops also considered ways of improving safety, including education, enforcement and bicycle facilities.

Safety and Location Criteria for Bicycle Facilities *Author:* De Leuw, Cather and Co. *Published by:* US Department of Transportation FWHA. *Available from:* National Technical Information Service, Springfield, Virginia, 22161. There are three reports under this title: (1) User Manual Volume I, 1976 (2) User Manual Volume II, 1976 (3) Final Report, 1977.
Together, they form the results of a research project set up by the FHWA which was designed to improve the quality and consistency of bikeway planning and design. Volume I deals with design, focusing on the process and details of laying out the physical features of bikeway facilities. Volume II deals with location criteria for bicycle facilities and the process of systematic planning for bicycles. The final report is a compendium of all the research activities undertaken.

Safety of Two Wheelers *Author:* Organisation for Economic Co-operation and Development. *Published by:* OECD. *Available from:* Her Majesty's Stationery Office, 49 High Holborn, London WC1. 1978
The OECD has gathered information from member states to compare accident rates and to identify what actions can and have been taken. This is a useful source of information for anyone wanting to study accidents across various countries.

A Study of Bicycle/Motor Vehicle Accidents: Identification of problem types and countermeasure approaches *Author:* K. Cross, G. Fisher. *Published by:* US Department of Transportation NHTSA. *Available from:* National Technical Information Service, Springfield, Virginia, 22161. 1977
The report of a research project designed to specify accident types and identify countermeasures which would reduce the number occurring. Ken Cross is widely known as the leading authority on this issue.

Technical Bulletins *Published by:* Geelong Bike Plan. *Available from:* Geelong Bike Plan, State Public Offices, Cnr Fenwick and Little Malop Streets, Geelong 3220, Australia.
This series of technical bulletins currently has six titles: 1. Bicycle Signs 2. Bicycle Accidents 3. School Bicycle Touring 4. Bicycle Surveys 5. Bicycle Enforcement 6. Bicycle Racks. Each bulletin is packed with valuable up-to-date information.

Ways of Helping Cyclists in Built Up Areas (Local Transport Note 1/78) *Author:* UK Department of Transport. *Published by:* Department of Transport, 2 Marsham St, London SW1. 1978
This is the most recent advice from the UK government on technical aspects of cycle route provision. The document brought together information gathered from local authority experience of providing facilities for cyclists in existing urban areas. It is essential reading for UK planners and engineers.

Woonerf (Residential Precinct) *Author:* ANWB, The Royal Dutch Touring Club. *Published by:* ANWB Traffic Department, Wassenaarseweg 220, Post Box 93200, 2509 BA, The Hague, Holland. 1980
This report describes the successful Dutch experiments with residential precincts. It gives design and construction details and traffic regulations for the precincts. It is well illustrated and the foreign edition is written in English, French and German. It is one of the best documents available and would be valuable for anyone concerned with the improvement of residential areas.

Woonerf in City and Traffic Planning, including planning for cyclists and pedestrians *Author:* Dirk H. ten Grotenhuis, Chief of the Traffic Department. *Published by:* Municipality of Delft, Oude Delft, 53, 2611 BC, Delft, Holland. 1979
Introducing an integrated approach to traffic planning, this report sets a framework for the development of residential precincts and includes a description of the Delft bicycle and pedestrian network.

Index

Note: numbers in italics refer to illustrations, figures, tables